ritain and Northern Ireland and of her other realms and ter

of all the Orders of Chivalry and Lord High Admiral of the United

Registrar of the Imperial Society of Knights Bachelor • Boy Bishop

nque Ports, Constable of Dover Castle and Admiral of the Cinque

er to the Duke of Normandy • Lord Archbishop of Canterbury and

per of the Great Seal, Keeper of the Royal Conscience and Speaker

velsby • President of Tynwald and Lord Bishop of Sodor and Man

Brother of the Hospital of Saint Cross • Sergeant at Mace and

rt • Hereditary Warden of Savernake Forest • Master Treasurer of

e Isles of the Sea • Lord of the Isles, Prince and Great Steward of

Prince of Wales, Earl of Chester and Duke of Cornwall • Knight

Military Knights and the Military Knights of Windsor • Officers of

f Arms and Secretary of the Order of the Garter, Norroy and Ulster

aster Herald, Windsor Herald, Maltravers Herald Extraordinary,

l Herald Extraordinary, Rouge Croix Pursuivant, Rouge Dragon

of Arms • Lord High Constable of Scotland and Slains Pursuivant

Admiral of the Western Isles, High Sheriff of Argyll and Keeper of

ert • Captain of Dunstaffnage, Hereditary Keeper of Dunstaffnage

Lord Warden of the Stannaries, Rider and Master Forester of the

Vice Chairman of the Prince's Council • Speaker of the House of

ster of the Rolls • Searcher of the Sanctuary and High Bailiff with

ancellor of the Duchy of Lancaster • Lord High Admiral of the Wash

Escheator, Clerk of the Markets and Admiral of the Port of London

l Companies of Skinners and Merchant Taylors • Tolly-keepers

er of Eton College • Choristers of King's College, Cambridge •

KEEPERS OF THE
KINGDOM

JUBILEE EDITION

KEEPERS OF THE
KINGDOM

JUBILEE EDITION

Alastair Bruce · Julian Calder · Mark Cator

CASSELL&CO

First published in the United Kingdom in 2002
by Cassell Illustrated

A CIP catalogue record for this book is available from the
British Library
ISBN 0 30 436201 8

Art Direction by David Rowley
Designed by Nigel Soper
Typeset in DeVinne
Printed and bound in Italy

Cassell Illustrated
2–4 Heron Quays
Isle of Dogs
London E14 4JP

The authors wish to thank everybody who appears in this
book for their time, patience, support and enthusiasm. Our
gratitude also extends to all those who do not appear but who
were responsible for setting up each portrait, often putting up
with months of badgering, pestering and endless letters. We
certainly enjoyed travelling around the country and meeting
so many different people. Finally, in completing this Jubilee
Edition, we thank The Queen and all members of the Royal
Family for taking part in this project.

Page 2: *The SYMBOLS OF SOVEREIGNTY await the Sovereign in the Throne Room at Buckingham Palace. The Imperial State Crown has a sapphire in the top cross, which came from Edward the Confessor's ring; below it hang Elizabeth I's pearl earrings. The massive ballas ruby, owned by the Black Prince and worn by Henry V at Agincourt, sits above the bright second Star of Africa diamond. The Sword of State was traditionally the monarch's personal weapon and is the symbol of both her authority and power. The Throne, with the Royal Cypher, was used when the Queen made her Oath during the Coronation in 1953.*

Opposite: *The QUEEN'S BARGEMASTER (in the foreground) and the ROYAL WATERMEN (see page 160), like their predecessors, are all experienced boatmen on the River Thames. Nowadays, conveying the monarch from Hampton Court to the Tower of London by barge is no longer necessary. In Tudor times, however, it was the safest route, and the multiple oarsmen made sure it was also the quickest.*

Contents

Introduction

HISTORY HAS LEFT ITS MARK ALL AROUND BRITAIN. The story of these islands can be read in the scars on the landscape, in its buildings, institutions, books, pictures, and in a wealth of archive materials. But it also lives today in the people who hold a collection of odd appointments, names and titles that give them the right to jobs that were created hundreds of years ago. The desire to uncover and revive some of the historic clues vested in these reminders of the past was the impetus for this book.

Despite the rapid pace of modernization, Britain still has the broadest spectrum of appointments in the world. This is partly because there has been no conquest since 1066 and also because the monarchy continues, changing but constant. This book describes the holders of over 120 such posts. Many of them still play a role on the national stage, while others do little more than carry their strange titles.

Quite often the bearers of historic posts have no idea of their provenance. Time has worn out the purpose of most of these jobs, but in every case there was once a real need for them. Each tells a story, whether of post-Roman Britain, the evolution of our separate kingdoms, the union of the country or the growth of empire. Most of the appointments no longer carry any real power, but they have survived because there has been no pressing need to destroy them. No revolution has ever completely swept aside the old order; instead, succeeding events have concealed history, just as plant life overwhelms deserted buildings.

Since the first edition of *Keepers of the Kingdom* was published in 1999, some of the appointments described in that volume have disappeared. This is a natural process, but hastened by a change in the national mood, which is moving away from an enjoyment of what might seem like anachronistic traditions. Few may mourn when old appointments are swept away, and fewer still may regret the constitutional changes that have reduced the powers of hereditary Lords. But none would applaud a similar destruction of the country's architectural treasures, such as its castles, churches and industrial buildings, that speak so eloquently of a shared past. By recording the many ancient offices that permeate our culture, this book seeks to preserve a fascinating aspect of our past, in case it disappears from view.

When Queen Elizabeth II was crowned in June 1953, she claimed her title by descent from a troublesome immigrant called Cerdic, who landed on the south coast of England with his band of warriors in 495. She also claims descent from King Coel of the Britons, Fergus the Great of the Scots, Rolf the Norman and Llewellyn of Wales. It is a well-known genealogy, but everyone who lives in her Realms has a family tree just as varied, wide and rich. Indeed, many of us share the genes of the warriors who helped Cerdic secure his throne. We are all products of the same mixed ancestry, and the ruled, as well as the rulers, played their part in the evolution of Britain. Hidden behind some of the ancient titles and rituals that exist to this day are stories of ordinary people who did extraordinary things. The titles that arose from their actions offer clues as to how power was wrested from kings and placed in elected representatives, leading to the parliamentary democracy we now enjoy.

For 50 years now, The Queen has been at the centre of public life in Britain, and, by convention, members of her family are expected to share the responsibilities that a monarchy entails. To this end, all of them hold a range of public appointments, reflecting their duties as Keepers of the Kingdom. For the first time, and for this special Jubilee Edition of the book, every Prince and Princess of the Blood Royal who is of working age has come forward to be photographed, in order to share the stories specific to each of their appointments.

Ancient titles survive because the monarchy continues. For example, Britain has a Chancellor of the Exchequer rather than a more prosaically named Finance Minister, but the responsibilities of the two are indistinguishable. The Lord High Admiral of the Wash, on the other hand, no longer has any duties, or illusions of grandeur: his title merely provides a clue to part of Britain's past, when it was his responsibility to keep the coastline safe from invasion. This task was already obsolete in the 16th century, when a properly organized navy assumed that duty, and these days the RAF does the job. Typically, no one ever formally announced an end to the Admiral's role – there seemed no need.

The office should be greater than the man – or woman – a fact often overlooked by those who serve themselves and not their appointment. The holding of office can also be fleeting and the ballot box can turn a prime minister into a mere backbencher or indeed out of parliament altogether.

Reactions to ancient titles in Britain today are mixed. The idea of men and women in ceremonial costume performing odd rituals sometimes provokes derision, and commentators are quick to pick up on this. It is sometimes said that without titles the nation would rise above the burden of its class history, and that it would be better if archaic names, such as First Sea Lord, were dropped in favour of something more modern, such as Chief of Staff (Navy).

Others, however, argue that if power is under democratic control, there can be no harm in the survival of traditions that enable us to understand our past, particularly when they are self-funding. Britain possesses something that many other countries seem to covet. It is understood that preserving history within an evolving structure provides a valuable fingerprint, which has touched almost every one of us living in these islands. This print survives because the country has modernized without feeling the need to rid itself of its past: it may often dislike that past, even detest it, but confidence in the future is sometimes best measured by a country's ability to live at ease with its history.

The kingdoms that became Britain wisely maintained their individual identities at the time of their union, and their history remains available to all of us. The anecdotes associated with them and their sometimes bizarre appointments bear retelling time and again: people generally enjoy a good story, and in the process may come to understand and respect little-known aspects of the past. Over the 50 years of the current Elizabethan Age few have attempted to share these stories. The holders of some appointments forget that their privilege involves a responsibility to explain the significance of their roles, and this has rightly earned the indignation of an excluded public. If the background to historic titles goes unexplained and people at large remain unaware of them, we will all eventually become alienated from our own historic inheritance.

This book clearly shows that the past can illuminate the present. Every title described in these pages reveals something of the nations and communities that presently form the United Kingdom of Great Britain and Northern Ireland, the Channel Islands and other Realms. Each title-holder shares with us the history that they embody. Their stories belong to each and every one us.

1 First Steps

from the early days to AD1150

BRITAIN'S CIVILIZATION developed from seeds that germinated in the disorder left by Rome's withdrawal at the onset of the 5th century. This disintegration of order and the tribal power struggles that followed were further stirred by the arrival of barbarian immigrants from the continent.

Power was the key to forming unity from anarchy. The leaders who emerged were mostly proven warriors who held sway for as long as they were victorious. This changed in the four centuries that followed as brawn gave way to statecraft, and a structure of kingdoms developed known as the Heptarchy. Kings demonstrated power by patronage, forming a loyal administration founded on the understanding that what was given could be taken away. The Heptarchic kingdoms developed systems for passing power from generation to generation, in which laws of heredity were justified by religion, and patronage was distributed with rights of inheritance. Land was divided into areas, called hundreds, and the Saxon kings appointed 'reeves' (administrators of land for the owner) to enforce their rule. Among them were shire reeves (sheriffs), who enforced the law and gathered revenues.

From around 789, the Anglo Saxon Chronicle records regular invasions of Viking warriors, who settled wherever they could land, particularly among the islands of Scotland and north-west England. The Isle of Man was one such strategic location, providing easy raiding access to the wealthy shores of England and Ireland. The Vikings who settled in the north-east of England were kept at bay by payment of the Danegeld, a punitive tax.

With the end of the time of chaos went the beliefs of the ancients. However, pre-pagan rituals, like saturnalia, were adopted by Christian missionaries, including the first Archbishop of Canterbury, who converted the Saxon courts. This brought about the elevation of children at Christian festivals, like the making of Boy Bishops. In Scotland, Ireland and Wales, Saints Columba, Patrick and David placed their indelible print upon subsequent offices.

The Heptarchy ultimately unified under the kings of Wessex and enshrined a democracy, albeit limited, in the Witenagemot, or council, that surrounded the King. St Dunstan, Archbishop of Canterbury, skilfully devised a coronation ceremony in 973 for Edgar, King of Wessex, that pleased both clerics and sheriffs. It remains essentially the same to this day, placing the king's authority subject to God, which was granted only with the Witen's will. The Church thrived, as did the sheriffs.

The influence of feudal government touched everything. It was this, and England's agrarian riches, that William, Duke of Normandy, won by conquest in 1066. The Conqueror ensured that the Witen approved his claim to the throne, and that Dunstan's ritual was used at his coronation. He then used feudal power to dominate a defeated people. All land was his, and was managed by others subject to his will and terms. Successful Norman knights were rewarded with manors and acreage, and in return they became responsible for enforcing William's laws, gathering his dues and providing whatever services he might demand. This duty was called sergeanty.

Government with reference to a council continued under Norman kings, though the Saxon magnates were soon 'cleansed' from the Witan, and Normans formed a new Curia Regis. The Byzantines had developed a feudal system of government distributing royal authority to great officers, and it was this that William I adopted. The Great Officers of State are still part of the constitutional arrangements in both England and Scotland.

The English Great Officers included the Lord High Steward, the Lord High Chancellor, a secretary in Norman times, and the Marshal. The latter, originally right-hand man to the Constable in handling military matters, is now Earl Marshal and remains the architect for England's greatest State occasions. Then there is the Chamberlain, who looked after personal administration, and the Almoner, who passed on the monarch's obligatory largesse. All these roles survive, though it is only at coronations that the title-holders are gathered together. They ensure that the monarch to be crowned is the selection of the country, according to law, and after the crowning they 'lift' the Sovereign into the Throne: the symbolic moment when possession is taken of the kingdom.

Under the Normans, forests, common ground in Saxon times, became private playgrounds for the king and his nobles, and wardens were appointed for forests like Savernake to enforce unique Forest Laws. Norman knights expropriated further territory; when the treaty with Wales expired, the

small, mountainous principality was also ripe for conquest, and the king supported the Marcher Barons in their quest to seize power and wealth in new territory.

The Saxons and Normans in these first steps unified the land under one system of effective royal government. To develop and administer the country, they established appointments whose holders derived their authority and their titular names from the land itself. Agricultural revenue was organized so that it passed from the peasant farmer up through a chain of tenants to the king. Just as the Conqueror's feudalism used great officers to govern the kingdom, so a similar grouping of officers was employed at every level down to the manor: a system that was to be the norm for seven centuries.

The evolution of power from the hands of many leaders into those of a single king followed a predictable path. Supremacy was attained gradually by treaty, defeat and consent. The process depended upon loyalty, and rested upon the need for legitimate status and continuity. This right to wield power was considered ultimately to come, through religious ceremonies, from God; and the motto of the British monarch, 'Dieu et mon Droit', 'God and my right', still echoes this idea today.

There have been many and various influences on life in Britain, and some of the rituals associated with them continue to this day. The Gorsedd stones of Parc Caergybi in Anglesey are called the 'altars of literature' and were once used as sacrificial altars by the ancient Druids. Amid these stones, the ARCHDRUID OF ANGLESEY, wearing a crown of laurel leaves and the blue sash of poetry or the green sash of music, continues to lead his fellow Bards in a celebration of Welsh culture.

Opposite: THE SOVEREIGN,
*with the Symbols of
Sovereignty (see pages 2
and 4), wears the thick
embroidered Robe of State,
made for the Coronation in
1953. The Diadem, which
was made for George IV to
wear before his crowning in
1821, comprises rose, thistle
and shamrock badges of
England, Scotland and
Ireland between Crosses.
The Collar of the Order of
the Garter, tied at the
shoulders, is made up of
roses within buckled Garters
alternating with golden
double lovers knots, from
which England's patron
saint, St George, is depicted
slaying the dragon. Queen
Victoria received the necklace as a gift during her
Golden Jubilee in 1887
from the 'Women of the
British Empire'.*

BRITAIN'S MONARCHY sparked from the
smouldering ruins of Rome's empire, which
had reached into the British Isles but never
conquered them all. During the Roman Empire's
decline, opportunities to attack the islands were
seized by barbarian tribes from the German plains.
Roman legions were unable to hold back these
warrior hordes and were forced to retreat, leaving
Britain in 409 to be picked over by an unending
stream of invaders, including Picts, Scots, Attacotti,
Franks, Jutes and Saxons. One such invasion force,
a group of Saxons led by Cerdic, landed on
Hampshire's coast in 495. Cerdic founded the
kingdom of the West Saxons, or Wessex, in 519 and
his direct descendant, Elizabeth II, continues the
unbroken line of succession that he established: a
line that follows the evolution of kingship from
warrior chief to constitutional figurehead. The
changes in fortune that affected this line of
succession over more than a thousand years can be
read in the titles that each ruler held.

Cerdic, like many rulers from the continent,
claimed his own legitimacy as King of Wessex by
descent from his eight times great-grandfather, the
God-king, Woden. Without this genealogy, pagan
society might have had little reason to respect one
man in preference over another outside the fact
that the order of precedence in this anarchy was
hammered out by brawn and military prowess.
Britain's invading tribes fought for their destiny
against the ancient Britons, whose reputed 5th-
century king, Coel the Old, is also numbered among
The Queen's ancestors. A nursery rhyme recalls that
he was 'a merry old soul and a merry old soul was
he'. Bardic genealogy declared Coel the descendant
of another god-king, called Beli Mawr, associated
with the Druids' Beltane, or May Day festival, which
is still a public holiday. At about the same time, the

Pictish king, Fergus the Great, ruled Albany, now
known as Scotland. He is a predecessor of Elizabeth
II through the Picts' favoured system of matriarchal
descent, a tradition that the Scots have always
recognised and respected.

For most of the second half of the first
millennium AD, Angle Land, or England, was
divided into a number of small kingdoms known as
the Heptarchy: similar divisions existed in other
parts of these islands. Christian missionaries
converted their monarchs by offering to replace
legitimacy, based on descent from Woden, with that
offered by the sacrament of unction. With Holy Oil,
the Sovereign, or supreme ruler, was anointed as
God's vicegerent on earth, just as Zadok the priest
and Nathan the prophet had anointed Solomon as
king in the Bible. Missionaries also confirmed a
genealogy, recorded in the Anglo Saxon Chronicle
around the year 840, that extends the line of royal
descent a further fifteen generations back beyond
Woden to Sceaf, the son of Noah and thence to
'Adam the first man and our Father, that is Christ,
Amen'. It was brilliant spin because it offered a more
venerable status and made regicide, killing the
anointed king, a sin. One consequence was that the
church in Rome gained influence over the titles
claimed by English kings.

Offa, King of the Mercians in the 8th century,
was the first monarch to claim all England under his
rule, as *Rex Totius Anglorum Patriae*. But Wessex
was flourishing at this time and in 973 St Dunstan
crowned its king, Edgar the Peaceable, as Emperor
of Britain, in a coronation ritual which has remained
broadly unchanged since and which was the basis of
that used for Elizabeth II. The Normans grasped
Saxon rituals to give their conquest of England
legitimacy in 1066. William I was crowned on
Christmas Day in Edward the Confessor's new

The Sovereign

Opposite: *Parliament gathers to hear The Queen's Speech from the Throne each year, in which* THE SOVEREIGN, *wearing the Imperial State Crown and surrounded by other symbols of Sovereignty, her Court and diplomats, spells out the reasons for which she has assembled the Lords and Commons. She sits beneath the Cloth of Estate, a canopy behind the Throne that displays heraldic symbols of the Realm. Following the results of each General Election, the monarch entrusts her executive power to Ministers, who form Her Majesty's Government: they draft the speech from policy placed before the Electorate.*

abbey at Westminster, setting a precedent followed ever since. He styled himself *Willelmus Rex Anglorum* and his son prefixed this title with *Dei Gratia*, by grace of God, perhaps to add legitimacy to the conquest. Other medieval kings added to this with the dukedoms of Normandy and Aquitaine, as the vastness of possessions accumulated by Henry II and his wife Eleanor of Aquitaine made England the mere backyard of the Angevin Empire. Most of these territories were lost in a single generation by their son John 'Lackland' who, perhaps to make up for his losses, was the first to add lordship over Ireland to his title.

Edward I may have been nicknamed Scotorum Malleus, or Hammer of the Scots, but he never completely conquered the country. It was in Wales that his knights and a necklace of massive castles brought him success, with an end to the ancient line of Welsh princes. Edward's wife, Eleanor of Castile, produced a son at Caernarfon Castle in 1284 who was subsequently created Prince of Wales, beginning a new tradition. But since then the blood of the displaced princes, including Llewellyn the Great,

has found its way back into the genealogies of British sovereigns.

Edward III claimed France by inheritance through his mother, Isabella, who was the daughter of King Philip the Fair of France. The French fleurs-de-lis were added to the three lions of England on his coat of arms and he was proclaimed as *Rex Angliae et Franciae*. He also laid claim to the blue livery of France by dressing his new Knights of the Garter in dark blue robes. His claim to France led to the Hundred Years War and shaped England's diplomacy in Europe for generations. Even when the claim was technically made good by victory, at Agincourt in 1415, it was lost again within a generation. Despite this, the titular claim endured.

The Pope gave Henry VIII the suffix *Fidei Defensor*, or Defender of the Faith, for writing a polemic against Luther. The title, intended for Henry alone, was retained in a deliberate display of irony against the superiority of Rome by his successors. Following his marriage to Anne Boleyn, Henry made it treason not to recognise him as 'of the Church of England and also of Ireland, on Earth

Here Edgar was (of Angles wielder!) with mickle pomp to king yhallowed in the old borough Acheman's-chester, but those that dwell there in other word Bath name it. There was bliss mickle on that happy day caused to all which sons of men name and call Pentecost-day. There was of priests a heap, of monks much crowd, I understand, of wise ones gathered. And then was gone ten hundred winters told of rime (number) from the birth-tide of the illustrious king, the Lord of Light, but that there left then yet was of winter-tale, as writings say, seven and twenty; so nigh then was of the Lord of Glory a thousand run when this befell. And Edmund's son had nine and twenty (brave man of deeds!) winters in world when this took place: and in the thirtieth was hallowed king.

THE ANGLO-SAXON CHRONICLE

the Supreme Head' and he elevated Ireland to a kingdom in his title. This list of kingdoms was made complete in 1603, when Elizabeth I died and James, the King of Scots, came south to claim his cousin's titles in what was described as the Union of the Crowns. For the sake of uniformity, the ancient Scottish title was changed from 'of Scots' to 'of Scotland', thus ending a tradition which reflected that these monarchs were of people and not of land. Cohesion was achieved with the Act of Union between England and Scotland in 1707. For the first time since Edgar the Peaceable a head of state, Queen Anne, was described as monarch of Britain. In 1801 empty claims to France and Aquitaine were finally dropped, when the union of kingdoms was extended to include Ireland.

The growing Empire enabled Disraeli to persuade Parliament to create Queen Victoria Empress of India in 1876; a title that was dropped at India's independence in 1947. In 1927, following Ireland's division by Home Rule, Imperial possessions were re-defined when George V was styled king of 'the British Dominions beyond the Seas'. As the Empire dissolved, its affiliation was maintained through the formation of the Commonwealth of Nations, of which George VI was titled as Head. This family of former colonies, which ranged from independent republics, like India and Pakistan, to the self-governing realms that held the king still as their Head of State, was oddly named. 'Commonwealth' still echoed the Civil War, when Oliver Cromwell removed both crown and head from the anointed monarch in 1649, making himself Lord Protector of the Commonwealth.

When she inherited her father's crown in February 1952, Elizabeth II's titles were reorganised so as to reflect that she was individually Queen of many different nations: for instance Queen of Australia, of New Zealand and of Canada, countries that no longer have any constitutional ties with the United Kingdom. Therefore, while many countries each possess their own title for her, in Britain the coins still spell out the titles of Cerdic's successor as 'Elizabeth II.D·G·REG·F·D', representing *dei gratia regina fidei defensor*, or by grace of God, Queen, Defender of the Faith. Further changes may come as a response to devolution. At the opening of Scotland's new Parliament in 1999, the Presiding Officer hinted at restoration of the traditional title, Queen of Scots. It would be just another step in the path by which the title seeks to adapt in order to reflect changing needs. The role of the Sovereign is to serve the title and thereby to serve both the people and the constitution.

THE ABBEY TOWN of Bury St Edmunds grew up around the legend of a local saint and national hero, Edmund. An early king of East Anglia, Edmund was a pious but short-lived ruler, whose peaceful reign and virtuous life were cut short in 869 by marauding Danes. Although the English put up a valiant defence, they were outnumbered. Edmund was captured and, after refusing to renounce his faith or submit to his captors, was shot with arrows and beheaded.

His life and death bore all the hallmarks of medieval sainthood – tried and tested virtue, martyrdom and miracles. Immediately after his death, his severed head, which had been tossed into a thicket, called out in Latin 'Here, here', until it was found and restored to its body. More miracles followed at his graveside: the sick were healed, the wronged righted and the evil punished. Before long, the saint's body was uprooted from the site of his martyrdom and ceremonially buried closer to the living in the nearby town of Beodricesworth, later named Saint Edmundsbury.

News of the sainted King's virtuous life and miraculous death spread through Christendom. His shrine drew the faithful from far and wide. Medieval pilgrims would often embark on tortuous and treacherous pilgrimage trails, seeking salvation, enlightenment and miracle cures. The main attraction at every pilgrimage site were holy relics – saintly remains – often just glimpsed through peepholes in a priceless reliquary. Far from being ghoulish trophies or sentimental keepsakes, relics were powerful talismans, charged with sacred charisma, with the saint's virtu, or holy power to work magic and change lives.

Venerated pilgrimage sites like Bury went from strength to strength, attracting gifts from rich and poor. Donors gave sincerely, but also in a clear-sighted bid for salvation. Alms were part of holy currency – a good deed on Earth accrued interest in heaven. Religious donations also paid for the monks' devoted prayers – almost a guarantee of salvation. Small wonder, then, that the shrine of the sainted King should attract generous donations from great and royal patrons. King Cnut built a splendid Benedictine abbey in 1020, which in 1044 attracted another royal patron, Edward the Confessor, soon to be sainted himself. He helped house and support the brethren of the shrine by offering the royal manor of Mildenhall and a large liberty, or plot of freehold land. A generous gift, it covered eight and a half hundreds, or hides, so-called because 100 families were meant to live on one hide.

The abbey grew in fame and fortune, inspiring reverence and patronage even from unlikely royal patrons, such as the Norman invader, William I, who took a special interest in the Abbey, partly due to his regard for the able Abbot Baldwin. Not only did William think to appoint a Steward to look after the liberty, he also paid for his services by providing the royal manors of Lidgate and Blunham. After the first Steward, named Ralph, the title passed through various hands, becoming hereditary with the De Windsors in 1115. The office passed to various distinguished local families – the Hastings in the 13th century and the Howards in the 16th. A powerful Roman Catholic family, the Howards fell from grace in 1688 when James II was ousted by his Protestant son-in-law, William of Orange. Having lost the power to hold office, the family was forced to sell to Thomas, Lord Jermyn. Passed down the line, the office finally came to rest with the Herveys, Marquesses of Bristol who inherited in 1806. A local family, with deep roots in the area, the Herveys seem well placed to keep the ancient office and guard the hallowed ground of Bury's much-loved saint.

Opposite: The HEREDITARY HIGH STEWARD OF THE LIBERTY OF ST EDMUND holds a cartulary, containing copies of grants made by various kings and popes to the Abbey of St Edmund, which is undated but probably comes from c. 1350–1375. He stands beside two of the four crossing piers that once supported the tower of the abbey, begun in 1080 by Abbot Baldwin, at Bury St Edmunds in Suffolk. This is where St Edmund's body was enshrined; the fame and wealth this earned for the monastery led to special privileges from the Crown, including a 'liberty', jurisdiction over which his family has held stewardship for nearly two centuries, even though the ancient responsibilities have long since ceased.

Hereditary High Steward of the Liberty of St Edmund

SINCE ITS SAXON BEGINNINGS and into the 21st century, knighthood has maintained its cachet perhaps more than any other honour. Almost every child has heard about brave knights risking danger in pursuit of good – an image that evolved centuries ago from the Christian ideal of chivalry. Film, books and hearsay continue to underpin this romantic culture while the appointment is still used to reward modern merit.

The first Saxon Cnyhts [sic] were probably just young attendants in a large household because this is what the word derived from. The description evolved to define a man proved in the profession of arms and sworn to follow his master into battle. William of Malmesbury recorded the occasion when Alfred the Great knighted his grandson, the future king Athelstan, probably at Winchester: 'He had made him a knight unusually early, giving him a scarlet cloak, a belt studded with diamonds, and a Saxon sword with a golden scabbard'. The ritual involved became more elaborate with religious overtones – the candidate was required to fast and pray in order to purify his soul. Dubbing, or striking, of the shoulder with the flat of the sword blade was the symbolic gesture of affirmation that followed the vigil. This was sometimes called the 'accolade', which possibly derives from the embrace following the dubbing, and could be performed by priests, other knights or their ladies. Nowadays, the State controls the honour tightly and only The Queen, or someone appointed by her, can give the accolade.

The Crusaders who fought in the Holy Land tried to conduct their lives well. Sin and its punishment weighed heavily upon otherwise fearless minds and gave life to the Age of Chivalry. The hardy warrior lived by the rules of courtly conduct and sought also to be a gentle Christian. Chivalry was the source of romance at a time when almost everything else lacked grace. Chivalrous knights looked back into history for affirmation and found it in the legend of the mythical king Arthur.

In the fourteenth and fifteenth centuries two forms of knight took to the battlefield. The most junior rank, who earned their spurs by proving their ability in the skills of warfare, were created Knights Bachelor (a corruption of the Latin battalia, the exercises performed by soldiers), either immediately before or after a battle. They were given a triangular flag, or pennon, with two points in the fly and served under the command of a great Lord, as part of knight service. Sometimes, valiant knights were promoted on the battlefield: the points of their pennon were cut off and they became Knights Banneret, a title that ceased before the Reformation.

Knight Bachelor is now the most junior level of knighthood, a rank that is unique in that it remains exclusively male. In 1908 a voluntary society was formed to serve and protect their interests. The Imperial Society of Knights Bachelor is responsible for obtaining the uniform registration of every created knight and for maintaining the Register of Knights Bachelor. A Register of knights exists dating from the reign of James I, into which every knight given the accolade was entered, though it is thought the earliest registers date back to the 1250s. The roll of honour has included many illustrious names over the years including Francis Drake, Walter Raleigh and Christopher Wren. Knighthood still has an important place in modern culture, though many of today's recipients of the accolade are from the world of theatre and film. Sean Connery, the legendary James Bond actor, was fittingly knighted in the year 2000, thus fulfilling both the childhood image of knighthood and the contemporary view of achievement.

Opposite: Alfred the Great is supposed to have dubbed the first knight at Winchester, Hampshire, where this Great Hall of the old royal castle still houses Edward III's Round Table. At that time, the city was capital of Alfred's kingdom of Wessex. Henry VIII painted the table with the names of Arthur's mythical knights. Wearing robes of the Council, the REGISTRAR OF THE IMPERIAL SOCIETY OF KNIGHTS BACHELOR *carries the latest volume of the Register, which contains the names of all Knights dubbed during the last few decades, and the Sword of the Imperial Society, called 'Chivalry'. Around his neck hangs the badge of a Knight Bachelor.*

Registrar of the Imperial Society of Knights Bachelor

'Let a man humble himself till he is like this child, and he will be the greatest in the kingdom of Heaven.'

JESUS CHRIST

The Episcopal vestments, which have evolved from the symbols of Byzantium, – mitre (a hat designed to symbolize the Holy Spirit's tongues of fire), crozier (a shepherd's crook for guiding believers), pectoral cross and cope – are given to the BOY BISHOP *in Hereford Cathedral during his brief incumbency. Sitting upon a small cathedra, or Bishop's throne, the boy delivers his sermon on the Feast of St Nicholas. Behind is the tomb of a previous Lord Bishop.*

THE SUPREME sanctity and innocence of childhood is one of the central tenets of Christian philosophy. When Christ was asked by his disciples, 'Who is the greatest in the kingdom of heaven?' he called a child to his side and explained that unless they became like children they could not even enter its gates. Christ's birth was itself marred by the jealous rage of King Herod the Great, who ordered the massacre of all the young children in Bethlehem. Those murdered children became the Church's first martyrs, and the Feast of the Holy Innocents, as they were called, came to be celebrated soon after Christmas every year, on 28 December.

On Holy Innocents' Day during the Middle Ages, the Church did much to symbolically elevate children, drawing precedent from the pagan rites embodied in the ancient Saturnalia of pre-Christian Rome. From the 13th century onwards it became customary for cathedral choristers to select one from their number to be appointed *Episcopus Puerorum* (Boy Bishop), also known as Bishop of the Choristers or Bishop of the Innocents.

The Boy Bishop was nominated on 6 December, the Feast of St Nicholas. A period of theological preparation then took place until the Feast of the Holy Innocents, when the real Bishop handed over his pastoral staff to the child and installed him in the cathedra (bishop's throne). The Boy Bishop, assisted by two chorister Deacons, would preach a sermon, bless the people, then lead all the choristers around the cathedral close, singing carols to the priests for a reward of food or money. It is believed that this established the tradition of carol singers going from door to door.

During the Reformation, this tradition of elevating the Innocent over his Episcopal master was thought to be demeaning to God and was therefore banned. Henry VIII's daughter, Mary I,

removed the restriction, but it was reimposed during the reign of Elizabeth I. Only under Elizabeth II was it to be lifted on a more permanent basis.

In December 1973, a Gift Service was held at Hereford Cathedral for the Church of England's Children's Society. To mark the event, the cathedral's staff reached back into history and revived the appointment of a Boy Bishop, thus turning the clock back to the years before Henry VIII's reign.

The following year, John Eastaugh was appointed Lord Bishop of the diocese. Much taken with the idea of symbolically handing over his powers to a child, he proposed an annual appointment of Boy Bishop from among the cathedral's choristers, an idea that received support from the Dean and Chapter. Ten years later, ancient ceremonies last exercised in Tudor times were dusted down and the ritual took root. But it was in 1986, when the Royal Mail issued Christmas stamps depicting Hereford's Boy Bishop, that the appointment really came to the attention of the public, seemingly capturing the magic that marks Christmas while providing a colourful service full of symbolic meaning.

The revival of this ancient tradition has added a new poignancy to Christmas at Hereford. At Evensong on the Feast of St Nicholas, a procession of candle-carrying choristers leads the Boy Bishop into the cathedral. The Lord Bishop hands over his crozier, relinquishing his authority to the child. To the words 'He hath put down the mighty from their seat: and hath exalted the humble and meek,' the Boy Bishop is installed in the Lord Bishop's throne, before blessing the people. Powerful and moving, the ceremony is a lesson in humility to all who witness it, and is a profound expression of the fragile nobility and wisdom of innocence.

Boy Bishop of Hereford

IN THE 19TH CENTURY, archers of the Lord
Paramount of Holderness gathered at
Flamborough Head on Bridlington Bay in Yorkshire
and, for the last time, fired golden coins into the
North Sea. Legend has it that the Lord of the Manor
had once observed this custom every year, in order
symbolically to ward off the return of the Danes. As
he fired an arrow carrying this payment into the sea,
he is supposed to have uttered the words, 'If there be
a King of Denmark, this is our sign of loyalty.'

Such a ritual, if indeed it took place, demonstrates
the fear the Viking raids instilled over centuries in
the men and women who lived on England's east coast.
By 867 the Danes had established their rule over a
large area of north and east England that became
known, to the retreating Saxons, as the Danelaw. The
coins the arrows carried represented Danegeld, a tax
levied by the Anglo-Saxon kings from 868 to buy off
the Danes. The Danegeld was raised again by Alfred
the Great in 871 and regularized some hundred years
later by Ethelred II, known as 'the Unready'.

By the time the Danish ruler Canute was elected
king of England at Southampton in 1016, the
Danegeld no longer seemed necessary. Until 1163,
however, it continued to be periodically levied, to
raise funds for military campaigns. Indeed, it was in
order to collect this tax that William the Conqueror
compiled the Domesday Book. The Danelaw ceased
to exist soon after the Norman Conquest. However,
the unique administrative system introduced by the
Danes, which divided shires into thirds, or *ridings*,
and replaced Saxon *hundreds* with *wapentakes*,
survived until relatively recent times. Danish
customs from this region also survive and the jury
system arguably evolved from Danish practice.

The first Lord of Holderness was a beneficiary of
the Norman Conquest. In the north of England
discontent with Norman rule erupted into rebellion.

William resolutely put down this uprising and
redistributed the region's Danelaw land to his
friends. Among them was a Fleming named Drogo
de la Beuvriere, who was married to William's niece.
In 1071 Drogo was granted the lordship of the
manor Holderness, on the peninsula between the
River Hull and Bridlington Bay.

This rich prize was large enough to be subdivided
into a number of lesser lordships, as a result of which
the Lord of Holderness came to be described as Lord
Paramount, in order to reflect his status of overlord.
In return for the grant of this feu, William expected
Drogo to provide him with 350 archers, mounted
and on foot, whenever they were needed and to
supervise the gathering of taxes. Unfortunately
Drogo was no model friend to his king. Not only did
he kill his wife – possibly by accident – but he also
embezzled money. Fearing the king's wrath, he
escaped to the continent before William realised what
had happened. In 1086 the lordship was granted to
the king's brother-in-law, Odo of Champagne. The
title passed through various families until, in the
17th century, Charles II granted it to an ancestor of
the Constable family, who still hold it.

At its height Holderness was virtually a palatine,
with its own courts, sheriff and coroner. The Lord
Paramount was supreme within his demesne,
receiving dues from all the lesser lordships. His
courts had franchises over all shipwrecks, yielding a
considerable income from the treacherous local seas,
which are sprinkled liberally with the wreckage of
vessels ancient and modern. With the motive of
protecting such power, it is understandable that an
early holder of the title might have instituted the
superstitious custom of firing a coin of Danegeld
into the sea – because no Lord Paramount would
relish even the possibility of Viking longboats once
more rounding Flamborough Head.

Lord Paramount of Holderness

The LORD PARAMOUNT OF
HOLDERNESS *(left) gives a
golden coin to the Deputy
Warden of the Burton
Constable Company of
Bowmen for his men to fire*
*into the North Sea from
Flamborough Head as
Danegeld. This lapsed but
supposedly ancient custom
was probably intended to
keep the Danes away.*
*Flamborough Head was
named after an Anglo-
Saxon called Flein, who
built a fort here before the
Viking conquest in 867.*

WHEN SIR WINSTON CHURCHILL was appointed Lord Warden of the Cinque Ports in 1941, in the dark days of World War II, Britain was facing invasion. As the country's resolute wartime prime minister, Churchill was a wise choice by King George VI for this most ancient appointment, established to coordinate the defence of England's vulnerable south-east coast. *The Times* of the day commented, *'to this august tradition of Keeper of the Gates of England and Watcher of the English Seas, Mr Churchill now succeeds ... As the dauntless leader of the Nation in the moment of its greatest peril he can wear the symbolic dignity as no other man can do.'*

The threat of invasion then was as dangerous as ever the medieval monarchs had faced; on a clear day, German troops could be seen assembling on the French shore, just twenty-one miles away. For an island that sees itself as a fortress, the narrow Straits of Dover have always been a vulnerable point. With the disconcerting precedent of the Norman invasion of 1066, in which the Conqueror had gambled successfully on a favourable wind and an unopposed landing, the sea defences and a tireless Royal Navy were all that stood between Hitler and the coast of Britain. Along the shoreline, a thicket of barbed wire, navigation obstacles and thousands of vigilant sentries were a first line of defence.

As the name suggests, the Cinque Ports originally formed a group of five – *cinq* in French, which in this case the English pronounce 'sink'. They were a creation of military logic whose foundation predates any records, though the original five ports – from west to east, Hastings, Romney, Hythe, Dover and Sandwich – are described in an extant Charter of Edward I as existing as a federation back in the reign of Edward the Confessor. Collectively these ports were known

Lord Warden of the Cinque Ports, Constable of Dover Castle and Admiral of the Cinque Ports
(Overleaf) Admiralty Judge of the Cinque Ports

Cannon placed on the battlements of Walmer Castle, near Deal in Kent, look out across the English Channel towards France. This was once part of England's most secure line of defence against attack from the Continent. It was one of the fortresses built by Henry VIII to bolster the ancient Cinque Ports. Today, it remains the official residence of the LORD WARDEN OF THE CINQUE PORTS, who is also Constable of Dover Castle and Admiral of the Cinque Ports. The Silver Oar, the symbol of her centuries-old jurisdiction, is engraved with her special cipher. She wears a brooch, showing the Lord Warden's Oar within a golden chain.

as the 'head'; by the 14th century Winchelsea and Rye had also joined them. Meanwhile over thirty other ports became 'limbs', each associated with a particular head port, and often at some distance. For example, Brightlingsea (north of the Thames, in Essex), Sarre (north Kent) and Fordwich (well inland, on the River Stour) were Sandwich Limbs – and each year their Mayor Deputies still pay token 'Ship Money' to the Mayor of Sandwich.

Dover was, logically, the senior bastion of the Cinque Ports. Ever since the Romans made use of Dover – or Dubris, as they called it – as the fulcrum for their communication with the Continent, its geography has been seen as both convenient and impregnable. The lighthouse that the Romans built to guide their galleys still rises up within the walls of Dover Castle. The first fort to be built here was a Saxon one in the 4th century. Taking advantage of the massive 375-ft high white chalk cliffs, it was an ideal position for defence.

The first Constable of Dover Castle was Godwin, Earl of Kent, who was appointed in the 1050s. By the year of the Norman Conquest, 1066, King Harold II was Constable. In that year, three more Normans followed in the appointment: Bertram de Ashburnham, then William Peveril, and finally Odo, the Bishop of Bayeux and the Earl of Kent. A century later, in 1170, Henry II built a vast keep in the centre of the castle, which still stands today. It was evidence of the Normans' commitment that no further conquests would follow their own. It was also such a successful strategic location that Vice Admiral Sir Bertram Ramsay coordinated the evacuation of Dunkirk from its ramparts, while the town of Dover was the hub of military activity throughout the First and the Second World War.

There was no official navy during the medieval period, and the ships of the Cinque Ports effectively provided this service for the nation. According to a feudal agreement formalized in the 11th century, the Cinque Ports Confederation was expected to provide whatever ships and sailors the king needed for battle. Its vessels were used to carry knights and soldiers to war on the Continent, and, occasionally, were sailed towards enemy ships, lashed together so

that the combatants could fight it out on the open decks. In 1217, Hugh de Burgh led the Cinque Ports in defeating the French fleet at Sandwich, a victory that removed Prince Louis of France, who was then laying siege to Dover Castle. The Cinque Ports navy was so successful at controlling access to the south-east coast, and at generating revenue, that it became a law unto itself. Useful in war, it went on fighting in peace, in flagrant acts of piracy. By the 13th century it became imperative to place the confederation under formal authority. To achieve a strategic all-round defence, based at Dover, there had to be a coordinated policy under a single command.

Under a royal charter of 1278, a good feudal bargain was struck between the monarch and these towns. For their part, the Cinque Ports would generate harbour revenue for the national exchequer. They would also provide England's navy with ships and men to patrol the English Channel and secure the kingdom from invasion, and to convey armies to the Continent. This was a massive

Few of the titles, privileges and powers gathered by the Cinque Ports over the centuries have survived. One that has is the ADMIRALTY JUDGE *who still administers residual laws over maritime matters in the busy Channel. Dover was once a fortress against the French, but is now a principal link with the Continent. From its white cliffs the Judge has a commanding view and holds the symbolic silver oar, with the Lord Warden's cypher.*

commitment, which continued until the creation of a permanent navy in Tudor times. In return, the crown gave a degree of independence and considerable judicial privileges, along with the right to carry a canopy over the Sovereign at coronations – a role observed until the reign of George IV. Privileges granted included exemption from tax and tallage, along with such odd-sounding legal powers as 'soc and sac, tol and team, blodwit and fledwit, pillory, tumbril, infangentheof, outfangentheof, waives and strays, flotsam and jetsam and ligan' – in other words, extensive powers of local jurisdiction, of collecting taxes and tolls, the authority to try cases involving bloodshed, fugitives from justice and thieves, and the right to keep unclaimed goods, wreckage and salvage. The ports also acquired the right to hold a portmote, or parliament, to which came representative mayors from each of the original five and the two 'ancient towns' of Winchelsea and Rye.

The last time the Cinque Ports were active as a naval power in England's seafaring history was during the defeat of the Spanish Armada, in 1588, when Dover provided a ship manned by several hundred men to serve alongside others commanded by Sir Francis Drake.

Overall command of the Cinque Ports Confederation lay with the Lord Warden, a post established in 1268, who acted as a virtual palatine governor within his considerable domain. The Warden's appointment was combined with that of Constable of Dover Castle later that century, which further strengthened the monarch's control.

As Admiral of the Cinque Ports, the Warden also exercised full maritime jurisdiction. The coastline faces out over what has become in peacetime one of the busiest sea passages in the world, and some of the maritime laws of the ancient Cinque Ports still apply in this infamous sea lane. In the event of infringement or dispute, the Admiralty Judge of the Cinque Ports deals with the matter on behalf of the Lord Warden. Cases are still heard in the Cinque Ports' Court of Admiralty, which is extremely ancient, perhaps more so than England's High Court of Admiralty. The Court originally sat at Sandwich or in the chapel at Dover Castle, which itself survives from Saxon times, though it now finds space in a modern courtroom. Its office of Marshal – whose holder carried as symbol a silver oar – has now merged with that of Judge.

The nation's defence policy has long since ceased to rely upon the contribution of the Cinque Ports. Gradually the shape of the coast has changed, through erosion, flooding and the accumulation of silt. All of the seven head ports but Dover are now silted up; some are even inland now that the shore has shifted its position. Today the post of Lord Warden is only titular, but it is considered a distinguished honour and is conferred by the Sovereign for distinguished service to the Crown. There is an official residence at Walmer Castle, a fortress built by Henry VIII between Dover and Sandwich, and the Lord Warden still oversees Dover Castle as Constable.

The title has been borne by many great figures, including Winston Churchill. It seems doubly fitting that the Lord Warden appointed in 1978 was the Queen Mother, who, as a contemporary of Churchill, acted as Queen Consort to George VI throughout World War II. As she spends time each year at Walmer Castle, she perhaps remembers when the beaches below its walls were a thicket of barbed wire, watched over by vigilant troops guarding against invasion.

'A people which takes no pride in the noble achievements of remote ancestors will never achieve anything worthy to be remembered with pride by remote descendants.'

LORD MACAULAY

THE ANCIENT RULES state that the Dame de Rosel, who lives in the north-eastern corner of Jersey, like all the Seigneurs before her must be ready at any time to ride into the sea, up to her stirrups, in order to meet the Duke of Normandy's boat. She must then carry the Duke ashore, so that the ducal feet remain dry. Throughout the visit she must be available, at close quarters, and serve as Butler. Finally, when the stay is over, she must ride back into the surf and convey her overlord back to his boat.

This rule is a relic of the feudal system imposed so stringently following the Norman invasion. *Fiefs*, or areas of land, were granted to deserving knights, called Seigneurs, in return for services rendered to the overlord. Mostly these services amounted to providing the duke with trained knights on demand, delivering revenue and maintaining order. Failure to fulfil these obligations would render the land forfeit.

It was in the year 933 that the Channel Islands became part of Normandy. At that time, the barbarian northmen, or Normans, who had run amok through most of coastal Europe for four centuries, had only been recognised as legitimate settlers for 22 years. In a treaty between their chief, Rollo, and the king in France, Charles the Simple, the Dukedom of Normandy was established. Following an unsuccessful invasion by the neighbouring Bretons, a primitive treaty annexed the Channel Islands to the new Dukedom. The dukes of Normandy became kings of England in 1066 and the duchy all but disappeared in the 13th century. But the British Sovereign still reigns over the Channel Islands and is affectionately referred to there as 'Our Duke'. Thus a close relationship exists between Britain and the Channel Islands, through the person of a shared monarch, but the islands remain outside the United Kingdom.

Ducal visits to the Channel Islands have always been rare and they still are, by modern standards. When they took place in medieval times, the journey was made by boat over the shortest navigable distance. This meant landing on the island's eastern shore, which faces the mainland. There are no deep harbours here; instead the coastline is made up of shallow tidal bays with beaches and occasional outcrops of rock. Such conditions are not without danger, so it was quite sensible to have support waiting on the shore to give assistance, especially as the boat needed to be kept off the rocks and far enough away so as not to beach itself in a falling tide. The Seigneur of Rosel's servants would have kept a constant vigil over his shoreline and the sight of a boat flying the ducal banner would probably have triggered the community into action.

The name Rosel derives from the old French word *roseau*, meaning a reed, and was probably imported to Jersey by the first Norman settlers there. Ingram de Fourneaux was the first recorded Seigneur and for one and half centuries, it was held in fee by the Barentin family, after Henry III gave Drouet Barentin 10 *livres* of land and the manor in 1247. The Dame de Rosel's family, the Lemprières, came to the manor in 1376. This was when Raoul Lemprière was successful in petitioning Richard II for a special licence to leave Brittany and settle in Jersey. Most of the old feudal rules have been abolished, but a few rituals survive: when The Queen, as Duke, visits now, she arrives by plane, and at the bottom of the steps waits the Dame de Rosel who, as Butler, serves Duke Rollo's descendant.

Opposite: For more than a thousand years the Seigneurs de Rosel have been ready to gallop into the sea, up to their horse's girth and stirrups, in order to carry the visiting Duke of Normandy ashore from the ducal boat. Traditionally the vessel landed here, in Archirondel Bay, a favourite landing place for smugglers facing the shores of Normandy. The DAME DE ROSEL, *pictured here wearing the red heraldic banner with three golden eagles, has inherited this feudal duty from her ancestors.*

Dame de Rosel and Butler to the Duke of Normandy

I N AD 597, AROUND THE TIME that the history of the Anglo Saxon people was starting to take shape, St Augustine, with about 40 monks, arrived at Thanet in the south-east of England on a mission dispatched by Pope Gregory the Great. They faced a dangerous task, but at the court of Aethelbert of Kent the king's Frankish wife Bertha was a Christian and she made the monk from Rome welcome at the church of St Martin outside Canterbury.

The mission was successful and, that same year Augustine baptized the king and many of his people. In 601 a grateful Pope sent Augustine the Pallium, a simple scarf woven from lambs' wool that symbolized the Pascal lamb carried on the shoulders of the spiritual shepherd. It was also the symbol of his authority to act as Metropolitan over all the Christian churches in Britain. Augustine set up his cathedra, or episcopal seat, in Canterbury as the first archbishop. A marble cathedra, probably 13th century, still stands in the cathedral behind the high altar, and has been used to enthrone an uninterrupted line of successors to Augustine.

One of the most famous incumbents of the see was Thomas Becket. As a clerk in the household of Archbishop Theobald he was groomed for high office. In 1154 he was appointed Chancellor of England to assist the young King Henry II. Immediately they built a strong friendship. Thomas raised taxes for the king's wars in France and fought for him on the battlefield. Believing this loyalty was his forever, against the wishes of the cathedral monks Henry appointed Thomas to the see of Canterbury when it fell vacant in 1162, hoping that Thomas would work with him to reduce the Church's power and privileges. But the king was outmanoeuvred, as Thomas began to oppose him on a range of issues, including the demand to bring the Church courts under secular authority.

The king issued the Constitutions of Clarendon, which sought to assert secular law over the clergy, and to supervise their relationship with Rome. In 1164 he also brought charges against Thomas over his conduct when Chancellor. Thomas fled to France, hoping to gain papal support, returning in November 1170 with the dispute still unreconciled. A month later four knights, believing they would earn the king's favour, murdered the troublesome Archbishop in his cathedral as he was on his way to vespers.

The murder sanctified Thomas and strengthened the Church, in particular the see of Canterbury. Pope Alexander made Henry do penance at Becket's tomb. By the Accord of Winchester in 1172, whereas England's other archbishop, of York, would be Angliae primas (Primate of England), the Archbishop of Canterbury became *totius Angliae primus* (Primate of All England). Following Henry VIII's break with Rome in the 1530s, the monarch took over the role of the Pope in England. The new Church was anxious for effective leadership in difficult times, and it was Thomas Cranmer, as Archbishop of Canterbury, who played an important part in its reforms. Elizabeth I and her early Stuart successors recognised the importance of an episcopacy whose hierarchy they could control, and this too confirmed Canterbury's supremacy.

Today, membership of the worldwide Anglican communion still requires acknowledgement of Canterbury's position as 'first among equals', although some Anglicans from outside Britain challenge this because they feel excluded from the possibility of filling St Augustine's cathedra. In 2001 a new bishop, of Lambeth, was appointed to advise on this worldwide responsibility. The Archbishop presides over the Lambeth Conference, an assembly of Anglican Communion bishops held every 10 years.

The LORD ARCHBISHOP OF CANTERBURY kneels in front of St Augustine's throne at Canterbury Cathedral where he and most of his predecessors were enthroned. At his side lies a simple archiepiscopal crozier, or shepherd's crook. The desecrated shrine of St Thomas Becket stood where the Primate of All England prays. The grandeur of the principal cathedral in the Anglican Church has witnessed the religious troubles that have been the constant concern of 103 Archbishops of Canterbury.

Lord Archbishop of Canterbury and Primate of All England

The LORD HIGH
CHANCELLOR *is able to sit
in the Lords, even when he is
not a Peer , because he sits
on the Woolsack, which is
technically not part of the
Lords Chamber, at*

*Parliament in Westminster.
If he is a Peer and wishes to
speak in a debate he must
move from the Woolsack to
the top of the Earls' bench,
thereby reflecting his senior
position in the House. The*

*Mace is placed behind him,
as is the Great Seal in its
purse, which is his symbol of
office and authority from the
monarch. Queen Victoria's
throne and Cloth of Estate
provide the chamber's focus.*

BEHIND A TRELLIS IN THE COURTS of Ancient Rome sat a scribe, called the *Cancellarius*. Powerful, reforming but illiterate Norman kings needed secretaries, and appointed a *Cancellarius*, or Chancellor, to the job. From these humble beginnings, the appointment has become the highest-ranking secular office in Britain, responsible for issues affecting the Executive, the Legislature and the Judiciary of which the Lord Chancellor is head. Monarchs have always appointed their Chancellors, though since executive power moved from the Crown to Cabinet government, this choice has been made on the advice of the Prime Minister, who then takes precedence beneath the Lord Chancellor.

The advantage of literacy, a skill largely monopolized in medieval times by the Church, was that in a world of law driven by documents, reading and writing gave access to power. Saxon royalty legitimized its correspondence by using seals, a practice that William I continued. As these Great Seals were deposited with the Chancellor in his chancery, every important document passed under his gaze. His scrutiny became a formalized responsibility when he was named Keeper of the Great Seal. When a new Chancellor is appointed, his powers do not become effective until the Sovereign hands over the Great Seal. The new one, first used in 2001, follows tradition by being formed of two six-inch matrices, but for the first time no longer shows the monarch on horseback in impression.

Few appointments can boast three saints called Thomas. However, Henry II appointed his mentor and friend, Thomas Becket, as Chancellor in 1155 – the first Englishman to achieve high office under Norman rule. The other two were Thomas de Cantilupe, who served Henry III, and Thomas More, who, when Speaker, was celebrated for standing up for the rights of the House of Commons to his predecessor, Cardinal Wolsey. No Chancellor has probably ever wielded as much power as Wolsey did. But power so dependent on the whim of King Henry was not secure, and when Wolsey fell from favour, no appointment could save him.

Ironically, justice and its good administration have been the Chancellor's principal responsibilities ever since he issued writs on behalf of the king. Inevitably, responsibility for the administration of the courts followed, and consequently almost all Chancellors have had a good grounding in law. Most senior appointments in the judiciary have been made on the recommendation of the Lord Chancellor, and he is also responsible for introducing legislation concerning judicial reform. However, as it is vital for good government that Parliament and the judiciary remain separate, the role of an appointed and unelected Chancellor, holding executive power as head of the judiciary, is an accidental result of history, which must be vigilantly scrutinized.

As Keeper of the Royal Conscience, the Chancellor assumes the Sovereign's responsibilities for those unable to help themselves. One commentator describes his duties thus: '…visitor, in right of the king, of all hospitals and colleges of the king's foundation, and patron of all the king's livings…the general guardian of all infants, idiots and lunatics, and has the general superintendence of all charitable uses in the kingdom'. These responsibilities have now largely been farmed out to the courts.

It is in Parliament that the Lord Chancellor is most evident. He is Speaker of the Lords, but one who has little to do in a House that regulates itself. Every year during the State Opening of Parliament, reflecting that he was once the eyes and ears of the monarch in that place, it is the Chancellor who presents the Sovereign with her speech.

Lord High Chancellor of Great Britain, Keeper of the Great Seal, Keeper of the Royal Conscience and Speaker of the House of Lords

THE MANOR OF SCRIVELSBY COURT in Lincolnshire has been neither bought nor sold since it was given by William the Conqueror to his friend Robert Marmion after the Battle of Hastings in 1066. It remains in the hands of Marmion's descendants, but the house has changed a good deal. Nonetheless, it bears witness to one of the most romantic family stories in the kingdom.

From here, at most coronations and in order to fulfil the terms of the Conqueror's grant, knights have ridden as Royal Champions to Westminster, ready to stand and die for their king. In the words of the grant, written in Edward III's reign: 'The manour of Scrivelsby is holden by Grand Sergeanty, to wit, by the service of finding on the day of Coronation, an armed knight who shall prove by his body, if need be, that the King is true and rightful heir to the kingdom.'

Norman justice offered the bizarre appeal process of trial by combat, in which people could prove their innocence by felling a fully armed knight without appropriate weaponry. The dukes of Normandy made use of specially selected knights to stand in and do combat on their behalf, especially to challenge anyone doubting their right to rule. Robert Marmion had been that knight in Normandy, and, in the heady days following the defeat of Harold, the Conqueror offered him Scrivelsby on this condition. It was a challenge and Marmion accepted.

Surprisingly, no descendant of Marmion has ever been called to fight for his master. However, when the challenge was made at the coronation of George III in 1761, the crowd fell silent: rumours abounded that Bonnie Prince Charlie was in London and would do mortal combat with the Champion.

The Marmions grew strong with the benefit of Royal patronage and became powerful barons. Earl Philip Marmion was a staunch supporter of Henry

III throughout his troubled reign, but his demise meant confusion for the inheritance of the Marmions. The Earl produced only daughters, so the inheritance had to be divided, the eldest taking Tamworth as her dowry, while the younger retained the estate of Scrivelsby. She married Sir Thomas de Ludlow, and their grand-daughter's marriage to Sir John Dymoke in 1350 brought the Champion's duties to the Dymoke family, which still holds them to this day.

In return for putting their lives ceremonially on the line, Champions retained the estate of Scrivelsby and were given generous perquisites. They included a horse, 'the best but one' available from the Royal stable; a fine saddle, armour and furniture for the horse; a complete suit of armour for the Champion himself, including a shield and lance; 20 yards of crimson satin; and the gold cup and cover with which the Sovereign drank his health. Strictly, these gifts were only his if combat ensued but, as no King ever wanted a poorly turned-out Champion, no expense was spared on his knightly panoply or the caparisoning of his horse.

The last time a Dymoke was called on to answer a challenge to the king was in 1821, at the coronation banquet of George IV. The doors of Westminster Hall were opened and Dymoke, flanked by Great Officers of State, rode in to throw down his gauntlet. The Garter King of Arms read the challenge and this was repeated three times. The armour of Champion and horse worn on this occasion now stands as the principal feature in the restored St George's Hall at Windsor Castle.

Coronation banquets no longer take place in Westminster Hall, so neither does the Champion's ceremonial entry. Instead, for the last four coronations the Champion has carried the Union Flag or Banner of England.

The gauntlet on the lawn at Scrivelsby Court in Lincolnshire was last thrown down in 1821 to challenge any would-be detractors of George IV. The QUEEN'S CHAMPION no longer has to ride in armour to coronations and risk mortal combat for the monarch in order to keep his land; instead he has the privilege of attending and carrying the Union Flag.

Queen's Champion, Lord of the Manor of Scrivelsby

THE WORLD'S OLDEST PARLIAMENT in continuous use is on the Isle of Man's Tynwald Hill, off the north-west coast of England. Set on a high plateau, the mound is made up of four large ascending steps over what was probably a Bronze Age burial site. But, since the late 970s when Godred I was king, it has been a place of assembly where law is made and justice given out, while providing a forum for the Manx people to have their say.

'Tynwald' derives from a Norse word meaning 'parliament field', and the site's design is similar to that of a *thing-völlr* (law-hill), where Celtic chiefs were probably inaugurated according to the rite of tanistry, whereby power passed into a new chief when he stood over the burial site of former rulers.

Every 5 July, the Tynwald still assembles on the ancient hill by St John's Church. This gathering brings the Manx community together. The year's legislation is read out by the Deemsters (judges of ancient origin), and if any Act is not read out, it lapses immediately. Freemen look on while Coroners, Parish Captains, Members of the House of Keys and the Legislative Council gather to hear the promulgation.

There are three seats on the top level of Tynwald: the first is occupied by the Lieutenant Governor representing the Lord of Man (who, since 1765, has been the Sovereign); the second seat is the Lord Bishop's; and the third was added in 1990 for the President of Tynwald. This new appointment, decided by election, was created in response to the constitutional need both for a democratic representative of the people of Man and to separate the executive from the Sovereign's representative. Before the Crown bought the island and the Sovereign became Lord of Man, the Lordship was given in tenure. In token of his fealty he presented a cast (pair) of falcons at every monarch's coronation.

President of Tynwald and Lord Bishop of Sodor and Man

The Lord Bishop of Sodor and Man, who tends to the souls of this windswept tax haven, still holds the last remaining Viking barony. It is not known when the first bishop established the Cathedral of St Germain on the island. Legend suggests that St Patrick and other Celtic saints made visits in the 5th century, possibly they establishing a bishopric on Man. However, little evidence of Celtic life survived pagan Scandinavian invaders.

Viking raids caused havoc along the Scottish coast, as the Norsemen established territorial holds in Shetland and Orkney, which they called the Nordreys, and in the Hebrides, known as the Sudreys. Early in the 9th century Viking longboats beached on the shores of Man, which their men plundered and then settled. They established jurisdictions that evolved into eight feudal baronies, and the Barony of Jurby is still held by the Lord Bishop. This may be the oldest ex officio barony in the British Isles. It is the original source of his continuing right to membership of Tynwald's court.

Such power gave one medieval bishop authority to test the guilt of witches. He tied them to the keel of a boat and rowed them from Peel across the bay to St Patrick's Isle. It was a no-win situation for the victim: death proved innocence, while survival meant guilt, punishable by death.

Bishops on Man were subject to the archbishops of Trondheim, who created the diocese of Sodorensis and Mona. ('Sodorensis' derives from the old Norse kingdom of the Sudreys.) Even after the island was handed to Scotland in 1266, the ecclesiastical link with Norway was maintained: although Norway's authority has lapsed, relations are still friendly.

The Manx respond to criticism of the Tynwald by pointing out the stability it has given the island. As the records show, the names of its members have changed little over the centuries.

Opposite, left: Standing on the ancient Tynwald Hill, a mound that was cut into steps centuries ago and where the oldest parliament in the United Kingdom still meets, is the Senior Messenger. His case holds legislation that must be read out here before it can become law. The PRESIDENT OF TYNWALD, *who wears robes similar to those of the Lord Chancellor, is a relatively new appointment created to help the Isle of Man's parliament deal with 21st-century requirements.*

Opposite, right: St Germain's Cathedral on St Patrick's Isle near the town of Peel was once the seat of religious power in the Isle of Man. The island's Viking heritage is reflected in the BISHOP OF SODOR AND MAN's *title and in the ancient Viking barony he still holds.*

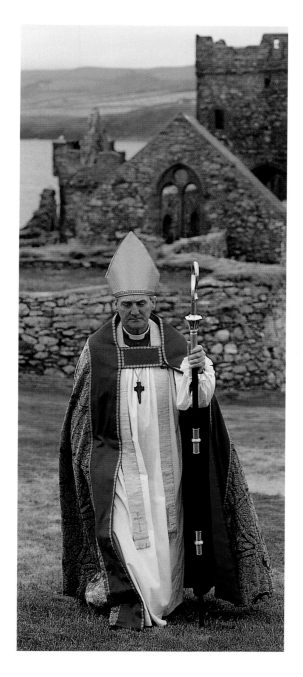

'I stole away to St John's, for to see one last time the ancient ceremonies of Tynwald Hill, and secretly to take from its lowest round, one little handful of that earth which has seen, maybe, and heard more history than any other spot on the island.'

THOMAS KELLY, 1827, BEFORE ECONOMIC DISTRESS DROVE HIM FROM THE ISLE OF MAN

ON THE OUTSKIRTS OF WINCHESTER is a thriving 12th-century welfare organization, perhaps Britain's first sheltered housing, certainly England's oldest almshouse.

The colossal Norman tower of the Hospital of St Cross rises above the lazy River Itchen. When Henry de Blois walked this riverbank in c.1133, he was not only Bishop of Winchester and Papal Legate, his half-brother was king and he was one of the country's wealthiest men. But England was enduring 'the Anarchy', and food was scarce. The legend goes that a milkmaid carrying a small child came into view, and, momentarily, he thought that they were a vision of the Madonna and Child. He was therefore attentive when she implored him to help her village. So, in the name of *Sancta Crux* (the Holy Cross), de Blois established the Hospital of St Cross to provide accommodation for 13 brethren, a number to match Christ and the 12 disciples. He appointed a Master to administer the endowment and provided resources to feed up to 100 poor people each day. The brethren (the Poor in Christ) lived out their days in security, with no further care than preparing their souls for the next life.

In the 12th century St Cross was administered by the Knights Hospitaller, and before every crusade knights would assemble and pray there. The brotherhood founded by de Blois therefore wear black gowns with silver crosses, from the arms of the Kingdom of Jerusalem, established during the crusades.

In 1445 a second brotherhood (the Brethren of Noble Poverty) was established. Its members wear dark red gowns and a silver badge engraved with the hat of their founder, Cardinal Beaufort. He was another wealthy Bishop of Winchester, closely connected with the Lancastrian Plantagenets, who wanted to provide for impoverished noblemen, particularly those in his own family.

The Master is no longer politically influential, and neither does wealth come with the appointment, but his domestic and pastoral responsibilities are unchanged. He administered payments from across the country, which included dolphins from Lincoln, and when the village of Twyford failed to pay up, the inhabitants were excommunicated. One notable royalist Master was forced to flee after Charles I's execution: his place was given to one of the King's judges, but he was reinstalled after the Restoration.

As a boy, Henry de Blois had entered the Cluniac Order. Cluniac monks believed in supporting travellers. To this day, all visitors to St Cross can ask for the Wayfarers' Dole which he instituted. This consists of beer and bread and is given to anyone who asks for it. Recipients find welcome and shelter in the medieval quadrangle as they drink their bitter beer, and the Brethren go peacefully about their business. Beyond the walls, the roar of the M3 motorway is audible. It beckons non-residents to move on, just as Jerusalem beckoned the Crusaders from this place of safety 800 years ago.

In the Brethren's Hall of the Hospital of St Cross, just outside Winchester, the MASTER OF ST CROSS is the head of this Norman almshouse where two brotherhoods are housed. Representative Brothers, *one from the ORDER OF NOBLE POVERTY (in red) and one from the HOSPITAL OF ST CROSS (in black), wear distinctive badges that have passed from brother to brother over the centuries.*

Master of St Cross, Brother of the Order of Noble Poverty and Brother of the Hospital of St Cross

The borders between legend and fact become increasingly blurred as the centuries unfold. Saxon history may benefit from having been recorded in the *Chronicles,* but little else remains of a period from which few parchments were adequately stored to survive the vicissitudes of fire and flood. In this vacuum, Ripon dates its antiquity from the gift of a Bugle Horn by Alfred the Great, King of Wessex, in 886. The meaning of 'bugle' has changed over the centuries, but in this instance (and originally) it meant 'wild oxen', the horns of these creatures being used to make the instruments. Although King Alfred's involvement is hard to prove, the Horn has survived. Like a witness whose testimony threatens to go either way, it could confirm or upset Ripon's claim to antiquity.

As the Horn is now extremely delicate, three others have been added over the years to the Hornblower's collection. They share a demanding schedule, with one being blown each evening at the four corners of the Market Place Obelisk and outside the Mayor's House. This signal commemorates the start of the Watch, an important responsibility undertaken by the Wakeman.

A Charter issued by James I in 1604 enshrined the need for a Hornblower and, perhaps foreseeing the potential risks the Wakeman might face, also gave provision for a Sergeant at Mace and two Stave Bearers to provide close protection.

The Charter specifically instructs the Wakeman, whose role has evolved into that of today's Mayor, that he 'shall cause a horn to be blown every night…at nine of the clock at the four corners of the cross… And if it happen any house or houses be broken…and any goods to be taken away…then according to old custom the Wakeman for the time

being shall make good.' Having to compensate from his own pocket anyone robbed during the night was a powerful incentive to ensure the night patrols were thorough.

It is worth remembering that civil obedience in the country at large during the 17th century was maintained by Sheriffs and other men-at-arms available for military duties. This system was seldom reliable, but for people living in the aftermath of the Reformation, the Charter made Ripon an attractive place. The promise of security at night and the benefit of insurance should the need arise helped the city develop. It was a reputation that helped attract a community, and it is a tradition that, despite the arrival of a nationwide police force, Ripon chooses to maintain. It may no longer do more than help the city and its police set their clocks, but it still attracts visitors who wish to feel part of an unbroken tradition.

The original Charter Horn is now a venerated object, its original form almost completely hidden by the protection of velvet and silver clasps, and it hangs from a baldric, or belt, covered in the emblems of earlier mayors. Nonetheless, it is carried before the Mayor when both are guarded by the Sergeant at Mace. Perhaps Ripon will take advantage of carbon-dating to discover how ancient its Horn really is. Few believe that the result would confirm an ox's death in 886. However, if it proved to be from that date, the 9th-century Charter and the legends surrounding one of England's oldest customs and appointments would take on renewed importance. In their wake further legends might take shape – perhaps even that Alfred the Great felled the animal himself. But history is no ally to Ripon here: it would seem that the king was busy fighting elsewhere that year.

Opposite: The baldric worn by the Sergeant at Mace, *who stands beside the obelisk in Ripon's Market Place, has 61 silver shields carrying the names of the city's mayors from 1570. From it hangs the Charter Horn supposedly presented to the town by Alfred the Great. The* Hornblower *uses a more recent instrument, as the original is now fragile.*

Sergeant at Mace and Hornblower of Ripon

In 1087 WILLIAM RUFUS reneged on his father's treaty with Rhys ap Tewdwr, the King of Deheubarth. This treaty had held the English border with Wales in peace because it kept the land-hungry Norman barons in check. But with Rhys dead, peace gave way to land grabbing violence. All along the Welsh border, from Chester down to the River Severn, the Normans advanced with small armies across the *Marchiae Walliae* (marches or boundaries of Wales). They deposed the Welsh rulers by sword or drove them into the hills. Their reward was land over which no English king had ever ruled, and consequently they owed no fealty to the Crown. Instead they held *Jura Regalia* (sovereign power) which was theirs by conquest.

One of the furthermost outposts grabbed in this way was Cemaes, one of the seven *cantrefs* (hundreds) of Dyfed. Taking its name from the Welsh *camas*, meaning 'river bend or sea inlet', it included the land around the town of Newport. The people here were well used to war and had endured Norse invasions before Norman ones. Wales itself endured a culture of domestic battles between rival princes. They had also heard tales of William I's recent progress, at the head of a vast army, to nearby St David's.

A Norman named Martin de Tours supposedly landed at Fishguard. The natives bombarded his ships with boulders as they lay at anchor, forcing him further east 'where the harbour was on the flat and safe from projectiles from above'. The King's Antiquary was sent to Wales in the 1530s to record the country's history: he wrote, 'one Martin de Turribus, a Norman, won the countrey of Kemmeys in Wales about the tyme of King William Conqueror, and that this Martinus foundid the abbey of S. Dogmael in Kemeis and that he lyith buried in the quier there'.

This was an endless saga for Cemaes, caught in the fray between Anglo-Norman and Welsh interests that, with the nationalism of the great Princes of Gwynedd in conflict with Norman and Plantagenet aggrandisement, could never be compatible. Cemaes was merged into the County of Pembroke, for a long time the possession of English kings.

It was not until 1536 that Henry VIII gave equal status to the Welsh under the Act of Union between England and Wales. The Act ended the independence of the Marcher Baronies, bringing them into the shires and creating new shires in the north. Cemaes was merged fully into Pembrokeshire, though the barony structure remained to administrate the community, as it did throughout England until councils took over.

William Owen, 14th Lord Marcher of Cemaes, was born in 1469 and lived to be 105. As a young man he did well in his legal training at the Temple and met up with Lord Audley, who made him 'Clerk of the courts of Cemaes for the rest of his life'. Audley had recently had the barony returned to him, was not much interested in it and was thus happy to offer it in security against a loan from Owen.

The Owen family still hold the Marcher Barony and considerable powers over its 22,000 acres. The Lady Marcher describes it as 'quite hard work in that we hold a Court Leet which meets three times a year in the Llwyngwair Arms pub, where it's met for hundreds of years. It deals with things like water, grazing, boundaries and travellers, and I always try to be there. Each member of the Court Leet still swears an oath of allegiance to me and The Queen, which dates from about 1400. Every November, I appoint the Mayor of Newport. The appointment is agreed between myself and the Court beforehand. At the Court Leet I place the chain of office round his neck and he gives me a red rose in fealty.'

Lady Marcher of Cemaes and Mayor of Newport

The river bend and sea inlet that gave Cemaes its name is now overlooked by the town of Newport on the west coast of Wales. From its castle the LADY MARCHER OF CEMAES can keep an eye on the community's affairs and choose the MAYOR OF NEWPORT from one of three names put forward by local people. She confirms her choice by giving the Mayoral Chain to her nominee. He gives her a red rose.

IF THE CONTENTS OF THE *Battle Abbey Roll* are to be believed, then Richard Estormit, or Esturmy, fought with William the Conqueror at Harold's defeat in 1066. By 1083, the *Exeter Book* shows him living in the area that the Saxons called the Wood of Savernoc. The Domesday Book describes him three years later as a servant of the king and occupying land which, in 1050, was owned by Aluric, who may have been warden or guardian of the forest. Whether the appointment came with Aluric's land or not, from this date until the family ran out of male heirs in 1427, the Esturmys are described as either Wardens or Chief Foresters of Savernake Forest.

Savernake, near Marlborough in Wiltshire, was subject to Forest Law and therefore exempt from Common Law. Its regular courts, or Eyres, required the attendance of the Warden. There he would receive, among other rents and fines, his equipage consisting of saddle, bridle, sword and horn. The 29th Warden said that, 'Today Richard Estormit's …saddle and bridle are dust: his sword is lost to us, and perhaps rusted away… It is, therefore, of peculiar interest to be able to see and handle the horn – "their great hunting horn, tipped with silver" – …which very possibly was Richard's own'. This horn is now in the British Museum. No longer will the Wardens be able to fulfil their ancient obligation 'to salute His Majesty with a blast of the Esturmy horn' whenever the Sovereign comes to Savernake. This practice derived from the traditional fanfare that began the hunt when the king arrived for a day of sport.

The Esturmys proved determined protectors of their royal masters' interests, particularly against the barons intent on deforestation. In 1225 Henry of Cluny and Thomas of Kennett attempted to take over royal land by Perambulation (walking a boundary to make a claim to land that falls within it). Within two years Geoffrey Esturmy had routed

their claim. However, the Forest Eyre of 1330 confirmed perambulations that reduced Savernake to 16 square miles.

The last Esturmy died in 1427, his inheritance and bailiwick passing through his daughter to the St Mawr (Seymour) family, who saw the forest contract further in the reigns of Edward IV and Henry VII. However, the family fortunes seemed set for recovery when a daughter of the family, Jane, became the favourite wife of Henry VIII. Her son, Edward VI, became a useful nephew for Edward Seymour, first Duke of Somerset, who appointed himself Lord Protector of the Realm, the apogee of the family's power.

In 1675, the 5th duke died. Knowing that this would make Elizabeth Seymour a wealthy heiress, the 20-year-old Thomas, Lord Bruce, made marriage with her his target. Perhaps surprisingly, this union was happy, and on moving into Tottenham House, Bruce's first act was to appoint a Seymour relative as Ranger of Savernake. In 1747, after spending time with his uncle at Tottenham, Thomas Brudenell inherited the estate and Wardenship.

The greatest achievement of this family inheritance is that it has managed to maintain an hereditary office for nearly a millennium when the Wardenship has always depended solely upon the good will of changing sovereigns. On the few occasions when individuals have slipped from favour, or possession has been vulnerable through minority, forgiveness or rescue was always forthcoming. In these situations responsibility was generally passed temporarily to the Constable of Marlborough. While today's Warden closes the gates for one day each year, to retain the legal independence of Savernake, for the rest of the year it is open to anyone who wishes to enjoy the ancient groves of the only forest in Britain that is still in private hands.

Hereditary Warden of Savernake Forest

In the beech wood at Savernake Forest, planted by Capability Brown, the WARDEN *blows a replica of the Esturmy Horn, which came over with his forebears and William the Conqueror in 1066.*

'When my father blew it for King George VI, he was standing inside the entrance hall at Tottenham House, and it was found afterwards that he had set all the dogs barking in Durley, a good half mile away!'

29TH HEREDITARY WARDEN OF SAVERNAKE FOREST, DESCRIBING THE ESTURMY HORN'S LAST ROYAL SALUTE

In 1119 A GROUP OF KNIGHTS undertook to protect pilgrims travelling to and from the newly conquered Holy Land. They gathered others into a religious community, calling themselves the Poor Fellow Soldiers of Jesus Christ, and took oaths of chastity, obedience and poverty, while dedicating their swords to the Patriarch of Jerusalem. Twenty years earlier, the First Crusade had captured the Holy City and established the Kingdom of Jerusalem. Its king, Baldwin II, gave the knights lodgings beside the mosque of al-Aksa, otherwise known as the Temple of Solomon, from which they took their name as the Knights Templar. They were one of the three great military Orders associated with the Crusades.

In the 12th century the Knights Templar in England established their base in an area of London now called the Temple. Here they constructed the Round Church on the model of the Holy Sepulchre in Jerusalem. It was consecrated by Patriarch Heraclius in 1185, probably in Henry II's presence. The international influence of the Knights Templar grew dramatically, and with it their wealth and their need of lawyers. By 1312, the Knights Templar fell from grace. They then became tenants of the Knights Hospitaller, who in turn came to an end with the Dissolution. As a result, in 1539, the Crown took back the freehold of the Temple, which finally became the lawyers' possession by grant of James I. However, several of its buildings were destroyed by the Great Fire of 1666.

When in 1207 Canon (Church) Law prevented the clergy – who had hitherto provided all educated legal practitioners – from undertaking temporal business, laymen were required to practise law in the secular courts. Magna Carta stipulated that the King's courts must be at Westminster, so a suitable place was needed to house, teach and administer the growing number of lawyers: Inns of Court provided the answer. Lawyers were trained, fed and lodged there as reward for their service. Two were established in the Temple, called the Inner and Middle Temples, and records show that both associations were operational by 1388.

The Inns of Court are incorporated companies, deriving their constitutions from precedent, in a manner similar to the Common Law they practise. The Benchers, sometimes known as the Masters, are the senior members of the company. Each year, they elect one of their number to be Master Treasurer and act as chairman of the governing body. Treasurers have held this position since the end of the 15th century. Both Temples are responsible for the ancient Round Church and its nave, an extension consecrated in the presence of Henry III in 1240.

The Round Church is a reminder of the Templars' ancient traditions, and its tombs stand as monuments to some of their greatest exponents. The somnolent black figures represent Knights of the Temple of Solomon and supporters of the order. Among them is William Marshal, the 1st Earl of Pembroke, whose surname derives from having shared the title of Marshal of England. His life is a phenomenal record of chivalry. Having at first supported Henry II, he was pardoned by his errant son King Richard I, then swore fealty to the Lionheart's brother, King John, and finally acted as regent to Henry III.

The principal ecclesiastic at the Round Church is called the Master of the Temple. He is appointed under letters patent from the Crown, which carry an implicit authority that all lawyers recognize. Similarly, the Knights Templar had no argument when Edward II's sheriffs arrived at the Temple to arrest their master in England, William de la Mare, on 9 January 1308.

Master Treasurer of the Inner Temple

The MASTER TREASURER OF THE INNER TEMPLE *is elected to chair his fellow Masters, or Benchers, for a year, and leads a legal community that has occupied London's Temple* since the Middle Ages. Much of the Temple's Round Church survived the air raids of the Second World War, though there was considerable damage. So also did the 13th-century figures on the tombs of Knights Templar, including that supposed to portray William the Marshal, who served four kings, from Henry II to Henry III.

2 Organizing Chaos

1150–1485

THE FIRST CENTURY of Norman rule in England was a time of consolidation. After a brief period of calm following their first arrival, the Norman kings began their subjugation of Wales, gained influence over the Scots, and, in 1169, invaded Ireland. The Domesday Book of 1086 recorded more than 13,000 settlements in England. The king and his 300 Rentiers, or tenants-in-chief, ran the feudal system and lived off the revenues of estates; at the bottom of the scale came the Villani (villeins), who owned only allotments, and the Cottars, who held small landholdings.

The feudal structure gave rise to powerful Rentiers, who increasingly challenged royal authority. Civil chaos often ensued, as the king, the large landowners, and the Church struggled for ascendancy, and the ideological balance of power in England shifted away from the king during this period. The titles described in this chapter have been chosen with these three competing factions in mind. Some of the titles survive from the earliest parliaments of the mid-13th century, and others are those granted to significant tenants-in-chief.

The tenants who enjoyed the riches of the great feudal estates were often tasked with important duties. Medieval kings in England and Scotland divided up their shores into admiralties, placing the security of the coastline under supervision. The invasion by Louis of France in 1216 had been a reminder of the country's vulnerability, and it was decided that every cliff, cove and port should be supervised. One family was charged with the security of the area around the Wash, and their descendants still farm the lands that originally came with this job.

The barons forced King John to sign Magna Carta in 1215, a charter that pruned royal power and guaranteed certain rights to his subjects. The Master of the Rolls was responsible for maintaining this document, and all other legal records, and although his function and position have changed radically through the years, the pipe rolls that recorded all judgements remain an archive of the law to this day.

Henry III also had to accept some restrictions on his power. When he made a commitment to invade Sicily, he placed a massive burden on the English exchequer. At this the country rebelled, under the leadership of Simon de Montfort, and the king was forced to submit his powers to scrutiny by a form of representational parliament. The members met at Westminster Abbey, rebuilt by Henry as a mausoleum for the lately canonized Edward the Confessor. The parliament made the abbey the focus of national life, and it was granted special privileges by the king. Among them was the right to grant sanctuary to fugitives, administered by the High Bailiff and Searcher of the Sanctuary.

Robert the Bruce's Scots army won the Wars of Independence against Edward II on the field of Bannockburn in 1314. Afterwards, the Treaty of Arbroath was dispatched to Rome, and the Pope recognised Scotland's sovereignty. Bruce took Scotland's castles under centralized Scottish royal control, and responsibility for them was dispersed through feudal means to loyal lieutenants. Their duties became dressed with titles like Governor, Constable or Keeper. Bruce also appointed the chief of the Hay family, who held lands and influence on the east coast, as Lord High Constable. One of the responsibilities of the post was the monarch's personal safety, and the appointment was made hereditary.

After Edward III came to the throne in 1327, overseas expansion became a political objective. The king planned to claim the crown of France by inheritance through his mother, but he could not go to war without security at home. To achieve this he leant upon the discipline of knighthood, which was a royal honour that had been vested since Saxon times upon proven warriors. The Church had used these knighted warriors during the crusades as the basis of its military organisation, and had obliged them to take additional oaths that encouraged loyalty to the king. Edward gathered round him the most powerful of these knights, and, by reviving the legend of King Arthur and the knights of the Round Table, he created a quasi-religious order of chivalry, called the Garter, made up of people on whom he could depend.

The medieval sciences of genealogy and heraldry flourished due to these matters of war and land, as their administration called for proof of inheritance, birth and ownership. Vibrant heraldic symbolism was developed to differentiate knights in battle. Monarchs entrusted disputes about privilege, position and status to their Great Officers of State – Lord Lyon in Scotland and the Constable and Marshal in England; each was assisted by officers of arms, who held important military and diplomatic responsibilities.

As the years passed, the merchant cities of London and York thrived as they traded with Europe, and livery companies developed a unique structure. As wealth increased, successful speculators and merchants pressed for special privileges, and monarchs, benefiting from their successes, were quite willing to grant them their requests. The City of London's wealth-based democracy developed its own court, charged with security, justice and revenue raising, and this court reflected the Crown's own blueprint of officers. The wealth that came from Cornwall's tin also commanded special privileges, granted with the caveat that an officer appointed by the monarch controlled their activities. This prevented the development of any separatist tendencies within territory so close to France. To tie Cornwall still closer, Edward III granted it to his son as a duchy.

For another son, John of Gaunt, Edward III revived the palatine status of the County of Lancaster as a dukedom. This gave authority for devolved powers, so the Count Palatine could administer his own laws. It was not always easy to remove feudal grants from those elevated to such power, however, and Lancaster later became the base for a challenge to the king's power. Lancastrians happily gave their loyalty to their Count Palatine, and supported the cause of Gaunt's successors, who adopted the red rose as a symbol, through the Wars of the Roses.

The Church's influence grew through these years, because educated priests ran the complex apparatus of the State; but their influence was threatened by the Black Death, which reached England around 1348. The plague was caught by clerics ministering to the sick, leading to a shortage of literate people. To check this dearth, and to continue the education of the laity, especially the poor, two great benefactors established important foundations: William of Wykeham founded Winchester College, and a century later Henry VI endowed Eton and King's College Cambridge.

The Wars of the Roses, and aristocratic factionalism, destroyed much of the structure that had been carefully amassed around the Crown. It was only with the end of this civil war, in 1485, that a powerful monarch like Henry VII was finally able to regain the initiative and recreate a strong kingdom.

Strachur, on Scotland's west coast, is not far from the ancient Dalriadic fortress of Duncconnel in the Isles of the Sea. The Hereditary Keeper and Captain of Duncconnel in the Isles of the Sea *wears a symbolic key that indicates possession of the island, which his ancestor tricked from the Lord of the Isles in the 14th century. This title was revived in the 1980s. Stitched to his Maclean tartan suit is the star of a knight of the Order of the Thistle.*

Opposite: *The LORD OF THE
ISLES, PRINCE AND GREAT
STEWARD OF SCOTLAND
wears the uniform of
Deputy Colonel-in-Chief of
the Highlanders (Seaforths,
Camerons and Gordons) in
the inner quadrangle of
Holyrood Palace in
Edinburgh, Scotland. It
was here that David I – who
appointed the first High
Steward of Scotland – had
his vision of a white stag
with a holy rood (cross)
between its antlers. The stag
supposedly instructed him
to build a monastery, which
was later rebuilt as a royal
palace by James IV. The
star on his left breast is the
insignia of the Order of the
Thistle, Scotland's senior
order of chivalry, which was
reconstituted in 1687 –
though some claim it evolved
from an earlier Order of St
Andrew, in 809.*

BACK IN MEDIEVAL TIMES, the Great (or High) Steward of Scotland had the job of maintaining the king's household and of protecting his interests in his absence. The post was first granted by David I in the 1130s to Walter Fitzalan, the younger son of a Norman baron who had become friends with the king in England. David, the youngest son of Malcolm III and St Margaret of Scotland, had grown up under the protection of the Norman court in England where his sister, Matilda, was married to William the Conqueror's youngest son, the future Henry I. It was a web of alliances between two distrusting neighbour countries, which did not last. But, during his stay at the English court, David learned about the civilising effects of both a strong Church and a feudal system of landholding . When David inherited the throne in 1124, he set about modernising Scotland, with Walter's help, imposing the feudal system and encouraging the spread of a vigorous Church. On Walter's death, the title of High Steward passed to his descendants, who used the alternative spelling Stewart as a family name.

In 1290 the Scottish throne was cast into turmoil by the death of the infant Queen Margaret of Scotland (the Maid of Norway), on her way to be married to the son of Edward I of England. Edward I intervened, claiming to be Scotland's overlord, and so sparked the Wars of Independence. James Stewart, the 5th High Steward, championed the rival claim, which put Robert the Bruce on the throne in 1306. In gratitude, Bruce gave his daughter, Marjorie, in marriage to James's son Walter. This marriage was significant because, when the Bruce line had no heirs on the death of David II, Walter's son Robert (7th High Steward) inherited the throne as Robert II in 1371. As a result, the office of Great Steward gave its name to the Royal House of Stewart (spelled Stuart after about 1567). In 1469,

by an Act of the Scottish Parliament, the hereditary office that was now vested in the king was conferred on 'the first-born prince of the King of Scots forever'. Since then, heirs to the throne of Scotland have been known as Prince and Great Steward of Scotland.

Lord of the Isles, another ancient title inherited by heirs to the Scottish throne, stems from an old Viking title Rí Innse Gall (King of the Isles), dating from the 9th century, when the Norwegian Vikings ruled the Scottish Western Isles (and the Isle of Man). In the early 12th century, Olaf, King of Mann claimed the title Lord of the Isles and in about 1140 the warlord, Somerled, married Olaf's daughter. As a result of this union, Somerled later claimed the title, after gaining control of the whole area and finally invading the Isle of Man and deposing Olaf's son and successor, Godfrey, in 1158. In 1164 Somerled was defeated and killed by King Malcolm IV, and therefore subsequent descendants of Somerled, who became the Macdonalds, ruled the Isles as vassals of the King of Scots.

John Macdonald (c.1326-87) was the first to be actually described as 'Lord of the Isles'. During the unfolding conflict with England in the early 16th century, James IV of Scotland became so exasperated with the intrigues of John Macdonald, the 4th Lord of the Isles, that he stripped the title from him, and James V formally annexed it to the Crown in 1540.

As heir to the throne of Scotland, the heir apparent to the Crown inherits three further Scottish titles: Duke of Rothesay, Earl of Carrick, and Baron of Renfrew. When in Scotland, he is known as The Duke of Rothesay, a title created by King Robert III in 1398. Robert the Bruce held the earldom of Carrick before he became king in 1306, and the Barony of Renfrew was named after land granted by David I to Walter, who was the first High Steward in Scotland.

Lord of the Isles, Prince and Great Steward of Scotland, Duke of Rothesay, Earl of Carrick and Baron Renfrew

QUITE HOW SUCH A STRANGE ITEM as a garter became the symbol of the oldest and most senior order of chivalry remains a mystery, but the Order is now over 650 years old and its badge crops up everywhere, even on cereal packets and marmalade jars. In fact, wherever the Royal Arms are shown, the Order's dark blue buckled belt with its golden motto neatly encircles the shield.

The actual date of the Order's foundation is unclear, as are the events leading up to it. What we do know is that Edward III encouraged chivalry among his nobles, leading them into great wars and celebrating victories with banquets, wine and women. The motivation for the Order's creation was political but its inspiration came from the legend of King Arthur and his Knights of the Round Table. As early as 1344, Edward told his court that a new Round Table of knights would be mustered for jousting tournaments. There would be two teams of 12: he would lead one, and his son, the Black Prince, the other. The meetings would take place at Windsor, where halls suitable for the festivities were to be built.

No sooner had the building work begun than Edward was off to war, this time to claim the French throne for himself: after all, his mother was the late king's sister. Aware of how quickly domestic problems could develop in his absence, he knew that conquests must be delivered to keep the barons in check. First his son achieved success at Crécy in 1346, then Calais fell into Edward's hands. Needing to secure his supremacy on his return to Windsor, he evolved his embryo Round Table into an order of chivalry, specifically one that imposed a grave oath of loyalty upon the membership. Few dared to break such oaths in those superstitious times.

The knights' symbol was then, as it is now, a blue garter marked in gold with the motto, 'Honi soit qui mal y pense' (Shame to those who think evil of it). Blue was the French royal colour and its use was a deliberate slight to the French and underlined England's claim to their throne. The motto's provenance is less easy to define. Possibly the fanciful story of Joan, Countess of Salisbury losing her garter while dancing and causing laughter among the courtly onlookers could be true. Edward supposedly picked it up, tied it round the heroic Black Prince's leg and uttered the words that became the motto of the Order. Other sources say it was Edward's queen who dropped her garter and the motto was how she replied when Edward said it would one day be a symbol of reverence. However, the most tantalizing theory is more recent: it points out that witchcraft was still practised in the 14th century and that the garter would have been recognized as a symbol of coven membership. Edward therefore defused a potentially hazardous situation by stepping in to save a lady's embarrassment.

The Order of the Garter has evolved to suit the needs of successive monarchs. The Tudors, anxious to legitimize their dynasty by currying favour with foreign monarchs, used it as a powerful political tool. Henry VIII's excesses led to the most frequent use of Degradation, a ritual that humiliated any treasonable knight: his banner, sword and helm were thrown from their position above his stall in St George's Chapel, to be kicked by heralds out of the gates and into a ditch.

Today, the Order includes among its members former prime ministers, retired generals and admirals, and a number of familiar ducal names. Recently, the statutes were altered to include ladies.

Founded at the onset of the Hundred Years War, the Garter's livery of dark blue mimics the royal colours of the defeated French. This KNIGHT COMPANION OF THE MOST NOBLE ORDER OF THE GARTER, *robed in mantle with collar and Great George Star, and carrying his ostrich-plumed hat, also holds the Garter worn by his ancestor, the Duke of Wellington, who was the last man to lead an English army to victory over the French. This portrait was taken in the Waterloo Gallery, part of the 'Iron Duke's' town house known simply as 'No 1, London'.*

Knight Companion of the Most Noble Order of the Garter

The Military Knights of Windsor, and their Governor, have their roots in the College of St George, created by Edward III in 1348. The College was founded as a fraternity of priests and laymen to serve at Windsor Castle in St George's Chapel, which had been founded by the king as the spiritual centre for the Order of the Garter, founded in the same year. It was Edward's wish, expressed in letters patent, that the College fraternity should include 26 bedesmen, or men of prayer – from the Old English *bed* for prayer. The bedesmen were to be appointed by the Knights of the Garter from among Army veterans – referred to initially as *milites pauperes*, or impoverished warriors, men who had lost everything while fighting for king and country. In return for living expenses and accommodation, the bedesmen, dressed in simple red cloaks with St George's red cross on a white shield, were to pray daily for the king and the Knights Companion. They were expected to be beyond reproach and subject to a forfeit if nothing less than diligent in their duties. Bachelors or widowers were preferred as less likely to be distracted by worldly or family duties.

Dubbed the Poor Knights, though actual knights were seldom appointed, they lived up to at least part of their name. Throughout the medieval and early Tudor years, their funding was haphazard, with rarely more than two or three Poor Knights in post. The situation improved after the Reformation, when proper financial provision for their upkeep was put in place to ensure that there should be 13 Poor Knights, one of whom was to be appointed as the Governor.

Houses were built for them beside the castle walls in the 16th century from the stones of Reading Abbey, with later additions and improvements, such as drains and extra windows prompted by the Prince Consort. But, by the early 19th century, the Poor Knights were agitating for change of a different kind. In the early 1800s, satirical verses in the local press had made mockery of their title with their embarrassment undiminished by the anachronistic red dress that they still wore on official occasions.

The success of a petition to William IV put an end to their humiliation in 1833, allowing them the dignity of a new title: the Military Knights of Windsor. Other changes were more superficial but of no less importance: their uniform, for example, was changed to that worn by Unattached Officers, men unaligned to any regiment. The black trousers (to which a red stripe was added in 1897), a scarlet swallowtail coat (with gold epaulettes bearing the insignia of their former rank), a crimson sash, black sword belt (changed to white under Edward VII) and a cocked hat are still worn today.

Indeed much remains the same. The Military Knights continue to live in the rows of houses built for them 500 years ago against the inner side of the wall of Windsor Castle, opposite St George's Chapel. They still pray regularly each Sunday for the Sovereign and the Garter, and are recruited entirely from retired Army officers. Reflecting this, their Governor, since 1906, is always a retired major-general or lieutenant-general, whose remit has widened since 1964 to include the post of Lieutenant-Governor of Windsor Castle. They may now be appointed not by the Knights Companion but by the Sovereign (in discussion with the Ministry of Defence) but they still sit where their predecessors did, beneath the Garter Knights, in the lower stalls of the choir. All remains just as Edward III intended with a significant exception: wives may now live in the ancient lodgings too.

Governor of the Military Knights of Windsor

Beneath the massive Round Tower of Windsor Castle, in Berkshire, the walls of the Lower Ward contain the homes of the MILITARY KNIGHTS OF WINDSOR. The Knights are all military men, just as the foundation intended, and they still maintain an ancient obligation to pray for the Sovereign, the Order of the Garter and its founder, King Edward III. They are headed by the GOVERNOR OF THE MILITARY KNIGHTS OF WINDSOR *(third from right)*, who is distinguished by a golden belt and who lives in the Mary Tudor Tower, beneath which he stands.

HERALDRY, WITH ITS strident colours, romantic beasts and strange language, provides a bright illustration to European history. Since the Middle Ages, its symbolism has been used to celebrate, identify and associate people from the nation's story with buildings, documents and possessions. The earliest Heralds, in the 12th century, were little more than criers who announced jousts at tournaments, but by 1350 they were responsible for arranging royal events, negotiating with foreign rulers and delivering proclamations. Knights were recognized by the coat of arms displayed on their shields and the crest on their helmets. Heralds soon acquired expert knowledge of these insignia and became responsible for recording arms and controlling their use. The rapid develop-ment of heraldry in Europe brought the need for regulation and control. Two separate bodies were established in Britain: the College of Arms regulates the heraldic system in England, and the Court of the Lord Lyon King of Arms administers heraldic law in Scotland.

There are 13 full-time officers at the College of Arms, known as Officers in Ordinary, who are split into three ranks: Kings, Heralds and Pursuivants. They specialize in genealogical and heraldic work, and are assisted by part-timers called Officers Extraordinary. The Kings administer vast areas and have the right to grant armorial bearings in the monarch's name. There are three Kings, the chief of whom is Garter King of Arms, who also has additional responsibilities for running the Order of the Garter. Next in order of seniority is Clarenceux King of Arms, whose province is England south of the River Trent. The third King, known as Norroy and Ulster King of Arms, has jurisdiction over the counties north of the Trent and in Northern Ireland. Norroy is short for 'north king', and the title dates from 1276. The realm of Ulster was added in 1943.

The Heralds are Chester, Lancaster, Windsor, York, Richmond and Somerset, all founded in the 14th and 15th centuries. The Pursuivants, or apprentice Heralds, include Bluemantle, named after the Garter's robe, and Rouge Croix, Rouge Dragon and Portcullis, all appointed by the Tudor Henrys.

Heraldry in Scotland is controlled by the Lord Lyon King of Arms, who is assisted by three Heralds and three Pursuivants. He is a Great Officer of State and a judge, with his own Court of the Lord Lyon. He is appointed by the Sovereign and answers to no one else. The Lord Lyon has unique control over the granting of armorial bearings and of the recognition of clan chiefs. Scotland's State ceremonies are the Lord Lyon's responsibility and he advises the First Minister where necessary. He also makes all Royal Proclamations from the Mercat Cross in Edinburgh.

The Lord Lyon sits in judgement on any abuse of heraldic law that is brought to his Court by his Procurator Fiscal. His is the only Court of Chivalry in regular use and it is totally integrated within the national legal system. Grants for armorial bearings are made at his sole discretion, and if evidence of inheritance can be proved, the original grant may be altered for the grantee's descendants. He instructs the Lyon Clerk and Keeper of the Records to enter these grants in the Public Register of All Arms and Bearings in Scotland. Proven family lines are likewise recorded in the Public Register of all Genealogies and Birthbrieves.

Officers of Arms in Scotland and England are now the guardians of the way the State celebrates itself, evolving traditions to reflect changing needs. They are the professors of ceremonial provenance, and the guardians of the national armoury and pedigree. They exercise the Sovereign's authority in granting new arms just as they have since the Middle Ages.

Officers of the College of Arms and Lord Lyon King of Arms

The ruins of Slains Castle, on top of Scotland's eastern cliffs, stand close to the original fortress of the powerful HIGH CONSTABLES OF SCOTLAND. SLAINS PURSUIVANT wears the tabard of his master, showing the three red shields on a silver background that flew over de la Haye's men at the 14th-century Battle of Bannockburn. It was at this battle that his bravery earned the family their hereditary appointment. The Earl of Erroll carries the High Constable's silver baton and wears the tartan of the Hay clan, of which he is Clan Chief.

Considering that the Hays of Erroll have frequently supported the losing side in royal history, it is remarkable that they have held on to the most powerful hereditary appointment in the land, Lord High Constable, for so long. But their high principles and independent spirit were wisely directed in support of Robert the Bruce at the Battle of Bannockburn in 1314, where Sir Gilbert de la Haye proved a loyal and effective supporter. The grateful king, who believed only a miracle would win him the battle, made Gilbert the Constable of Scotland and decreed the title to be hereditary.

Constables appeared in all the western courts that adopted Byzantine Court administration and customs. It implied military command and, in Scotland, asserted jurisdiction which superseded that of ordinary courts over offences committed within a certain distance of the monarch or Parliament. Two centuries before the Hay family took the title, the first appointee mentioned was called Edward, who served both Alexander I and David I in the 12th century. He was referred to as Chief of David's Knights.

The Constable commands the Doorward Guard of Partizans, the oldest body guard in Britain, and holds a silver baton as a symbol of his office. The appointment takes precedence above all titles bar those of the Royal Family.

The Chiefs of the Clan Hay, who became earls in 1452, held court in Slains Castle. Their large household, as befitted their station, included an officer of arms named, not unnaturally, Slains Pursuivant. When Robert Bruce's male heir had no children and his daughter's son, by Walter the High Steward of Scotland, became king, the Constable became more powerful yet. With the Steward's title now merged into the Crown, more responsibilities were passed to the Constable. Thus, when young Mary, Queen of Scots was married to the Dauphin of France, his duties included acting as Lord Lieutenant for most of the country in their absence.

Although the Hays often found themselves on the losing side, these were honourable defeats. Two Constables fell in combat fulfilling their obligations against the English army – first defending Bruce's son, David, at Neville's Cross in 1346, then at Flodden Field in 1513, when most who marched south with the king never returned. Catholic loyalty led them to lose again, twice. First they supported a Counter-Reformation plan with Philip of Spain to overthrow Elizabeth I and place a 'converted' James VI on the united throne. This fouled up James's plans so badly that the king felt honour bound to blow up Slains Castle to appease Elizabeth's envoys. On the second ill-omened occasion, during the 1745 Jacobite Rebellion, Lady Erroll, believing herself to be Constable to Bonnie Prince Charlie, sent her sons to fight for his cause.

When James VI left Holyrood for London, the Constable's role altered. In the absence of the King, responsibility for protecting his person and the Verge of his palace switched to the Council. A new job title was consolidated in 1681, with a ratification in favour of John, the 12th earl, and establishing his title as Lord High Constable. These changes reflected the inflation in court titles then current on the Continent, particularly at Versailles, where levels of deference were becoming a cloying art form. The English Constable was similarly prefixed for James VII/II's coronation. This title had been held by the de Bohuns, as Earls of Hereford and Essex; it passed to the Staffords (Dukes of Buckingham) until Henry VIII merged it with the Crown. It is now revived only 'from sunrise to sunset' on the day of a coronation.

The Errolls, along with the Dukes of Hamilton, are also Assessors to the Court of the Lord Lyon.

Lord High Constable of Scotland and Slains Pursuivant

A SON WAS BORN TO James II, king of Scots, in 1455 and was christened James. The new heir provided security for the Scottish succession at a time when the fortunes of the Stuart dynasty were improving. To enhance this period of stability, a new peerage was established: one of these new peers was Colin Campbell of Lochawe, who was created the first Earl of Argyll in 1457. The new earl already had plenty of titles; among which he was Keeper of the Royal Castles of Carrick and Dunoon and by 1470 this list of responsibilities extended to include Dunstaffnage Castle as well, for which he appointed a cousin to be Captain (see page 64).

Just as James II's government of Scotland appeared to be in strong royal hands, disaster struck. In 1460 James attacked Roxburgh Castle in order to remove the English Lancastrians who were occupying it, but during the campaign, a cannon exploded beside him and he was killed. His death placed James III on the throne, aged nine, and the boy's mother became Regent. Among his other guardians was the new Earl of Argyll and it was not long before this position of loyalty was rewarded. In 1464, Argyll was appointed Master of the Royal Household before becoming Lord Chancellor as well. His son too held the post of Master until he died at the head of James IV's right flank in the battle fought against the English at Flodden in 1513. In 1528 the third Earl was made hereditary Master of the Royal Household and it has been held by each Argyll since.

The third Earl also became Lieutenant of the Borders and Warden of the Marches, thereby protecting Scotland from attack from any direction. In addition, he became Heritable High Sheriff of Argyll and by 1514 he was signing his name as High Justiciar. This title too was made hereditary and thereby placed the Argylls in a position to profit from the judicial system: a benefit that could never

last and which was largely surrendered to Charles I, on condition Argyll could retain Justiciarship over Argyll itself and the Western Isles. By Act of Parliament in 1633 the king, who promoted the Earl to Marquess, thereby consented to two hereditary appointments: these were High Justiciar of Argyll and, perhaps the most romantic, Admiral of the Western Isles. However, since 1747, when heritable jurisdictions were abolished, the import of this admiralty was reduced to a mere symbol.

However, the Marquess tried to serve too many masters. He declared loyalty to Charles I but led the Covenanters, a popular movement that rose against the king's interests in Scotland. After the king's execution, Argyll actually crowned Charles II, at Scone, only to turn his coat by assisting in the proclamation of Oliver Cromwell as Protector soon after. Little wonder that, after the Restoration in 1660, Charles II saw him tried for High treason and hanged. His son, the 9th earl, also stood for the Protestant Faith and was sent for execution by King James VII, against whom he had led the Scottish contribution to Monmouth's Rebellion. Loyalty to Crown, on the one hand, and Faith, on the other, presented a challenge to any family in the following centuries, however, the Argylls managed to do both. In addition, they kept their appointments, and in 1701, Archibald Campbell, 10th earl, was raised to the rank of Duke. His son and successor was one of the first two officers promoted to the rank of Field Marshal in the British Army, a rank also held by the 5th Duke. The 8th Duke was a Cabinet Minister and the 9th Duke as Marquess of Lorne married Queen Victoria's daughter, Princess Louise.

The duties of the Hereditary Master of the Royal Household are now just ceremonial, but the Royal Navy, in particular HMS *Argyll*, still fires a salute to the Admiral of the Western Isles.

Opposite: Beside the Brannie Burn, in Glenshira, near Inveraray, Argyll, the MASTER OF THE ROYAL HOUSEHOLD *carries the red velvet rod of his office. This is sprinkled with thistles and topped with the Sovereign's crest, which shows a lion wearing the 'Honours Three': the crown, sword and sceptre of Scotland. In his left hand the Master clasps the High Justiciar's symbolic sword. On his jacket can be seen silver buttons in the form of silver salmon – ancient symbols of the highest status whose origins are lost in the mists of pre-Christian mythology.*

Hereditary Master of the Royal Household, High Justiciar of Argyll, Admiral of the Western Isles, High Sheriff of Argyll and Keeper of the Royal Castles of Carrick, Dunoon, Dunstaffnage, Sween and Tarbert

THE 13TH-CENTURY FORTRESS at Dunstaffnage was once a vital strategic defence guarding Scotland's vulnerable western approaches. Within its impregnable-looking walls is the residence of the Hereditary Captain, a descendant of the first person appointed to the post in 1490.

Before Ewen MacDougall, the Lord of Lorne, built this castle around 1250 to keep Norse raiders at bay, legend has it that a series of strongholds stood on this promontory. Local folklore suggests that one built by the mythical King Ewin existed here before Julius Caesar arrived in Britain. It has long been said that the Stone of Destiny, used at the coronation of Scots monarchs and removed for that reason by Edward I to Westminster, originally rested here, until Kenneth MacAlpine, the king whose marriage to a Pictish princess united Scotland, moved it to Scone. When The Queen was recently advised to return it to Scotland, there was speculation that it might return to Dunstaffnage.

Such was the strategic and historical significance of Dunstaffnage, and the importance of the Lordship of Lorne it governed, that when its occupant MacDougall foolishly resisted Robert the Bruce in 1309, the King attacked, took possession and appointed Arthur Campbell as Constable of the fortress. Constable evolved into Keeper, an appointment that the Argyll family retain. In the 15th century, the Earl of Argyll subcontracted responsibility for the castle to his cousin, creating the new title of Captain.

This was no free gift. While it brought a reasonable acreage and income, and later included a golden key as a ceremonial symbol of office, it involved clear responsibilities. A charter signed by the 9th Earl to his kinsman, the 10th Captain, in 1667 outlines them: 'holding our said Castell of Dunstaffnies and ever keeping and holding therein six able and decent men with armour and arms sufficient for warr and keeping of the said Castell'. In addition, the Captain had to provide the Earl with free access and lodging if required, and pass on certain rental payments. His family became known as Clann Aonghais an Duin (Children of Angus the Dun) – a reminder of the provenance of the word 'clan'.

Scottish clans were bitterly divided by religion during the Reformation – a situation that polarized when some supported the Jacobite claimant to the throne against George I, the Hanoverian king, in 1714. Clans and their septs, or junior branches, were forced to take sides in the civil war that followed. In each case there was self-interest involved. Over some 50 years passions rose and once again Dunstaffnage was found to be strategically useful. The Captain was holding the castle for George I when the Old Pretender (the son of James II) planned to land there and claim the throne in 1715. Weather and circumstances saved Dunstaffnage from becoming the focus of the uprising's first assault.

In 1746 the Captain had to fulfil his duty of garrisoning the fortress in the build-up to the Battle of Culloden, when every available redcoat was scouring the shores for Bonnie Prince Charlie. Later that year its dungeon received the bold and romantic Flora Macdonald, who risked so much to row the Prince to safety on Skye.

When Argyll claimed the Captaincy back from the Children of Angus the Dun, the case went before a judge, who upheld the Captain's position as heritable Captain but underlined Argyll's superiority as Keeper. He also ruled that, to keep the title and the land, the Captain was required to spend three nights a year in the fortress. Since the fire in 1810 this has meant passing some Spartan nights in a bare, unfurnished building.

Opposite: To maintain his livelihood and fulfil the ancient responsibilities given to his ancestor, the HEREDITARY CAPTAIN OF DUNSTAFFNAGE meets his obligation of spending a night locked within the ancient walls of Dunstaffnage Castle on Scotland's west coast. With his key of office resting on the mantelpiece, this descendant of Angus the Dun wraps himself in Campbell tartan and fortifies himself with whisky against the cold and the castle's heavy-footed ghost. So attached is he to this ancient castle that he even spent his honeymoon here.

Hereditary Captain of Dunstaffnage

THE RIVER OUSE, which flows south-eastwards into the River Humber and the North Sea, provided York with all the geographical advantages necessary to become a significant trading centre. Successively a Roman, Anglian and Viking trading town, it became a bishopric in the 620s. A century later the early church also established one of its two English archbishoprics here in 735. Before the Norman Conquest, York had grown to become a significant merchant city trading with London and Rouen. However, the Norman Conquest led to several local rebellions, which were brutally suppressed by William the Conqueror, though the damage was short-lived and the city was flourishing again as a major trading port by the early 12th century.

York's location was too important for the Normans to ignore for long and gradually the city, its population and its trading patterns were re-established. A system of guilds developed, starting with the Weavers, who received their Charter in 1163: a sign that wool in its raw state was already being superseded by woven cloth as the principle export. Some years later, in 1212, the city was given powers to regulate itself. This meant that all traders wishing to do business in the 13th century first had to become freemen of the city, thereby establishing allegiance to the burgesses and agreeing to observe the rules of commerce. By this time, York merchants were trading as far afield as the Baltic and Spain.

The merchants built their hall in the 14th century, close to the quay on the bank of the Ouse, and it provided a meeting point, a centre for religious worship and for distributing charity and a place for doing business. The fraternity staged religious plays at Corpus Christi and funded a hospital for the unfortunate. In 1430, Henry VI granted a royal charter to the Mistery of the Mercers of York, 'mistery' being the medieval word for handicraft. In this document, the role of Governor is first referred to, and apart from some Masters during the 15th and 16th centuries, the appointment of Governor has always led the Company through its evolution.

By the 16th century, competition from the Hanseatic League reduced York's revenues and it became more difficult to compete against London. The merchants' fortunes only revived with the Charter they bought from Queen Elizabeth in 1581. This incorporated their fraternity into the Society of Merchant Adventurers with a Governor who was directed to regulate its monopoly over business, which ensured a growth in wealth sufficient to fund trading all over Europe, from Russia and the Baltic to the Mediterranean. Business was interrupted by the Civil War, which placed York between the warring factions, and the Hall became variously a barracks and a storage for munitions.

The monopoly survived until the 18th and 19th centuries, when it became increasingly difficult to restrain traders under the terms of an Elizabethan charter. The Municipal Corporations Act of 1835 ended all guild restrictions and there was little that the new generation of industrial Governors could do but to evolve the Company's role to meet new requirements if it was to survive and remain relevant. This they did successfully, providing a conduit for members to lobby Parliament, establishing a short-lived stock exchange and returning to the original role of providing a social focus for the commercial community of York. The city's new industries, particularly confectionary, have provided resources and many of the recent Governors, each of whom supervises the continuing charitable work of the ancient foundation and seeks to sponsor and encourage new crafts and small traders in the city.

Governor of the Company of Merchant Adventurers of York

CORNWALL'S WEALTH LIES UNDERGROUND – at least that was once the case. Its deposits of tin provided the county with a status sufficient to establish its own coinage, courts and parliament. It even provided sufficient temptation for the Romans to set sail from Gaul and conquer England.

The mines, now abandoned, once generated considerable income for the Crown and gave Cornishmen a strong negotiating hand, which brought them immunity from taxation, a unique royal status and a special governor.

The wealth that the miners produced gave them self-confidence and a sense of independence that eventually disturbed the faraway English king into action. In 1198, Richard the Lionheart sent William de Wrotham to end this independence. Wrotham was given special powers and the title Lord Warden of the Stannaries (*stannum* is the Latin word for 'tin'). He imposed order and codified the ancient stannary laws in a peculiar jurisdiction for Cornwall. This legitimized the Stannary Parliament, which Lord Wardens had power to convoke and preside over. Twenty-four Cornish stannators met four times a year in Truro, while the Devonshire stannators met at Crockern Tor on Dartmoor. Everything other than issues concerning life, limb and land fell within the remit of these parliaments, and their decisions were upheld through the Stannary Courts.

One hundred and forty years after the first Lord Warden established this powerful viceroyalty, Edward III further recognized Cornwall's unique status and wealth by creating a duchy, consisting of much of the county and some other lands, and then conferring it on his seven-year-old son, the Black Prince. This was England's first dukedom, a possession intended to provide the heir with an independent source of revenue which the Lord Warden was directed to run. This situation has not changed – the duchy still provides income for Prince Charles as Duke of Cornwall – although the duchy's possessions and income have altered out of all recognition.

Henry III granted the Forest of Dartmoor to his younger brother, along with the earldom of Cornwall, and thus, in 1337, it became part of Edward III's new duchy. At the same time, the Lord Warden was charged with responsibility for Dartmoor's extensive forest and chase, famous for its dwarf oaks: in particular he supervised the Venville tenure by which people held fishing or grazing rights on the land. It would be a full-time task today.

The Lord Warden's principal duties remained the governance of the independent-minded medieval miners, who endured hideous conditions and great danger. Among the privileges they could apply to him for was the right to Tin-Bound – stake out territory and work it just as Gold Rush prospectors did in the USA several centuries later. Cornwall, rich in tin and copper, provided opportunities for fortunes to be made – not least for the Lord Wardens.

Miners were excused the obligation of fighting for the King abroad. However, their skills could be summoned to burrow beneath the defences of a besieged castle. Whenever stanners were called up, they served only under the Lord Warden's command.

Previous Lord Wardens include Sir Walter Raleigh, appointed by Elizabeth I to administer the duchy with no duke, and Prince Albert, Queen Victoria's consort, who turned the estate into a model of efficiency.

The Lord Warden now supervises 129,000 acres spread across the south-west and elsewhere, along with residential property in London and a portfolio of other investments. One of the few reminders of Cornwall's once-flourishing tin industry is in the Latin roots of the Lord Warden's title.

Opposite: *Tin – the Romans wanted it and for centuries Cornish-men dug for it, even beneath the Atlantic waves. Its quality was checked by 'coining' under the auspices of the* LORD WARDEN OF THE STANNARIES. *Once virtually an independent governor in the far-flung peninsula, today he still ensures that the Duke of Cornwall gets his income. However, tin is too expensive to mine in Cornwall now, and most mines are flooded including the shafts beneath these cliffs at Botallack, in Cornwall.*

Lord Warden of the Stannaries, Rider and Master Forester of the Forest and Chase of Dartmoor, Keeper of the Prince's Privy Seal and Vice Chairman of the Prince's Council

THE RITUAL OF dragging the Speaker to his chair recalls centuries of tension between executive royal power and a determined Commons. Ever since Simon de Montfort forced the profligate Henry III to submit to a representative assembly which, under Edward III, became the constitution's third arm, the House of Commons has grown in stature and influence. It has gradually wrested power from royal hands and deposited it in the arms of universal suffrage. But doing so was not easy and the task of conveying the House's decision to furious, sometimes autocratic and tax-hungry kings often fell to the Speaker.

The first person to hold the office, and the first Speaker to make demands of his monarch, was Sir Peter de la Mare who, in 1376, was sent by the Commons to confront Edward III. He protested at the king's mismanagement of the war with France, and demanded an end to heavy taxes and the impeachment of certain ministers. Finally, he insisted that an audited account of royal expenditure be submitted to the Commons forthwith. Speaker Peter was soon staring at the world through a set of iron bars and a new parliament was summoned to reverse these impertinent demands.

Few Speakers were more worthy of their position than William Lenthall, whom Charles I had appointed to the office because he believed he was malleable and likely to do his bidding. Lenthall's test came on 4 January 1642, during the Long Parliament, when the king ignored convention and burst into the House of Commons to arrest five of its Members. Failing to discover them in the chamber, the monarch's chill blue eyes fell upon his Speaker, and he demanded to know their whereabouts. The House held its breath but Lenthall's answer was, 'I have neither eyes to see nor tongue to speak in this place but as this House is pleased to direct me, whose servant I am here'. His reply foreshadowed

Charles's fate at the hands of the House and also ensured that no Sovereign would ever set foot inside the chamber again. After the king's execution in 1649 Parliament was supreme, and although Speaker Lenthall held no real power he was the first man in the State.

Unlike most other medieval appointments, which have diminished in importance in the centuries that have passed since their creation, the office of Speaker has grown in relevance, in line with the power of the democracy that it embodies so potently. However, this very democracy is also perhaps the greatest threat to the Speaker's role as defender of the right of Members of Parliament to challenge the Executive. In the past, the monarch was the Executive, while the Commons and the Lords existed to hold the Crown to account. But with the removal of power from both monarch and Lords to the Commons, and as a result of countless democratic reforms, a conflict of interest has emerged almost unnoticed. Executive power is now vested in Ministers, almost all of whom sit in the Commons. And perhaps because power and office are always attractive, it is argued that many Members of Parliament show greater energy in pursuing promotion onto the Executive's front bench than they do in questioning the Executive Government's legislation in the House. In addition, the Speaker may only impose rules that Members themselves have passed and these can be changed at any time. The relationship between this office and the Executive has therefore changed fundamentally since the time of Speaker Lenthall; and it could be argued that the independence of the Commons as a separate body to hold the Executive to account has been compromised.

The effectiveness of the Speaker's office derives from the extent to which its holder is able to ensure this independence – and from the regard in which he

Speaker of the House of Commons

or she is held. Certainly, popular respect has been enhanced in the media age by the examples set by fine parliamentarians elected by their fellow legislators. Resting on the tenets of fairness and impartiality the Speaker, who suppresses personal party bias, is chairman of the Commons: responsible for ensuring orderly debate and protecting the privileges of the House and the interests of minorities. A range of considerable powers and duties, many of which are shared with the Lord High Chancellor (see page 33), are merged in the appointment. Under the Parliament Acts, which reduced the authority of the Lords, the Speaker can decide which Bills do not go to the Upper House for consideration – and which will become law even when they are rejected by their lordships. This apolitical and balancing role means the Speaker holds a position that should be above the political mainstream, yet very much part of it.

The Chamber of the House of Commons in London was rebuilt after it was bombed in the Second World War. The SPEAKER *sits in the chair given by Australia, one of the Commonwealth's gifts to the 'Mother of Parliaments'. Speakers are 'dragged' to this seat because once this was a dangerous post to hold.*

'Think of what our Nation stands for, Books from Boots and country houses,
Free speech, free passes, class distinction, Democracy and proper drains.'

SIR JOHN BETJEMAN

ALCESTER HAS MAINTAINED its ancient Court Leet for more than seven centuries, an enduring example of the feudal system by which England was regulated. Originally every feudal manor was run like this one. Alcester's Court Leet no longer performs the functions that once kept it busy in administration throughout the year. The members' former duties have now been taken on by local government and related agencies. However, the regular gatherings in Alcester's Town Hall, itself dating from the 1600s, give a good insight into life before councils. They also provide a good example of how the great estates were run in England, from the arrival of feudalism until quite recently. The officers created at a local level echoed the great officers of state in function: it was merely the more limited scale of their operations that distinguished them.

The manorial system reached its prime in the 13th century, at about the time Alcester began keeping records of High and Low Bailiffs. The first appointee was called Roger the Bailiff.

At the centre of this simple feudal system of interdependence would have been a manor house and church with the homes of other inhabitants clustered around. The Lord of the Manor divided out the ground to his tenants, either for rent or in return for military service. Each field was divided into manageable strips a pole (5½ yards) or yard in width, known as *virgate* or yard-land, which extended to contain an acre of land. In that way the Lord, himself the proprietor of land given by the Crown in return for certain duties, was able to meet his obligations upwards while granting a livelihood to those below.

In addition to freemen, the manor would have its share of natives, villeins, bondmen and holders of *virgates*. This social structure implied a complex balance of mutual responsibility according to wealth and position. In simple terms, everyone owed service

and deference to their social superiors, ultimately to the King, who owed his deference only to God. In return, the benefits of security and justice trickled back down. When this operated in balance, the feudal system worked very well. Sadly, greed, self-interest and other human failings often damaged it.

The Steward was responsible for both accounts and the courts, and represented the Lord of the Manor. The Bailiff collected the rents and services,

Lord of the Manor of Alcester

as many still do for the Councils that took over from the manors. The Constable was responsible for keeping order, and this is why, when Robert Peel established the police force in Britain, he gave the name constable to the lowest police officer and divided policing into constabularies.

The other appointments varied from manor to manor according to what was grown and sold there. Bread, meat, fish, ale and leather obviously formed the ancient economy of Alcester, and today, when they meet, each appointee carries a symbol of office that is linked to the job title.

The Court Leet no longer has any official responsibilities. Instead it raises money, which it then distributes to local good causes.

The Lord OF THE MANOR OF ALCESTER (seated) is surrounded by one of the few remaining Courts Leet and Courts Baron – forerunners of town councils. From left to right they are: the Bread Weigher, two Fish and Flesh Tasters, two Ale Tasters, Marshal to the Court, Constable, High Bailiff, Surveyor of the Highways, Hayward, Steward of the Manor, Immediate Past High Bailiff, Searcher and Sealer of Leather, Brook Looker, Chapelayne to the Court, Town Crier and Beadle and the Low Bailiff.

EFFECTIVE MEANS OF TRAVEL are essential to the maintenance of power, as monarchs have always been aware. Harold II, for instance, marched his infantry from Stamford Bridge to Hastings when he heard of the Norman invasion. William, Duke of Normandy, on the other hand, moved his army and horses by ship, thus keeping them fresher for battle. The outcome is seared into the national memory.

Ever since man learnt how to break a horse's will to his own, there have been few more reliable forms of transport. Horses have carried knights into battle, conveyed messengers from one court to another and enabled monarchs to survey their territory. Indeed, the Normans ruled England from horseback. This was reflected in the increasing prominence given by Kings to their Marshals and Keepers of Stables. During successful campaigns in Scotland and Wales, Edward I's Keeper supplied his king's insatiable demands for new horses through a network of studs both north and south of the River Trent, the traditional dividing line between the north and south of England.

Edward III's claim to the French throne was the catalyst for a war that lasted 100 years. John Brocas, a Gascon noble who had survived two royal coups and the murder of Edward II, was sent to Gascony to procure a local supply of horses. By turning procurement into an efficient military operation, he secured victory for English at Crécy and later at the siege of Calais. The grateful king knighted Brocas and created him Master of the Horse.

At Agincourt, Henry V placed even greater demands on his Master, John Waterton. He had to find horses for the long autumnal march through France and the battle at Farfleur, while also maintaining the garrison's horses on the Scottish border prior to departure. Waterton retired soon after the battle. His three successors had all seen action with Henry V at Agincourt, serving among the 'happy few' on St Crispin's Day.

Following victory on Bosworth Field, Henry VII appointed Thomas Brandon as Master of the Horse. His instructions were to run an efficient, frugal stable but to ensure that it could meet the demands of Tudor pageantry. (Display of royal splendour was a vital art of statecraft.)

Henry VIII's Master at the Field of the Cloth of Gold was Sir Henry Guildford, chosen partly because his horsemanship would not rival the King's. He followed immediately behind Henry, leading the King's second charger, as was the custom. The job well done coincided with a wealthier court, so the Master became better paid and more powerful.

The Earl of Essex, one of Elizabeth I's ill-fated suitors, acted as her Master for 14 years. He was given many other lucrative appointments besides but he still managed to reorganize The Queen's studs. He was one of five Masters to die on the scaffold.

Others too have managed to combine demanding jobs with their duties as Master: John Claypole served Cromwell, and the 4th Duke of Devonshire was Prime Minister. The Master of the Horse was a powerful political appointment and, until 1782, proffered the holder Cabinet rank, membership of the Privy Council and a peerage. Thereafter it was a Government appointment, changing with each ministry, until 1924, when it became permanent.

The Master now has nothing to do with the acquisition of new horses for the army or running the Royal Mews for the monarch. His role is purely ceremonial – to accompany The Queen on his white charger whenever horses are involved.

For the moment, the post of Master is held by a Peer, but soon it may seem more relevant to appoint the Crown Equerry to the role, thus reuniting a once considerable rank with real responsibility.

Master of the Horse

In Windsor Great Park, with the Castle to the right of the trees, the MASTER OF THE HORSE *rides his charger, St Patrick. The golden cords hanging from his right shoulder are called* aiguillettes *and symbolize the ropes he once used to tether the monarch's horse – perhaps while hunting here. The Master, who originally procured horses for royal travel and battle, now has a reduced role. He keeps close to the monarch when horses are about – usually on ceremonial occasions.*

Few professions generate more paperwork than the law. The archive produced by lawyers over more than a thousand years is huge and it all needs to be stored. The individual appointed to do so needs to understand the history of law in this country and the wealth of material involved.

The legal structure imposed on England by the Romans held sway for three centuries. When the Saxon kings of Wessex superseded the Romans, they introduced what we know today as English Common Law. This is not embodied in legislation but derives from the precedent of common custom and judicial decisions that derive from legislation.

Following his victory over Harold II, William the Conqueror shrewdly chose to respect the country's existing laws and waited for the Witenamegot (high council) to 'elect' him as king – a vote he was unlikely to lose.

English Common Law applied to the whole country and was quite distinct from any laws imposed at local level by barons. Its emphasis on precedent allowed earlier judgments to be introduced as evidence in legal arguments, so it was essential for all judgments to be recorded by scribes and stored for future reference.

A reference in *The History of England's Chancery* states that parchment rolls containing the most important judgments and decisions were being stored in Chancery as early as 1199. By the time John de Kirkby was appointed *Custos Rolulorum* (Curator of the Rolls) in 1265, it was a full-time job to keep them in order.

Reflecting the growing importance of this archive, the status of its custodian increased during the early 14th century. By the end of Edward I's reign, the title Master of the Rolls was in use and its holder was allocated funds for a household. At this time the Master was both a senior judge and an administrator; responsible for running the courts and a group of other judges.

In 1377, Edward III recognized the importance of the post by granting the Master a splendid residence called the House for Converted Jews, just off Chancery Lane. Perhaps because of the gradual accumulation of vellum rolls, this residence became an office and then an archive. Its site is now occupied by a vast Victorian building where, until recently, all significant documents of State, apart from Acts of Parliament, were stored along with the ancient rolls. Among them are the Coronation Rolls, the only contract that sovereigns sign, obliging them to rule according to law, as Henry I promised in 1100. This collection came to be known and administered as the Public Record Office, with the Master of the Rolls as its custodian.

In the 18th century the Master of the Rolls was second in judicial power only to the Lord High Chancellor. Indeed, sometimes the Master sat as Vice Chancellor. For 50 years in the 19th century he had his own Rolls Court, but needs have changed, and now the Master presides over the Court of Appeal, dealing with civil rather than criminal matters.

The 1990s have seen further change for the Master and his rolls. The constant need to assess information and store it more effectively meant upheaval for the Public Record Office. Most of the documents were moved to Kew, leaving the Master responsible only for the Chancery Records. His title survives, however, despite the alteration in his responsibilities. This is partly because continuity and precedent form the basis England's system of justice and partly because he still has a latent responsibility for the rolls. But mainly it survives because it sounds better than President of the Court of Appeal, which more accurately describes his role.

Master of the Rolls

Until their transfer to the
Public Record Office at Kew,
government records had
been stored here in the Rolls
Estate, which lies between
Chancery Lane and Fetter
Lane in London, since the
Middle Ages. Historically,
the MASTER OF THE ROLLS
was not a judge but the
Keeper of the Parchment
Rolls, or 'king's filing clerk',
supervising storage in the
Sovereign's Chancery.

Westminster Abbey is England's pantheon. It has been inextricably linked with the country's fortunes since Edward the Confessor founded it in lieu of making a pilgrimage to Rome in the 11th century. Its monastery was dissolved by Henry VIII, and the collegiate body, governed by a Dean and Chapter, was founded by Elizabeth I in 1560. This history has made it arguably the most prominent ecclesiastical building in the country, attracting visitors influential and disreputable alike.

To deal with this wide range of people the Dean made some non-clerical appointments – the High Bailiff and the Searcher of the Sanctuary (now combined in a single appointment) along with the High Steward – who acted for the monastery when it was deemed either politic or dangerous for the clergy to do so directly.

The High Bailiff was a policeman whose job was to keep order in the Abbey's bailiwick – a considerable task as the Abbey then owned most of the land that now constitutes the City of Westminster, including Buckingham Palace, the Houses of Parliament, Soho and the West End. Maintaining law and order was particularly important because the royal court attracted development and an increasing population. The only areas outside the High Bailiff's jurisdiction were the immediate precincts of the Abbey and the Sanctuary.

For millennia there had been a belief that holy places offered both spiritual and physical refuge in their Sanctuary. The Anglo-Saxon king Aethelbert codified Christian Sanctuary at the start of the 7th century, and subsequent Canon Law allowed those accused of violent crime a period of grace within Sanctuary. In fact, many churches had a Peace-Stool beside the altar for seekers of Sanctuary. Edward the Confessor granted Westminster Abbey the right of Sanctuary, but many rogues and criminals abused the privilege. Dean Stanley wrote that 'The precincts of the Abbey were a vast cave of Adullam for all the distressed and discontented in the metropolis, who desired, according to the phrase of the time, to "take Westminster".' Indeed, so bad did the surrounding neighbourhood become that it was known as the 'Devil's Acre'. Among well-known fugitives who took Sanctuary were Elizabeth Woodville, the wife of Edward IV, who was escaping Richard III, and Henry VIII's court poet John Skelton, who hid there after his satirical verse about Cardinal Wolsey backfired. Sanctuary covered an area bounded by Tothill Street, Horseferry Road and the River Thames. This area was later policed by the Searcher of the Sanctuary, who checked that all within the defined area had a legal right to remain.

The High Steward had to be a man of gravitas and diplomacy able to negotiate on behalf of the Abbey with the State. This role became necessary after the Dissolution of the Monasteries and the establishment of the Abbey as a Royal Peculiar (a church owing allegiance directly to the Sovereign rather than to a bishop of archbishop). At one time, the Abbot had the right to sit in Parliament, but Deans were not accorded the same privilege. However, they are still entitled to sit on the steps of the Throne. The first High Steward to be appointed by the Dean and Chapter was Sir William Cecil in 1560: he became Elizabeth I's trusted counsellor, which allowed him to advance the Abbey's interests.

As the City of Westminster grew in importance, the Abbey's ancient influence was eclipsed. However, attempts by the City Council to let the Mayor take over the High Steward's role were resisted. The Dean and Chapter said 'it was of great importance to them that their Lay Arm, so to speak, should not be cut off'. The High Steward is still able to lobby on behalf of Westminster Abbey.

Opposite: The Chapel of St George is at the heart of Westminster Abbey's unique area of sanctuary. THE SEARCHER OF THE SANCTUARY, who wears a fur-trimmed, claret-coloured gown, is also the Abbey's HIGH BAILIFF. He once policed fugitives hiding among the pillars of this influential place, while the HIGH STEWARD did his best to advance the interests of the Abbey.

Searcher of the Sanctuary and High Bailiff with the High Steward of Westminster Abbey

THE QUEEN'S REMEMBRANCER, along with the Chancellor of the Exchequer, are the only two appointments that survive from the time of the medieval Court of the Exchequer. The first Remembrancer was Richard of Ilcester, appointed by Henry II in 1154 'to put the Lord Treasurer and the Barons of the Court of Exchequer in remembrance of such things as were to be called upon and dealt with for the benefit of the Crown'.

The Remembrancer represents an authority that is impossible to ignore – the Court of the Exchequer, which has now evolved into HM Treasury and the Inland Revenue. Its power has been enforced since medieval times by the barons of the Court of the Exchequer, in particular by the Cursitor baron, and the Queen's Remembrancer now performs the duties of that baron.

The Remembrancer still receives feudal debts on the Sovereign's account. Each year he receives two symbolic debts owed to the Crown by the City of London. The first 'quit rent' is a strange payment, made since 1211, a few years before King John signed the Magna Carta. The payment is for a scrap of wasteland called the Moors near Bridgenorth in Shropshire, and is paid off by providing two knives, one sharp and one blunt. The first was used to cut 'tally' sticks out of hazel rods, and the other to etch the debts between two people. The sticks were split and handed to both parties to act as unalterable evidence of the debt owed. The second symbolic debt was first paid to the Exchequer of Henry III in 1235. This was for 'The Forge', a tenement near St Clement Danes, which can no longer be identified. The payment is settled with six horseshoes, of the size worn by warhorses, and 61 nails, each laid out on the chequered cloth of the Exchequer.

The Remembrancer is also custodian of a seal of office that The Queen hands to the politician chosen to be Chancellor of the Exchequer. The appointee becomes Chancellor from the moment he receives it and remains so until the moment he delivers it back. If there is a resignation or a change of Government, the Queen's Remembrancer must hurry to No. 11 Downing Street so that this exchange can take place, because without it business in the Treasury and Exchequer Court cannot proceed.

The title of Queen's Remembrancer is one of the most ancient appointments of the legal hierarchy, but represents much more than something that has passed. The office is still responsible for the preparation of the nomination of High Sheriffs; for suing in the Courts for all fines and sequestrations imposed by the House of Lords, the Court of Appeal and the High Court; for the enrolment of the appointment of Commissioners of Customs and Excise; and it is before the Queen's Remembrancer that the Lord Mayor of London makes his declaration on Lord Mayor's Day. In addition to this, since the Queen's Remembrancer Act of 1859, whoever holds the title has also presided over the annual scrutiny of the coinage of the realm.

The Remembrancer's main job, however, is the onerous one of Senior Master of the Supreme Court, Queen's Bench Division, whose task is to administer the Central Office of the Supreme Court. This is where commercial and maritime law, serious personal injury, breach of contract and professional negligence actions are heard. The Senior Master hears relevant cases in their interlocutory stages as a judge in that Division. He is also the Prescribed Officer for election disputes and the Registrar of High Court judgements.

The word 'exchequer' comes from the chequered cloth that covered the table in the 12th-century Court of Exchequer and helped illiterate people understand their accounts visually when counters were moved from square to square. This cloth was recreated at a studio in London's Clerkenwell. The QUEEN'S REMEMBRANCER, *usually a senior lawyer, has duties both real and symbolic, most of which relate to monies and services due to the Crown, including the odd payment of horse shoes, nails, and sharp and blunt knives. Atop his wig is a baron's tricorn hat, which symbolizes that the Court of the Exchequer was once filled with barons.*

Queen's Remembrancer

Beside the high altar in Westminster Abbey lies the tomb of Edmund Crouchback, Henry III's younger son. Crouchback was so called because he wore a cross on his back as an act of faith during the Crusades. He had much to be grateful for, as the Pope had invested him as King of Sicily when he was only 10 years old. This investiture proved both expensive and troublesome for his father as it led to discontent in England, and ultimately to Simon de Montfort leading an uprising called the Barons' War. The King defeated the barons in 1265, seized their estates and gave some of them in northern England to Edmund. Two years later the boy became Earl of Lancaster, and in 1284 his mother gave him the Manor of Savoy on the north bank of the Thames.

Edmund's descendant Blanche, daughter of the Duke of Lancaster, married her distant cousin John of Gaunt, the son of Edward III. Through this marriage, he inherited her considerable possessions and subsequently became Duke of Lancaster himself. His palatinate powers allowed him to appoint a Chancellor to act as judge in the courts, with a Sheriff and Justices to assist. However, during the Peasants' Revolt of 1381 his palace at Savoy was destroyed, and later his son, Henry Bolingbroke, was banished from the kingdom. When John died in 1399, Richard II seized the Duchy and its possessions.

That summer, a fisherman recognized the commander of a small flotilla sailing into the Humber, and he ran to the village shouting, 'Our noble lord the Duke of Lancaster is come to claim his inheritance.' So began the exiled Henry's quest for Lancaster, which became a first step to the Crown itself. Within months both were his, and he declared that the County Palatine should be held separately from the Crown. In order not to leave the Duchy bereft of his leadership, Henry elevated the Chancellor to be chief administrative officer. This arrangement was confirmed by Edward IV, who enacted that the Duchy would be held 'for ever to us and our heirs, Kings of England, separate from all other royal possessions'.

The Duchy was a valuable source of income to the Lancastrians during the Wars of the Roses, sufficiently so for Henry VI to endow both Eton College and King's College, Cambridge. When the white and red roses finally conjoined following both Richard III's defeat at Bosworth and Henry VII's marriage to Elizabeth of York, the new king confirmed the Duchy's status, with the support of Parliament, as a possession of England's monarchs but separate from the Crown. This is why The Queen is also Duke of Lancaster, and why the Duchy's Chancellor, originally responsible for administering its land, courts and appointments, became a member of the Cabinet.

The Lancaster Inheritance brings with it a considerable income for the Sovereign. The net amount goes to the Privy Purse from which The Queen is given an allowance to cover her private expenditure; any profits are taxed. The Chancellor chairs the Duchy Council, which advises him on the Duchy's administration, and he is responsible solely to the Sovereign for its affairs. He also draws up short lists of Sheriffs for the new regions that represent the old County Palatine, namely Lancashire, Greater Manchester and Merseyside. The Duke shows her approval by pricking the names on the list with a bodkin.

The Prime Minister now appoints the Chancellor, whose real business is always set by the administrative programme of the elected government. There have been pressures to remove a title which is perceived by some to be arcane but there remains a real role to play in the affairs of the Duchy.

Opposite: The old Palace of Whitehall has all but disappeared. However, Cock Pit Passage is still a major thoroughfare in the Cabinet Office, the workplace of the Chancellor of the Duchy of Lancaster. *The ducal lands he ministers for in Parliament are owned by The Queen, who is Duke of Lancaster. Over them flies the Duke's banner, which belonged to Edmund Crouchback and shows England's three golden leopards on a red field. This design is 'debruised' with a three-pointed blue 'label', each point marked with three gold fleurs-de-lis. The Red Boxes carry official papers and are marked with each minister's title.*

Chancellor of the Duchy of Lancaster

On the Wash's eastern shore is the parish church of St Mary the Virgin at Old Hunstanton. Beside it, in January the village pond freezes over and there is no relief whatever from the cold when the heavy church door closes the visitor inside its voluminous interior. Idle gas-heaters and rattling window panes struggle unsuccessfully to keep the icy wind at bay.

Wandering round the aisles, the evidence is clear that this is the pantheon of one family. It was built by them, nurtured by them, and their mortal remains have been laid to rest here for nearly 800 years. Beside the altar, under worn carvings of heraldic achievements, lies Henry le Strange, his plaque dated 1485; in the North Aisle an altar tomb, covered with an intricate brass, celebrates the life of Roger le Strange. Plaques everywhere refer to others in the line, including Henry L'Estrange Styleman le Strange, who restored this freezing building (or desecrated it, depending on your view of Victoriana). What these memorials do not record is that the le Stranges came to England long before any surviving memorial can attest: their arrival in this corner of Norfolk, where they governed the coast as Lord High Admirals, was for a vital purpose.

Roland le Strange supposedly left Brittany during the first decade of the 12th century. The attraction for many who crossed the Channel at this time was adventure. Duke William of Normandy's son, Henry, had seized the throne. Seeking riches and land, many knights came to assist in his coup, anticipating the rewards that success might bring. Henry had two elder brothers. The eldest, Robert Curthose, was made Duke of Normandy on the Conqueror's death, while England's Crown was given to the next son, William Rufus. The latter, however, was killed in a hunting accident in the New Forest. Henry was present at the death of his unfortunate brother and, perhaps not surprisingly, seized the opportunity to take the throne. Robert attempted to claim his birth-right but was promptly imprisoned for life. Many Norman knights founded their fortunes on the abundant gifts bestowed upon them by Henry I, in order to secure their loyalty. With this new wealth Roland also found himself a wife, the eventual heiress of Hunstanton.

Lord High Admiral of the Wash

Proving the family's knightly worth in the campaigns against Wales, John le Strange became Supreme Commander of the Marches in the 13th century. And it was around this time that the Plantagenet monarchs reviewed the administration of England's vulnerable coastline, establishing admiralties vested in noble families as part of their feudal obligation. The Welsh wars had proved the le Stranges competent and they were given authority over the Wash. Surviving documents confirm little more than the existence of the title that went with the job, but these land-based admiralties were usually responsible for preventing smuggling, administering courts and controlling shipping.

None of these responsibilities remain with the le Strange family: over the centuries, as monarchs and governments chose to administer things differently, each has been assumed by other authorities. Nothing now remains but the title and the land.

The Lord High Admiral today is as peaceful and unassuming a man as you could meet; nowhere in his bearing can be seen the swaggering bravado of his medieval ancestors. The son of a vicar, it was through his mother that he inherited the Admiralty and, with the hall gone, he now lives in the village of Hunstanton.

Nearby, a lighthouse stands sentinel above the cliff, its famous coloured layers making the rock face appear like the walls of Constantinople. From it can be seen the open wildness of the Wash, with the flat landscape of Lincolnshire acting like a slipway for the endless penetrating winds. The commanding view from this place clearly shows why the le Stranges chose Hunstanton to control this Admiralty.

Standing on the beach at Old Hunstanton in Norfolk, where the family have lived since the time of the Domesday Book, the LORD HIGH ADMIRAL OF THE WASH *wears the uniform of an admiral of about 1800. The uniform has no connection with the appointment, and was worn for this book. He owns all the land from the high-tide mark to as far as he can throw a spear. This land-based admiralty, responsible for supervising the security of the Wash, was given to the le Strange family in the 13th century.*

THE QUEEN HAS BEEN LORD HIGH ADMIRAL of the United Kingdom since 1 April 1964. On that day the Board of Admiralty, consisting of Their Lordships the Commissioners, ceased to exist, their duties subsumed into the Joint Chiefs of Staff in the Ministry of Defence, where the three service chiefs report to the Chief of the Defence Staff, the senior serving officer in uniform.

The boardroom of the Admiralty remains in use, however, because the business of Admiralty continues. From here the Royal Navy, which won supremacy at sea for Great Britain and explored much of the globe, was sent forth 'By the Commissioners for Executing the Office of Lord High Admiral of the United Kingdom of Great Britain and Ireland, etc'. Two roles that survived the establishment of the Ministry of Defence were those of the First and Second Sea Lords. The First Sea Lord had also become Chief of Naval Staff during the First World War, while the Second Sea Lord also became Commander-in-Chief, firstly of Portsmouth and more recently of Naval Home Command (see page 186–7).

In medieval times, the English navy was supplied by the Cinque Ports under the same feudal system by which the monarch administered the land: the barons of these wealthy Channel ports served the King by supplying ships. In Henry III's reign, they were expected to supply 57 fighting vessels with 1,197 men and boys for 15 days at sea every year, after which the King would pay the expenses. Unfortunately, this feudal fleet tended to engage in piracy, and while travelling to Flanders in 1297 they attacked and demolished 20 ships from Yarmouth as Edward I looked on in horror.

The first Admiral of all England was William de Leyburn in 1294. When John Beaufort, son of John of Gaunt, was appointed the first Lord Admiral in

1406, he ruled a navy dependent on men who were pressed into service by gangs who seized them from the streets. (This practice continued until the conclusion of the Napoleonic wars in 1815.)

By the reign of Edward III, the Lord Admiral's duties and jurisdiction were fixed: he selected the ships offered under the feudal system, and chose the officers who would take them to sea. In fact, choosing captains to take command remains a responsibility of the First Sea Lord to this day.

Manning the navy remained a problem for many years. Indeed, Henry IV was forced to apply to private enterprise in the 15th century to protect his shores. Eventually, Henry VIII reorganized the navy completely, placing it upon the foundations that govern it still. He built ships with the money he plundered from the Dissolution of the Monasteries and established the Navy Board in 1546, chaired by the Lord Admiral and his deputy, the Lieutenant of the Admiralty. (It was not until 1623 that the title Lord High Admiral came into being.)

When James II was Duke of York and Lord High Admiral, he was served by the energetic reformer Samuel Pepys, who acted as his Secretary. After 1688 power passed from the Navy Board to the Admiralty Board, created in 1690 by William III, who appointed nine Commissioners to act as if they 'were the Lord High Admiral'. Chief among these was the political post of First Lord of the Admiralty, until 1806 sometimes occupied by senior admirals. From this time on, the senior serving officer on the Board of Admiralty was called First Naval Lord, a title that evolved into First Sea Lord. The appointee thereby became the senior serving officer in the Royal Navy.

The post of First Sea Lord survives as a link with the past, and also because geography does not change; Britain remains an island and needs a strong navy to protect the nation's interests at home and abroad.

Opposite: The Admiralty Boardroom in The Admiralty, off London's Whitehall, is dominated by the weather-vane that still spins with the wind to indicate whether it is 'Fair for France'. The ornate carvings by Grinling Gibbons are rich in naval symbolism, including ropes and anchors, astrolabes and bearing rings. It was in this room that plans were drafted for Captain James Cook's exploration of the globe. The FIRST SEA LORD now directs a vastly different navy from the one that Cook served, but it is one that values its history and the discoveries of its commanders.

First Sea Lord and Chief of the Naval Staff

CONTRARY TO COMMON BELIEF, Dick Whittington was led by his cat neither to riches nor to the mayoralty of London, but his appearance in pantomimes resulted from legends born from his life of splendid wealth, all of which he bequeathed to charitable causes. His enduring, if re-invented, reputation as Lord Mayor put the appointment on the map. In truth, Richard Whittington was no poor boy made good but the third son of a Gloucestershire knight, a mercer by trade, and while still young, already successful enough to make substantial loans. In 1397 he began his first term as Lord Mayor, a post he filled four times, being Mayor of Calais as well. When he died in 1423, having loaned money to three kings (Richard II, Henry IV and Henry V), he left a fortune. Since he had neither wife nor child to inherit, all of it went to charity, being used to build a new prison at Newgate, almshouses for the Mercers' Company, repairs to St Bartholomew's Hospital and more.

The City of London has a history of wealth and generous giving. The best merchants in the country based their businesses within the protection of the walled city, established as Londinium by the Romans in AD 43. It was later overlooked by the turrets of William the Conqueror's Tower of London, from whose ramparts William's successors saw the sort of wealth they could only dream of, being paraded by merchants who were organized into trading guilds or livery companies. Because this business brought revenue to the Treasury, royal cupidity was kept in check. However, the relationship between kings – who had power but never enough money – and the City – whose power existed only because it had money – was a tricky one.

Twenty-three years after the Battle of Hastings in 1066, the first recorded Lord Mayor, Henry FitzAlwin, is described as Chief Magistrate of the City. In a Charter of 1215, King John directed that the citizens of London had the right to choose, every year, someone 'faithful, discreet and fit for the government of the City' to be their own Mayor, who was then to be presented to him and swear fealty. As a result, each new Mayor made the journey upriver from the City to the royal court at Westminster, a tradition that evolved into what is known today as the Lord Mayor's Show. Edward III, who reigned from 1327 to 1377, appointed the Lord Mayor to be Escheator for the City. This means that the mayoralty receives the possessions of all who die without wills, or whose estates are seized for treason; 200 years later, Edward VI extended this appointment to include neighbouring Southwark.

The Lord Mayor is also Clerk of the Markets: its markets have always been the lifeblood of the City and they still are today, although the staples of life – such as sugar, coffee, meat, cloth and other tradeable items from across the globe – have given way to the financial services industry. Moreover, since London, like many other ports and coastal areas, needed an admiral to keep its waterways secure, the Lord Mayor became Admiral of the Port of London.

The Lord Mayor's title should not be confused with the new appointment of Mayor of London, which came into effect in 2000, following devolution of certain powers by Government to the Greater London Authority. Whereas both are elected – the former being one of the first democratic appointments in England – the Lord Mayor has authority only within the original boundaries of the City of London. The medieval City walls were surrounded by open countryside, but London has since grown to cover a vast urban area that embraces a population of many millions. The new Mayor is directly elected by this wider community

Opposite: The PAGEANT-MASTER must control the largest annual procession in England – the Lord Mayor's Show. Starting in Princes Street beside the Bank of England, it takes the new Lord Mayor to the Royal Courts of Justice, in order to comply with King John's Charter of 1215 to the City. From the Pageant-master's neck hangs a badge that carries the City of London's arms and, below, those of the new Lord Mayor. His watch, which belonged to his predecessor (father), shows the importance of timing to his job.

Pageantmaster of the City of London
(Overleaf) Lord Mayor of London, Escheator, Clerk of the Markets and Admiral of the Port of London

to be an executive figurehead, leaving the Lord
Mayor to pursue his role of promoting the City of
London as the foremost financial centre in the world.

To enable him to do this the Lord Mayor inherits
a lavish infrastructure. His home, the Mansion
House, is almost lost among today's towering banks,
insurance companies and brokerage houses.
Nonetheless, it still remains a dramatic edifice, with
the ancient Guildhall nearby to provide an arena for
display. Numerous dinners and banquets are given
there, where guests include Heads of State and
Prime Ministers. In addition, the City's Livery
Companies – trade or social guilds which adopted a
uniform, or livery – are engaged in a wide range of
charitable activities, which provide a framework for
supporting a complex range of schools, hospitals,
homes, help groups and other national institutions.

It is the task of the Pageantmaster to plan the
annual Lord Mayor's Show, which has evolved out
of the old river processions that conveyed new Lord
Mayors to the monarch at Westminster. (The term
'floats' is still used to describe decorated lorries for
this reason.) Elaborate pageants developed after the
Reformation, when City Poets were paid to write
plays that expressed the Mayor's message to
Londoners and were performed in the streets.

In the 20th century the need to make the event
more professional, particularly for television, led to
the appointment of a full-time post. The Pageant-
master is responsible for bringing more than 5,000
people together in 120 serials, which include bands,
marchers, carriages, dancers and massive floats. He
has to ensure that what is the largest annual
procession in Britain performs exactly as he expects
and precisely to time, without rehearsal. Fireworks
mark the end of the day that ushers a new Lord
Mayor into Dick Whittington's shoes: the legacy of
duties and charitable patronage is perpetuated.

THE LORD MAYOR OF LONDON *stands in Guildhall Yard, in front of the City of London's Guildhall, which was built in 1411 as the centre of City government. He wears the Scarlet Gown, over which hangs a Collar of SS that dates back to the 1520s; it is probably the oldest still in use and may have belonged to Henry VIII's Chancellor, Sir (later Saint) Thomas More. It consists of 28 letters 'S' in gold, interlinked with enamelled Tudor roses and golden knots; from the Portcullis in the centre of the collar hangs the Jewel, or Diamond Badge, which holds a cameo of the City's arms in the centre. The Mayor is surrounded by his body guard, provided by the Company of Pikemen and Musketeers, which was re-formed in the 20th century for ceremonial duties and is part of the Honourable Artillery Company. To the left and leaning against the Church of St Lawrence Jewry is a Drumbeater with Musketeers. To the rear a detachment of Pikemen stand at the 'Have a Care' position; armed with pikes, they wear uniforms from the 17th century. To the right, holding the Leading Staff, is their Captain, who talks with his Lieutenant, at the edge of the picture. Both officers wear armour and have lace in abundance according to rank. The Guildhall was struck in December 1940, during the Blitz, when this part of London was heavily bombed.*

POPULAR BELIEF HOLDS that the idiom 'at sixes and sevens' comes from the the 15th-century quarrel between two of London's livery companies, formerly known as guilds.

The most successful merchants in town needed well-cut garments to display their wealth and rank. Among those who supplied these essentials were the medieval tailors and furriers. Although the complexities of Court dress were yet to establish themselves, successful men wore clothes designed to prove that they did not have to get dirty to make a living. Clothing was strictly regulated, not so much by the dictates of fashion as by etiquette. Too much fur trimming, some misplaced ornament or the wrong lining could bring about social downfall. Tailoring was therefore a discipline as well as an art.

Trade guilds had existed in London since the 11th century, but grew in importance when Edward III began granting Royal Charters to the most successful ones. The Charters imposed regulations, conveyed credibility and, in most cases, bestowed a valuable monopoly. The Taylors and the Skinners (as furriers were then known) were granted their Charters in the same year, 1327.

Only freemen could do business in the City, but membership of Chartered guilds improved their standing. They paid a fee to join, and gradually the guilds became wealthy and controlled the medieval market. In time, guilds of Drapers, Mercers, Grocers, Fishmongers, Goldsmiths, Haberdashers and Vintners joined the select companies of Taylors and Skinners.

Precedence had always caused bitter rivalry between the guilds: in fact, a bloody street battle broke out between the Goldsmiths and Taylors in 1226 during the Lord Mayor's annual procession to Westminster. Trouble flared again in 1483, this time between the Skinners and the Taylors. Their rivalry

was further exacerbated when each tried to usurp the other's monopoly, and committees of arbitration made biased rulings. The Taylors' great wealth also presented a challenge the less affluent Skinners. The eruption of hostilities between them in 1483 was therefore no surprise. As the Lord Mayor's procession of boats moved along the Thames, each livery company cast off behind him in order of precedence. The Skinners and the Taylors, jostling for sixth position, began a dangerous race which led to the clash of oars and vessels, and eventually to bloodshed. It was the Mayor himself who later arbitrated the matter, and he decided that the two guilds should alternate sixth and seventh positions each year. He also stipulated that, on approaching Westminster, they should lash their barges together and drink a toast to 'The Merchant Taylors and Skinners; Skinners and Merchant Taylors; root and branch, may they flourish forever'. In addition, the wise Mayor insisted that they entertain each other to dinner every year to engender good relations.

Few guild members are now engaged in the trades once undertaken by their companies. They tend instead to be the descendants of former freemen, new City professionals, or others desiring close affinity with the Square Mile's unique constitution. The Masters of the Skinners and Merchant Taylors are now concerned with running their guilds' valuable property portfolios and distributing some of the proceeds to charitable interests around the country. Each year they process with the new Lord Mayor in his annual show, without argument or tussle, at sixth or seventh position. The lesson in compromise and common sense that was imposed on them has been a fine and enduring example to business life through the ages. Indeed, the two companies and their Masters have now been happily at sixes and sevens for over 500 years.

Opposite: In the City of London's Skinners' Hall the exchange of two gavels, one marked six, the other seven, symbolizes the alternation of precedence between two City livery companies. In this case the MASTER OF THE WORSHIPFUL COMPANY OF SKINNERS *must take second place to the* MASTER OF THE WORSHIPFUL COMPANY OF MERCHANT TAYLORS. *The rivalry between those supplying fur trim and those in the tailoring business is now no more than an unhappy memory.*

Masters of the Worshipful Companies of Skinners and Merchant Taylors

THE SHIPS LANDING along the south coast of
England in 1348 imported more than cargo;
they carried rats that brought bubonic plague.
Within a decade, the Black Death, as it became
known, had killed off one third of the country's
population, before heading north to slaughter the
Scots. Clergy were among the worst afflicted
because they ministered to the sick and caught the
incurable illness in the process.

William of Wykeham, a priest who held some of
the most influential and profitable benefices
available, including Lord Chancellor and Bishop of
Winchester, witnessed the terrible effects of the
plague and decided to amend the situation in the
only way he knew how. He applied to the Pope for
permission to found religious houses, where prayers
could be said for him and his many patrons, and to
establish within them colleges for the training of
priests ready to replace those who fell in the plague.

On 26 March 1388 the first stones of what is
now known as Winchester College were laid.
William had been educated in the city and born
nearby, at Wickham, so this was an obvious place to
establish the college. As decreed by Pope Urban VI
in the bull granting William permission for this
undertaking, the College still provides for 70 'poor
and needy' scholars, many of whom are educated
on the income derived from wealth bestowed by
William. The school's social structure, laid down in
early statute, requires that boys of all ages live and
study together as familial units in Chambers, the
elder scholars encouraging and overseeing the
younger ones.

For several centuries, a particular responsibility
of the older boys was to provide light for the
communal rooms. From among the 14 boys in their
penultimate year, the senior boy in College, the
Praefect of Hall, nominated seven as *Custodes*

Candelarum (literally 'keepers of the candles'). In
the arcane vocabulary of the school, the word for
candle is 'tolly', a corruption of 'tallow', the mutton
fat from which the candles were made.

As the Headmaster explains, 'The Tolly-keepers
are best described by what they are not. They are
above juniors but not yet Praefects.' Under the
Senior Tolly-keeper, the seven boys were
responsible for keeping the school supplied with
tollies from the chapel vestry. When electricity was
installed, the tradition ceased, but it was never
formally abolished. To the surprise of some, a
modern generation of scholars has chosen to revive
the practice. Nowadays, the Tolly-keepers carry
candles into College Hall, where the boys have
eaten since scholars were first admitted to the
school in 1394.

William of Wykeham's principal desire, that
both Winchester and his theological establishment,
New College, Oxford, (known collectively as the
Winton colleges), would exist for eternity in order
to offer up prayers for his soul, was not achieved:
centuries of religious turmoil saw to that. However,
both foundations have survived to become centres
of learning that achieve consistently high
standards. William is sometimes called the 'father
of the public school system', and perhaps it is no
surprise, therefore, that Winchester College is now
one of the largest and best-known public schools in
Britain. After the Royal Commission of 1857, the
tradition of accepting entrants by patronage and
nomination was replaced by competitive
examination for the whole school. The original
College founded for poor and needy scholars
remains an elite within an elite. Although many
Wykehamists, as old boys are known, achieve
notable careers, few follow the path of their
founder into the Church.

Tolly-keepers of Winchester College

Before the advent of electricity, William of Wykeham's College Hall in Winchester College and the 'toyes', or studies, in which the 70 scholars studied required plenty of candles. The Senior Tolly-keeper, carrying the snuffer, organized six other TOLLY-KEEPERS *in this logistical enterprise. Today, the exercise is purely ritual.*

ON 21 MAY EACH YEAR, a group gathers in the Oratory of the Tower of London's Wakefield Tower for the Ceremony of the Lilies and Roses. On this day and reputedly at this place, Henry VI was murdered in 1471. 'Pure displeasure and melancholy' were blamed, but this was disingenuous because he died on the very night that Edward IV returned to regain his throne. It was a grim conclusion to Henry's troubled life. As a ruler, he had been naive, burying his head in the sands of pious abstinence and religious observance. Succeeding to the two kingdoms of England and France from his valiant father, Henry V, at the age of nine months, he was almost abandoned by his mother and left in the hands of Richard Earl of Warwick (the Kingmaker), who taught him 'nurture, literature, language and other manner of cunning'. Henry had a particular interest in education and he was the founder of Eton College and King's College, Cambridge, which were set up to provide a first-class grammar-school and university education for poor scholars.

Henry used money accrued by his father's confiscation of the alien priories (mostly monastic offshoots of French religious foundations), supplemented with funds from his Lancastrian duchy, and founded a college at Eton in 1440. The following year, on Passion Sunday, in the hitherto unfashionable university of Cambridge, Henry laid the foundation stone of King's College. This was originally dedicated to St Nicholas but renamed 'Our College Royal of Our Lady and St Nicholas'.

The first foundation was set in fields across the Thames below Windsor Castle, where Henry could watch it develop. Called the 'King's College of our Lady of Eton', its religious complement included a Provost, 10 priests, or Fellows, and four Clerks, known as Conducts. Though initially a Conduct was just a humble priest who did the lesser chores, the

title has now become the one used by the College's 'senior' vicar. The original religious members were constituted with six choristers, one schoolmaster, twenty-five poor and indigent scholars and an equivalent number of poor and infirm men; this was a religious house first and a school second. However, after two years, Henry reviewed these arrangements and the number of boys was increased to seventy (the number of Christ's first evangelists), while the bedesmen were reduced to thirteen.

The first Provost named in the foundation was Henry Sever but within a year the King had replaced him with William of Wayneflete, who was poached from Winchester College and later went on to found Magdalen College, Oxford. Today Eton College consists of a Provost, six Fellows, two schoolmasters, seven clerks, seventy King's scholars, ten choristers and a number of inferior officers and servants. There has always been a clear distinction between the King's scholars, known as collegers, who have received a free education under the provisions of the original charter, and the oppidans (from the Latin *oppidum* meaning town), who had to pay fees and secure their own lodgings in the town. The Provost remains a royal appointment, even if he need not be a clergyman, and the Fellows have evolved from priests to governors, a change formalized in 1870.

The Founder's Charter for King's College was illuminated in 1446, depicting Henry VI at prayer, joined by his combined Lords and Commons. Parliament is thus shown united, which it still was then, in offering praise to God, the Virgin and St Nicholas for the new College. By 1453, the constitutional detail of the College had been established. It was largely similar to that of Eton but here there was to be a choir of 10 men and 16 boys to sing the daily services in the chapel. The charter initially provided for a rector and 12

Henry VI's original charter for the foundation of Eton College provided for a religious complement of staff led by a PROVOST (centre foreground), who was originally a well-born priest. The Provost is assisted by a senior cleric, known as the CONDUCT. The staple business of this well-known school, opposite Windsor on the River Thames in Berkshire, is represented by the HEADMASTER and a scholarship boy, known as a COLLEGER.

Provost, Conduct, Headmaster and Colleger of Eton College
(Overleaf) Choristers of King's College, Cambridge

scholars, reflecting Christ and his disciples. The 12
boys were selected from the King's scholars at Eton
and placed on a roll for admission to King's College,
Cambridge. The successful candidates remained at
school until vacancies occurred at the university.
The Eton scholars were maintained by King's
College funds and after three years they succeeded
to fellowships.

As if predicting the magnificent evolution of
English sung liturgy, despite the coming Reformation,
Henry VI had provided for boys' voices to help
maintain the spirit of worship depicted in that first
illustrated manuscript. The number of choristers
has never changed. Whilst these are no longer 'poor
and needy boys', the doors are open for all to
compete by audition.

The chapel at King's was not completed until the
middle of the 16th century, though the choristers
sang from Foundation. Henry VI's popularity in the
country was not sufficient to survive the loss of
France or bickering among the nobles that he
foolishly favoured. The country fell into the civil
wars of the Roses and little building work
progressed. After holding a chapter of the Order of
the Garter at King's on St George's Eve in 1506,
Henry VII sent a chest of money, literally, to enable
the work to be completed, both as a shrine to Henry
VI and as a celebration of the new Tudor dynasty.
Plans for the murdered monarch to be canonized
were rejected by Rome; however, his memory was
venerated in stone, not only with chapels at both his
colleges but also at Westminster Abbey.

The close link between the two colleges is evident in
the visual similarities between the chapels at Eton and
Cambridge, where English perpendicular style finds
its most glorious expression. It is also evoked in their
similar heraldic arms. Each shows symbols of the two
kingdoms that Henry inherited, but where Eton shows
three lilies of the Virgin Mary, granted in 1449, King's
College has three white roses, which some say is for
St Nicholas. The group that gathers in the Tower of
London on the anniversary of his death for the
Ceremony of Lilies and Roses are members of both
foundations. They lay bunches of the flowers shown on
the armorial bearings of their respective colleges.

*Henry VI cleared a large
area of land on the Backs of
the River Cam, in the centre
of Cambridge, to provide a
magnificent setting for his
chapel at King's College,
Cambridge. Sixteen
CHORISTERS were
established to sing at the
daily services in the chapel.
They still wear top hats,
undergraduate gowns and
'Etons', which consist of
'bum-freezer' jackets and
stiff collars, when they go to
and from the chapel.*

3 Reformation and Fear

1485–1603

IN 1485, MOST OF THE GREAT office holders who had served Richard III were either killed or captured in the last great battle of the Wars of the Roses, fought between the houses of Lancaster and York on the field of Bosworth. Henry VII had proclaimed himself king the day before the fight, making traitors of the vanquished. With the power of kingship in his hands the first Tudor monarch of England set about re-establishing unified government and the monarchy, and ending aristocratic factionalism.

The Tudors were to reign over a period of considerable change. The European Renaissance reached England at this time, and the Reformation, which was a movement of revolt against Papal authority, also swept from Europe through England, Scotland and into Ireland.

Henry VII used his patronage to grant appointments on merit, not rank, though he sold some judicial appointments to the highest bidder, such as Master of the Rolls, and even put the Speakership of the Commons up for sale as he worked to fill the depleted treasury. Pragmatically, he formed a Body Guard from the most loyal of his soldiers as his first priority: there were still Yorkist claimants threatening his security, even though most had been killed by Richard. Now the oldest military body in the world, the Yeomen of the Guard still provides close protection to the monarch within England.

The Lancastrian King Henry VII married Elizabeth of York to unify his kingdom: by giving their daughter, Margaret, in marriage to James IV of Scots they also hoped to prevent trouble from the north. The child of this union, James, was named Prince and Great Steward of Scotland and the Lord of the Isles, a tactic designed to unite the warring western and northern isles with the crown after centuries of fighting. The Prince of Wales today still carries these titles.

The Scottish court was fundamentally similar to that of England and stood at the centre of a feudal structure, with its own officers of state. Many of these were phased out after the Union with England in 1707, but some survived, including the Keeper of the Signet, responsible for sealing all the king's business.

When Henry VIII, son of Henry VII, defeated and killed his brother-in-law James IV on Flodden Field in 1513, his nephew James V came to the throne in Scotland, and, after years spent as the pawn of his nobles, came into his own with a vengeance. However, after two marriages to strengthen the Auld Alliance with France, James's heart was broken by the disastrous Scottish defeat at the battle of Solway Moss, in 1542. He died leaving an infant daughter in the regency of his wife Mary of Guise. The infant, Mary Queen of Scots, was to provide the final Catholic bastion against Scotland's imminent Reformation.

Through the secular and spiritual changes of the English Reformation, Henry VIII brought about a daring and revolutionary realignment of economic power in England. It changed the nature of his kingdom, isolating it within Europe so that it looked further afield for expansion. By dissolving the monasteries, after his conflict with the Roman Church, he filled still further the treasury that his father had worked to restore. The countryside is decorated with monastic ruins that once witnessed the moral trials in which people decided upon a faith by which they would live or die. After the Dissolution in 1540, Henry took on many responsibilities once fulfilled by the monasteries. One such service was that offered by the Carter family as Guide over Kent Sands on Morecambe Bay.

Perhaps the greatest misperception of the period, a time which gave rise to some of the more extraordinary and portentous appointments in this collection, is that Henry VIII was a Protestant. Far from it. Indeed, the mere suggestion would have added your name to the State Executioner's list in this time of despotic judicial murder. Henry's own book on the sacraments resulted in one of the Sovereign's titles that, in its timing, is perhaps the most ironic: Defender of the Faith.

The devotions of monarchs on military missions, or progressing with their court through the country, presented problems throughout the period of the Reformation. To ensure no service was missed, the Chapel Royal, a sort of travelling clergy, followed the monarch, with a choir to sing the liturgies. This body felt the strain of changing doctrine directly, as the pendulum of creed swung violently through the reigns of Henry VIII and his three children, Edward VI, Mary I and Elizabeth I. Court composers too walked a spiritual tightrope, writing music for the Children and Gentlemen to sing at Anne Boleyn's marriage, but also when Mary led the church back to Rome and persecuted the Protestants, and then again when Elizabeth endured excommunication for returning the country to Protestantism.

The charitable foundations of Edward VI's Protestant reign, including St Thomas's Hospital for the sick and Christ's Hospital for educating the poor, were also caught up in religious rivalry. It was especially difficult for scholars, and the universities, to tread between each creed. In Oxford, the new Protestant status quo set by Elizabeth's implacable stand gave one of her supporters, Thomas Bodley, the opportunity to establish a library that now houses every book subsequently published in England. Playwrights and poets also had to adapt to the changing religious climate, and became key figures as the court's political apologists. This role was to grow in importance and led in 1668 to the appointment of a Poet Laureate.

The feudal system was increasingly strained in the face of modernization during the Renaissance in England. The Tudors, recognizing that feudal systems would not efficiently provide the militia they needed, pioneered a new method for summoning men to arms. They appointed officers, who became Lord Lieutenants, in each county to assist the existing sheriffs in both finding and commanding a militia. However, feudalism still had its uses. In 1565 Elizabeth I granted the island of Sark, in the Channel Islands, themselves remnants of the duchy of Normandy, as a separate fiefdom that still survives with its unique form of government to this day.

The pressures imposed on society by the Reformation were made more complicated in Ireland by the Plantation, a sponsored immigration, that would further strain relations in the coming centuries and where the missionary inheritance of St Patrick was claimed by both denominations. The Dissolution in England had displaced Church wealth and power, though the new Church of England was to be a fervent episcopal successor to Catholicism in the following century, championed by a new royal house. Towards the ending of Elizabeth's reign, the Scots king waited at Holyrood to inherit England's throne, his Protestant education poised to set the political agenda for an isolationist Britain set on unity and colonization.

Roman Catholic archbishops wear purple robes over their piped woollen cassocks. However, when they are Papal Nuncios the robe is made from watered silk. Pectoral crosses are worn by all bishops. The DOYEN OF THE COURT OF ST JAMES'S takes precedence over all other diplomats in the Court of St James, and operates from his nunciate in Wimbledon, London.

The Court of Chivalry in the College of Arms, which is in the City of London, has as its judge England's hereditary EARL MARSHAL AND HEREDITARY MARSHAL OF ENGLAND. *His gold baton with ebony ends copies the one Richard III gave his ancestor. He appoints the Kings of Arms, who alone can grant armorial bearings. This court waits to be used in this century: the last case to be heard was in 1954. The Earl Marshal's coat of arms, which is shown on all documents granting new arms, is on the wall (top right): note the crossed batons behind.*

Each year the Earl Marshal (or his deputy) takes control of the State Opening of Parliament. He also stands ready to plan state funerals and coronations, as such ceremonies have been the responsibility of the Marshal since the job, originally a military appointment, was first granted by William the Conqueror. The appointment came to the Howard family in the 15th century, shortly before the Battle of Bosworth Field.

The word 'marshal' comes from *marescalcus*, which in turn derives from *marah* (horse) and *calc* (servant). In the ancient courts of Byzantium, the Marshal was responsible for organizing the mounted troops under the Constable's command. Charlemagne adopted many Byzantine practices in his empire, which filtered into other emerging European state structures. England's first marshal was imported with the Normans in 1066.

In Normandy the Marshal had been a hereditary post for some time; in 1066 it was held by William the Marshal, whose family married into the Clares, and Gilbert de Clare was England's first recorded Lord Marshal at Stephen's coronation. When that line ended without male issue, the title passed via the eldest daughter to her husband, Hugh Bigod, Earl of Norfolk. The Mowbrays were presented with the first golden baton, still the Marshal's symbol of office, by Richard II, and they held it until Edward IV's reign, when their male line died out and the title merged with the Crown.

Richard III revived the title for Sir John Howard, son of Lady Margaret Mowbray, on 28 June 1483, and the Howards have been doing the job, with occasional interruptions, ever since. Sir John's detractors suggested that his appointment as Earl Marshal and ennoblement to the dukedom of Norfolk implicated him along with Richard III in the murder of the young princes at the Tower of London. Whatever the truth, Sir John Howard was undoubtedly one of Richard III's closest associates.

Two years later, the 1st Duke was killed with his king at Bosworth Field, while his son, Thomas, the 2nd Duke, managed one of the sharpest political moves ever, by switching sides and becoming a trusted courtier to Henry VII. He convinced Henry that serving two masters showed treason to neither, explaining his actions by saying: 'he was my crowned king, and if the parliamentary authority set the crown upon a stock, I will fight for that stock'. With similar diplomacy, his descendants weathered civil war, religious upheaval and autocratic kings, all the while maintaining their position, rank and Roman Catholic faith. The Howard family steered a path of survival through the reigns of succeeding sovereigns, suffering several attainders and some beheadings. In the ceremonial splendour that surrounded Charles II's Restoration, the King revived the Dukedom of Norfolk and the post of Earl Marshal, which he made hereditary.

Among the Marshal's duties is that of judge in the Court of Chivalry. Set up by Edward III, the Court retains jurisdiction over chivalric matters pertaining to rank, heraldry and conduct, but the only hearing in the last few centuries was in 1954. The Court's chamber is actually located in the College of Arms, another branch of the Earl Marshal's bailiwick. Here the Officers of Arms, appointed by the Sovereign on the Earl Marshal's recommendation, conduct heraldic business and support him with the development of national ceremonial to meet changing needs: they have the expertise to provide an understanding for the provenance and meaning behind all State rituals. With baton in hand, hereditary Earl Marshals conduct Sovereigns to their crowns, their parliaments and their graves.

Earl Marshal and Hereditary Marshal of England

Going to bed was a dangerous business for 15th-century monarchs. There were potential assassins everywhere, so the Yeomen of the Guard were drafted in to prepare the royal bedroom at night-time and then sleep at the door to keep it safe. Among the extant appointments still shared out amongst the men who line the Queen's ceremonial path are two that reflect this responsibility – the Yeoman Bedgoer and Yeoman Bedhanger.

As monarchs were also at risk of being poisoned, the Yeomen acted as food-tasters too. They generally carried dishes to the dining room from the kitchen and, as they set each one down, took a mouthful to prove it was safe. The Exon-in-Waiting (so called because he is a regular serviceman 'exempt' from his duties in order to serve in the Body Guard) still stands beside the Sovereign's chair at State banquets, just in case he is called on to taste again.

The Queen's Body Guard of Yeomen of the Guard were formed after the Battle of Bosworth Field in 1485, and are therefore the oldest military corps in Britain. Henry VII claimed his crown by right of conquest: indeed, it was supposedly lifted from a thorn hedge on the battlefield by Rhys ap Thomas, who placed it on Henry's head. The country, however, remained divided. To ensure his safety, Henry VII – inspired by the Scottish Guard kept by the French kings – organized 50 of his loyal archers into a company called the Yeomen of the Guard of Our Lord the King: they would protect him at his coronation and afterwards. Not since the reign of Richard II had a monarch felt it necessary to engage 'a furniture of daily soldiers' to be in constant attendance.

It was at the onset of the 17th century that the Yeomen of the Guard had their finest hour. Getting wind of a plot to blow up the Houses of Parliament, they searched the cellars and uncovered Guy Fawkes amongst some powder kegs. Since then, it has become a time-honoured ritual for the Yeomen to search the cellars by lantern light before the State Opening of Parliament to ensure the Sovereign's safety.

When Charles II established a standing army after the Restoration, he also put the Yeomen of the Guard on a proper footing with their own officers. This was in recognition of the service they had rendered during his years of exile; it also explains how the corps has given the Sovereign unbroken service since 1485. Nonetheless, it suffered the indignity of having to accept royal favourites, with no military experience, as commissioned officers. However, the corps again enjoyed prominence when it provided close protection for George II, the last British king to command an army in the field, at Dettingen in 1743.

Members of the Guard retain the title of Yeomen because they are all warrant officers or non-commissioned officers drawn from the Army, the Royal Marines and the Royal Air Force. Each must have an exemplary service record and hold a Long Service and Good Conduct Medal. The corps also includes five commissioned officers. They command the force under the Captain, who is the Government's Deputy Chief Whip in the House of Lords.

Many Tudors' ranks remain, including Clerk to the Check, now Cheque, who originally arranged duties but is now Adjutant as well, and therefore responsible for discipline. The Messenger Sergeant-Major, was trusted with delivering important messages and became the senior rank beneath the officers: today he is also Wardrobe Keeper, the Wardrobe being where the Tudor monarchs kept their stores.

The Yeomen of the Guard turn out for State functions, investitures and garden parties, as alert today for threats of terrorism as they were when they foiled the Gunpowder Plot in 1603.

Opposite: The oldest military corps in Britain, the Yeomen of the Guard, have been quartered in St James's Palace for centuries. Yeomen, Yeomen Bedgoers and Yeomen Bedhangers, with titles deriving from security tasks performed to protect sleeping Tudor monarchs, parade in Colour Court, while the Messenger Sergeant-Major *talks with the* Clerk of the Cheque and Adjutant. *The Yeomen last fought for Henry VIII in France.*

Messenger Sergeant-Major and Wardrobe Keeper with the Clerk of the Cheque and Adjutant of the Queen's Body Guard of the Yeomen of the Guard

It is still true that almost every swan living on the open waterways of Britain belongs to The Queen. Recent attempts to revoke this unique status have been overruled, and the Royal Household includes a post to maintain an historic tradition that retains a surprising relevance.

Since the 13th century monarchs have employed someone, known variously as Swan Keeper, Swan Master or Swan Marker, to protect these royal birds, and each has been supported by a Swanherd of qualified helpers. In medieval times harsh punishments were meted out to those who did the 'bird royal' harm. Stealing a swan's egg, for example, earned a year and a day in prison, while killing a swan cost the perpetrator a small fortune in wheat: the swan was hung by the beak with its feet just touching the floor, then the criminal had to pour out sufficient grain to envelop the whole bird. In 1895, unlicensed killing was punished by seven weeks' hard labour. Nowadays, stealing a tame swan is still larceny, and the Malicious Damage Act makes it an offence either to maim or kill one.

Many stories, romantic and otherwise, attach to swans, and their associations with royalty have brought them a prestige that has found its way into successive statutes. Edward IV, for example, restricted applications for ownership, of which there were many, to men with land exceeding a value of five marks. This did not, however, stem the flow of requests, which made it necessary to develop unique markings on the beak, called Cygninota, to distinguish one owner's swans from another's.

By the reign of Elizabeth I there were over 900 markings recorded, and each July new cygnets were marked according to the nicks and scratches on their parents' beaks. Any without markings belonged to the Sovereign. Those that could not be attributed to particular parents were given to the monarch or whoever owned the grass where they were found feeding. This practice of marking the birds was called Swan Upping or Swan Hopping.

When Edward IV was short of money, he applied to the City of London's Worshipful Company of Vintners for a loan. In return, a charter of 1473 granted them the right to own some swans on the Thames. A few years later the same privilege was granted to the Dyers' Company. Every July since then the Queen's Swan Marker is joined by the Markers belonging to the Vintners and Dyers, and their teams row along the Thames in six skiffs between Sunbury and Abingdon. As they pass Windsor Castle, the Queen's Swan Marker gives the toast, 'Her Majesty The Queen, Seigneur of the Swans'. In the 17th and 18th centuries, when great barges were still used for this ceremony, they provided an excuse for Swan Banquets, when the swan uppers feasted on roast cygnet.

Times are very different now, and swan upping is a hard week's work for the oarsmen, who are all licensed Watermen and Lightermen. The week remains a traditional event, but one in which conservation and education are also emphasized. Increased leisure activity on England's waterways has contributed to the reduction of swan habitats in many areas, and also reduced the number of birds. Swan upping provides the opportunity to monitor the welfare of the swan population on the River Thames. The information gathered is passed to Oxford University, which surveys the health of the birds – something that has improved significantly since the lead weights once used for fishing have been banned. The Queen's Swan Marker also has a national responsibility, confirmed by Statute, to advise on the birds' welfare.

Opposite: *The* QUEEN'S SWAN MARKER, *holding his Swan Hook, wears the royal livery of scarlet and gold, and sports a swan feather behind the Crown badge on his cap. The swans behind him (pen on the left and cob on the right) swim with their young cygnets on a quiet stretch of the River Thames at Cookham. As they belong to The Queen, the Seigneur of the Swans, they will be checked but not marked.*

Queen's Swan Marker

PAGEANTRY WAS A REGULAR PART OF LIFE for the first 26 knights who wore the garter emblem of Edward III's order of chivalry in 1348. The Order met annually at Windsor Castle on 23 April, the feast of St George. As the knights processed towards the chapel dedicated to St George within the Castle grounds, they were led by an Usher (from the Latin word *ussarius*, meaning 'doorkeeper'), who carried a black rod. When the knights were safely assembled, the door was closed and its security guarded by the same Usher.

The earliest reference to this door-keeping role is found in *Letters Patent*, dating from 1361. There it states that Walter Whitehorse, 'usher of the free chapel in Wyndesore Castle' received 12 old pence a day for life.

The Usher eventually became better known by the name of his staff of office, Black Rod, and moved as part of the court to attend the monarch wherever he might be. When a fire in 1512 forced Henry VIII to move from the Palace of Westminster to York House, Black Rod was left in the burnt-out remains and has stayed there ever since. Ten years later, he was given custody over 'all the doors where any councils are held, as well in Our High Court of Parliament, as in other places'.

The role of Usher has not always been straightforward. Henry Norris, who was Black Rod to Henry VIII, was also Groom of the Stole to Anne Boleyn. In her tragic fall from grace, he was implicated in the web of fanciful accusations that Thomas Cromwell concocted and was executed. Such a situation might not have arisen if he had travelled more with his monarch, as Sir William Compton later did. He fought with Henry VIII in France, and accompanied him to the Field of the Cloth of Gold. But he was still expected to keep up his Garter duties and arrest errant knights by tapping them on the shoulder using his black rod. If the knight were found guilty – almost a certainty in Tudor England – he would have to pay a then-hefty fine of £5.

Following the Restoration in of the monarchy in 1660, Sir Fleetwood Sheppard was appointed Black Rod. He was also steward to Charles II's mistress Nell Gwynn, and a *bon viveur*, who once invited the membership of the Commons into the King's cellar to drink a loyal toast. In 1698 Admiral Sir David Mitchell became the first in a continuing line of military men to be appointed to the role. This fulfils the edict of Henry VIII that Black Rod should be a 'Gentleman of Name and Arms'.

As recently as 1971, the role of Sergeant-at-Arms, who is responsible for discipline in the Lords, was merged with that of Black Rod, and he became Secretary to the Lord Great Chamberlain. The latter role fits in well with his responsibilities as a senior administrator for the Lords, and the influence Black Rod now exercises is greater perhaps than at any previous time. Every year, however, he returns to his roots at Windsor to lead the members of the Order of the Garter into St George's Chapel.

During the State Opening of Parliament, which is televised every year, Black Rod can be seen walking through the Palace of Westminster to the House of Commons, where, in time-honoured words, he conveys the Sovereign's command that the MPs leave their chamber and appear at the Bar of the Lords to hear the Queen's Speech. As he approaches the door, it is symbolically slammed as a reminder that the Commons fiercely guards its independence. Black Rod then gives three resounding knocks on the door with his staff of office. When it is opened, he utters the Queen's command that 'this honourable House...attend upon Her Majesty immediately in the House of Peers'.

The door of the House of Lords in the Palace of Westminster is guarded by BLACK ROD, *who holds the symbol of his office and wears his badge as an officer of the Order of the Garter on a chain around his neck. From The Queen's throne there is a clear view of Black Rod's progress towards the House of Commons, and the ritual door-slamming can be fully witnessed.*

Yeoman Usher of the Black Rod, Secretary to the Lord Great Chamberlain and Sergeant-at-Arms of the House of Lords

TWO MONTHS AFTER LEAVING Southampton in September 1415, and after a long march through the French countryside with Henry V and his army, the Children of the Chapel Royal sang a dawn Mass for the King and his knights in the cornfields beside Agincourt. The Chapel Royal was a travelling church, consisting of priests who ministered to the monarch's spiritual needs, and gentlemen and children who sang the services.

Ever since St Augustine converted Ethelbert of Kent in the 9th century, monarchs had been under considerable pressure to maintain their devotions, even while travelling. When journeying around their kingdom – the only certain way of holding on to the throne – and during times of war, monarchs always included priests and acolytes in their entourage.

Music has always been an important part of church ritual. Indeed, Edward I referred to choirboys in his Chapel Royal in 1303. It is also clear from these early references that monarchs undertook to educate the boys who had given their voices to help with royal worship, and arranged for them to study at Oxford and Cambridge once their singing days were over.

To obtain the best voices, pressure was brought to bear on cathedrals or nobles who had fine singers in their charge. Gradually, the Chapel Royal gained a complement of about half a dozen children. They were cared for and supervised by a Master of the Children, who, if necessary, accompanied them on the monarch's expeditions. The last major journey, involving 10 boys at tuppence a day, was to France in 1520 to support Henry VIII's display at the Field of the Cloth of Gold. However, boys of the Chapel Royal later travelled to Scotland in 1625 for the coronation of Charles I.

Nowadays, the choristers of the Chapel Royal are based at St James's Palace, where they moved in 1702, and are currently educated at the City of London School on scholarships funded by the monarch. In return, they sing at ceremonies that The Queen attends annually, such as the Royal Maundy Service and on Remembrance Sunday.

The Chapel Royal has attracted many eminent composers during its history, and the choristers still sing many of their commissioned works. In 1569, at a time when conflict between Protestants and Catholics beset the country, William Byrd, a former chorister of St Paul's Cathedral, and a Roman Catholic by inclination, was appointed organist to the Chapel Royal. He composed music that satisfied Elizabeth I and her Stuart successors, and left a large repertoire of anthems still in constant use. The German-born George Frideric Handel, who found the Hanoverian kings particularly welcoming, was also commissioned to write for the Chapel Royal. He wrote many choral works and also composed the music for George II's coronation in 1727, including the now-famous anthem 'Zadok the Priest'.

The Children of the Chapel Royal have seldom missed the chance to make mischief, especially when given licence by James I to act like policemen. He ruled in 1622 that 'No man whatsoever presume to wayte upon us to the Chappell in bootes and spurs', and the children were encouraged to fine offenders Spur Money. This is now ritualized into the Epiphany Service, when The Queen, following the example of the Three Wise Men, makes gifts of gold, frankincense and myrrh to Christ. One of the Gentlemen Ushers in attendance always wears spurs so that a chorister can demand a fine, but the boy has to recite the gamut, or scale, before the money is handed over. The 1st Duke of Wellington got away without paying when the boy who challenged him forgot this part of the ritual. That has never happened since.

Opposite: The CHILDREN OF THE CHAPEL ROYAL, *wearing State Coats, as prescribed in Charles II's warrant of 1661, gather in the Chapel Royal at St James's Palace in London, under the ceiling painted by Holbein. The trunks and suitcases show that they are ready to travel with the Sovereign whenever needed. Their predecessors even followed Henry V's retinue to the fields of Agincourt.*

Children of the Chapel Royal

Every county has had a Lord-Lieutenant since Henry VIII appointed the first in 1557. Originally responsible for maintaining local defence and civil order, the lieutenant (from the Latin *locum tenens*, meaning 'one holding a place for another') stood in for the Sovereign.

There is a buzz in the air. A small crowd has gathered. Many of them have Union flags and the police watch vigilantly while the royal car approaches. Around the main gate are well-dressed people ready to greet their monarch, but in front of them all is the Lord-Lieutenant. This is a scene played out all over the country by Lord-Lieutenants who are the first to welcome the monarch, her family or visiting heads of state into their particular county. Dressed in a quasi-military uniform, complete with top-ranking officer's sword and braid on their cap, they echo the role Henry VIII originally envisaged for them as local militia commanders. Having greeted the royal visitor and, as it were, handed over the county, the Lord-Lieutenant follows the visit and is the last to bid farewell. On the visitor's departure, he is once again back at the top of the county's pecking order.

The necessity for a lieutenant arose when 16th-century kings realized they could no longer rely on the feudal system to provide knights and fighting men in time of need. Instead, the money that manors paid in lieu of providing soldiers was centralized and used to found the beginnings of a standing army. The new Lord-Lieutenants were then expected to command the county militias, but their role altered as the army changed. However, they retained a special association with the Territorial Army, and took a leading role in the Home Guard, or 'Dad's Army', of the Second World War.

Until recently, most Lord-Lieutenants were local landowners from the county with large houses and grand titles. This suited the benevolent unpaid nature of their work, especially when their military role declined and only their position at the top of the county's social pyramid remained. There are still parts of the country where this style of lieutenancy is greatly valued and works well. Lord-Lieutenants support the broader life of the community within their county by supporting schools, charities and other good works. The people whom the Prime Minister today recommends to Buckingham Palace to become Lord-Lieutenants more closely reflect society at the start of the 21st century. Women are also appointed to the lieutenancy, but the title of Lord-Lieutenant is applied to whoever holds the position, regardless of gender.

Some Lord-Lieutenants are also appointed to be *Custos Rotulorum* (keeper of the records), the most senior civil officer in the county. Historically, this position gave the holder power to appoint senior officials, but now he or she is the senior magistrate in the county and presides over the Lord Chancellor's advisory committee for the appointment of lay Justices of the Peace.

Gloucestershire is first recorded with that name in *The Anglo Saxon Chronicle* of 1016, but it is probably older. The area technically became a county when Henry I granted it to his natural son Robert as an earldom, 'earl' being the Anglo-Saxon word for 'count', from which 'county' derives. Thereafter, Gloucester's royal associations made it the place to which medieval kings came for one of the three crowning festivals each year. Since the Domesday Book was compiled, the shire has radically altered its boundaries, but the Lord-Lieutenant and *Custos Rotulorum* is still the Sovereign's representative over land that includes the Cotswold Hills, the Forest of Dean and the Severn basin. The lush landscape supports dairy and fruit farming, and lots of sheep.

The Lord-Lieutenant and Custos Rotulorum *of Gloucestershire, once the commander of a large militia, wears a general officer's uniform with silver rather than gold braid. The county, which boasts the Forest of Dean, the Cotswolds and many sheep, has never lost its idyllic rural identity, for instance here at Colesbourne Park near Cirencester.*

Lord-Lieutenant and *Custos Rotulorum* of Gloucestershire

SINCE TUDOR TIMES, Trinity House has safeguarded Britain's busy river routes and rocky shores, guiding mariners safely through coastal waters with a coordinated system of beacons, buoys and other navigation aids. Today, the Corporation's responsibilities have vastly expanded to cover the coastal waters of England, Wales, the Channel Islands and Gibraltar. Its modern Lighthouse Service oversees 72 automatic lighthouses, 13 major floating navigational aids, including lightships and lightfloats, 45 radar beacons and 429 buoys. Trinity House also clears all dangerous wrecks, apart from HM ships.

The Corporation started out as a small medieval guild of mariners and navigators, who were active on the Thames from at least the 15th century, possibly earlier. The guild's fortunes changed radically when in 1513 Henry VIII decided to build the first Royal Dockyard at Deptford, upriver from the palace at Greenwich. The Comptroller of the Navy, Sir Thomas Spert, was put in charge of the project and recruited the expertise of Trinity House. When, one year later, the dockyard was opened, Henry VIII formally chartered the guild to make the Thames safe for mariners. The royal charter established a 'Guild or Fraternity of the most glorious and undividable Trinity and of St Clement in the Parish Church of Deptford Strond'. The new fraternity, comprising a Master, 11 Wardens and Assistants, could now legitimately demand fees for its navigation services in guiding or piloting boats to and from the sea.

The fortunes of Trinity House slumped briefly during Edward IV's reign, when many semi-religious guilds were dissolved, although the Guild survived by changing its name to 'Corporation'. Elizabeth I restored its lost privileges and the right to place beacons, marks and signs along the river Thames.

Initially, business expanded during the reign of James I, and, in 1604, the Corporation organised itself more efficiently into two classes: the Elder Brethren, who discharged operational duties, and the remainder or Younger Brethren, who assisted. After Charles I's execution, the royal Guild was dissolved until 1660, when Charles II revived its fortunes. The Corporation's restored powers and responsibilities were codified in a new royal charter granted by Charles' brother, James II, and drafted by Samuel Pepys in 1685. Growing income from its expanding business led to almshouses at Deptford, as well as a new headquarters, first at Ratcliff, then at Water Lane, and finally, in 1796, on Tower Hill, where Trinity House is the Corporation's London base today.

For Britain, the 19th century was a time of rapid expansion, and the speed of seagoing traffic demanded ever safer shipping routes. For the Corporation, also, responsibility and income increased, and in 1836, Trinity House was granted the right to set up a coordinated, nationwide navigation system.

Throughout the Corporation's history, its Masters have at times played a central role in promoting change or encouraging new technology and business. Two classic examples are the first Master, Sir Thomas Spert, and the first royal Master, Prince Albert. Appointed in 1850, at the height of Britain's naval and colonial expansion, Albert actively promoted the efficiency of England's beacons, improving the safety of her busy shipping lanes. It was Albert, also, who arranged for the Corporation to manage the Thames ballast, increasing its revenue. Since Albert's death, with the exception of his successor Lord Palmerston, all Masters of Trinity House have been princes, some of whom have also been professional naval officers.

Today, the Corporation continues to play a vital role in contemporary navigation. Trinity House also enjoys the unique privilege of guiding the Sovereign safely through home waters with its vessels.

Opposite: *Seafarers have constantly developed aids to navigation in order to sail safely around the globe. The* MASTER OF THE CORPORATION OF TRINITY HOUSE OF DEPTFORD STROND *presides over a Corporation that runs lighthouses, beacons and buoys, marking ports and rocks around the coasts of England, Wales, the Channel Islands and Gibraltar. These are maintained from* THV Patricia, *a model of which is shown. Elizabeth I granted the coat of arms that decorates the entrance hall at Trinity House in the City of London. The uniform worn by the Master recalls the old Royal Navy frock coat pattern, with bands of gold lace round the cuff, similar to that worn by rear-admirals. Trinity's badge is on the cap, buttons and sword belt.*

Master of the Corporation of Trinity House of Deptford Strond

So fast is the incoming tide at Morecambe Bay on the north-west coast of England that it can outpace a galloping horse. The ever-shifting sandbanks created by the waves are dotted with quicksand, but even those who avoid these pitfalls are likely to be ambushed by the sea's rapid return.

Good fortune, however, shines on a few, and these supposedly included the Roman governor Agricola, who successfully crossed Morecambe Bay with an army when heading north through Lancashire, and Robert the Bruce, who probably crossed in the other direction when leading his marauding invasion south. Many travellers risked crossing the broad sands and the unpredictable River Kent in order to shorten their journey, but the risk was high. Indeed, the Abbot of Furness Abbey petitioned the King in 1326 to investigate the great loss of life on the sands.

It is not known when the first guide was appointed to show travellers across the Bay, but the first recorded is Edmonstone in 1501. He was given a 10-acre tenement at Cartmell and described as the Carter upon Kent Sands. His successor, William Gate, was paid by the Prior of the foundation at Cartmell, which was an outpost of Furness Abbey. This bill was later picked up by the Priory of Conished. However, the future looked bleak when the Abbot of Furness was charged with treason for involvement in the Pilgrimage of Grace in 1536, an uprising in response to Henry VIII's doctrinal changes. The Dissolution of the Monasteries followed almost at once, and the vast abbey, the largest Cistercian foundation in the country, was surrendered, together with all its wealth, land and outposts, on 7 April 1537. In 1540 everything was transferred to the Duchy of Lancaster, including responsibility for paying the Guide.

One year after the Abbey was surrendered, Richard Carter was given the job, probably taking his family name from the appointment. He and his descendants drove a cart across the Bay for an annual payment of 10 marks until 1865, but it was dangerous work and led to the death of one Guide, William Carter, in 1672. A letter that his son wrote to the Duchy of Lancaster asking for a pay rise gives an insight to the Guide's life. He described the expense of maintaining two horses and reminded them that his father had lost his life saving two people from drowning. He also explained the hardships and hazards of wind, rain and fog while seeking fresh fording places over the constantly changing river. The plea earned him a sympathetic ear and a few extra pounds in his pay packet.

The Guide still lives at Cartmell, on Guide's Farm, where his predecessors have waited for centuries to provide an escort. The house is surrounded by laurel, both to protect it from the bitter winds and to provide 'brobs' that indicate safe routes across the Bay. Using his stick to test the sand, the Guide finds a safe path, every now and then pushing a brob into the sand, where it will stay as a marker until the tide has covered it many times.

After five centuries, today's Guide is just a telephone call away from helping travellers across the Bay, or taking large parties for a day on the sands. He teaches them how to identify the different types of sand, including caff, slape, slutch and quicksand, which constantly change. The last of these has inevitably made its mark in the local vocabulary: 'There is a saying, "It'll mire a cat," meaning that even a nimble cat would go down in such an area.'

The appointment is now funded by The Queen from her Duchy of Lancaster, and there is still a need for it. Although signs abound, some people still set off alone, ignoring the brobs. They learn the hard way that Kent Sands remain as dangerous as ever.

Queen's Guide over Kent Sands

'Brobs' of laurel, taken from
the bushes that surround
Guide's Farm, are placed at
intervals to mark a safe
route over the constantly
moving sands here in
Morecambe Bay on the

North West coast of
England. These remain in
place for several tides, but
the practice has endured for
at least five centuries.
GUIDES use their eyes, feet
and a stick to find a safe

crossing and have warned
for generations against
walking on the sand at low
tide. When the tide comes in
it can do so at the speed of a
galloping horse. No unwise
walker can escape.

In summer, the Norfolk Broads become a teeming mass of sailing boats and pleasure craft, but away from these crowds, the open and often empty countryside is punctuated by churches built to celebrate faith in God and the wealth of their benefactors.

Standing on what was once a holme (island) in the marshes alongside the River Bure in Norfolk is a crumbling, grey stone wall surrounding a dilapidated building. Its incarnation as a windmill is only its most recent one. These ruins are, in fact, all that remains of the only monastery that Henry VIII left untouched: indeed, he enhanced the influence of its Abbot by enshrining his office in legislation.

The Dissolution resulted in the dismantling of a monastic tradition that had then lasted for about seven centuries, and also saw the destruction of some of the most magnificent buildings in the kingdom. Their traditions of learning and devotion counted for nothing with Henry: it was their wealth, influence and power that he coveted.

When the representative of Henry VIII's Vicar General arrived at this monastery, the countryside was already filled with displaced monks, while burning monasteries illuminated the skyline. Abbot Rugge of St Benet's, awaiting the fateful knock, had no resource but prayer to protect his small community. The Reformation in Europe, together with the consequences of Henry's decision to wed Anne Boleyn, fundamentally disrupted society and severed England's links with Rome. Resistance to the new order was hopeless.

Fortunately for Abbot Rugge, the Vicar General had recently been a guest of the Bishop of Norwich, and witnessed a life of considerable opulence. By comparison, either through bad management or good fortune, the Abbey of St Benet was worth

virtually nothing. Its Benedictine inmates were living in poverty, and their pious example of religious life gave Thomas Cromwell, mastermind of the Dissolution, an idea. Instead of dissolving St Benet's, he persuaded the King to depose the Bishop of Norwich. The wealth of Norwich was taken into the royal coffers, and Abbot Rugge suddenly found himself enthroned in the vacated bishop's cathedra. St Benet's thus won the distinction of being the only abbey that Henry VIII did not dissolve, and by an extraordinary Act of Parliament in 1536 it was protected in perpetuity.

Unfortunately, this turned out to be just a handful of years. Bishop Rugge failed in his obligations to his former abbey, and gradually its buildings decayed and neighbouring farmers removed its stones. By the 19th century, all that remained was the ancient gatehouse, which was transformed into a mill, its sails obscuring the old monastery.

Over the years, the See of Norwich was filled by successive bishops who sat in Parliament and saw no advantage in continuing to use their monastic title, so it fell into disuse. However, this century has seen a change. Anomalies of history are now enjoyed, and there has been a will to revive old customs. Accordingly, the terms of Henry VIII's Act of Parliament have once again been put into effect: a vicar from a local parish now acts as Prior of St Benet-at-Holme, and he has 12 lay monks to assist him in his work. Since 1939 Bishops of Norwich have proudly assumed the title Abbot of St Benet's again, and each August Bank Holiday for the last 60 years, boats have brought a flood of pilgrims to join the Abbot for an open-air service. Thus, a unique title, granted by the King responsible for destroying so much, has kept St Benet's alive long after destruction. After a long abeyance, it has never been healthier than it is now.

Opposite: *Carrying satchel and crozier, the* ABBOT OF ST BENET-AT-HOLME *walks towards the West Gate of the once-great Abbey of St Benet-at-Holme, on the banks of the River Bure in Norfolk, previously the site of a 9th-century chapel founded by Suneman the Hermit. Behind the ruins stands a dilapidated windmill built from the stones of the Abbey's gatehouse. Among the notable people buried at the Abbey is Sir John Fastolff, a hero of Agincourt, who was Governor of the Bastille and Regent of Normandy.*

Abbot of St Benet-at-Holme

When Christ's Hospital moved from the City of London to Sussex in 1902, the 'Grecians' Arch' went too, and the architect incorporated it into the new building. Over a thousand scholars and children made the move, including the two years of sixth-formers, who, since the 17th century, have been called Grecians. One of them is now appointed from among his or her peers as Senior Grecian.

The roots of the school and its traditions lie in the 16th century. Nicholas Ridley, the Bishop of London, was a scholar of great standing. He preached on charity to the teenage King Edward VI, known as 'God's Imp', and his influence on the boy was profound. Ridley, who had already assisted the Anglican reformer Thomas Cranmer in preparing the new articles of faith, was set upon using the impressionable young monarch to spur forward the Reformation. As a result of the sermon, Edward gathered together the Bishop, the Lord Mayor and the Aldermen of the City of London and proposed the foundation of a substantial charity to put Ridley's charitable ideas into effect. Edward himself gave an endowment, and the monarch still contributes today.

With adequate funds gathered, three hospitals were established in 1552, each benefiting from the large legacy of vacant monastic buildings that Henry VIII had left behind. They were Bridewell for the 'Idell vagabondes', St Thomas's Hospital for the 'sore and sicke', which still operates on the south bank of the Thames opposite the Houses of Parliament, and Christ's Hospital, which was established to educate gifted children and originally occupied the buildings in Newgate Street from which the Grey Friars were evicted. The financial endowment was considerable, but within a month of Edward presenting the Charter in 1553, the sickly monarch was dead. England immediately became a hotbed of intrigue, as Bishop Ridley pragmatically proclaimed Lady Jane Grey the dead king's rightful heir. Her reign lasted for only 13 days, and she was succeeded by Edward VI's Roman Catholic sister, Mary, who burnt Ridley at the stake in 1555.

Religious turmoil made the first years of Christ's Hospital difficult to say the least. Queen Mary wanted to restore the building to the Grey Friars, but large bribes and an impassioned appeal by Friar John on the Hospital's behalf saved the day: he said that 'he had rather be a Scullion in theire kytchin then Stewarde to the Kinge'.

Despite the politics, the new school set about providing education for boys and girls with talent but no financial means to pay for decent schooling. The doors first opened to 400 children, some of whom were still infants. Most children stayed in education only until they were 12 or 13 years old, when the demands for clerks in the City drew most away to earn money for their pauper families. Those who remained were destined for Oxford and Cambridge, and their obligatory proficiency in Greek led to their being called Grecians. Within the school they were revered as intellectuals with their heads in the clouds.

The Christ's Hospital Girls' School is now the oldest school for girls in the country, having admitted its first 'poor young maiden child' in December 1554. Originally, charitable organizations proposed most of the children to be taken in and cared for. Even today, financial need is considered alongside academic ability in every application.

The distinctive uniform, worn by all scholars, earned them another name – the 'Blue Coats'. It dates from the foundation of the school and was possibly based on the habit worn by the displaced Grey Friars. The unmissable bright yellow socks were originally designed to keep vermin at bay; apparently, yellow is a colour loathed by rats.

Opposite: A statue of Christ's Hospital's founder, Edward VI, stands above the figures of four 'Old Blues' – Coleridge, Lambe, Middleton and Maine – in front of the school's new buildings in Sussex. The Senior Grecian sits with her books, while the school band, which plays at a parade before lunch, gathers round. All wear a uniform based on that of a Tudor apprentice.

Senior Grecian of Christ's Hospital

THE GREEKS STARTED the custom of crowning poets with laurels – the highest accolade in ancient Greece, as sacred to Apollo, the god of poetry and music. The fashion caught on in Rome, where not only poets and orators, but warriors, senators and emperors were honoured with glory laurels.

With the collapse of the Roman Empire, the custom lapsed, but the spark of epic poetry was kept alight during the Dark Ages by wandering poets who sang their songs of gods and heroes around the courts of Europe. With the revival of classical culture in the late Middle Ages, Latin poetry and laurels came back into fashion, initially at medieval universities, where classical scholars, such as John Skelton, were laureated in Roman fashion, and dubbed 'poet laureate'. The custom caught on at fashionable Renaissance courts, where favourite court poets were commonly called 'poet laureate' as a mark of regard. It was the job of court poets to sing royal praises and entertain the court. The successful were promised, and sometimes paid, a fee. Tudor court poet, Bernard Andreas, received an annuity of 10 marks for drumming up Latin verse for Henry VII. The rate went up under the Stuarts. Ben Johnson, whose lyrical masques entertained the Jacobean court for much of his life, enjoyed a life pension of 100 marks and a 'terse of canary wyne'. Although Andreas, Benson and his successor, William Davenport, were called 'Poet Laureate', the title was not formalised until Charles II appointed John Dryden in 1670.

An inspired choice, Dryden was a gifted narrator and political satirist, whose *Absalom and Achitophel* brilliantly satirised the king's political opponents. Although often labelled a turncoat, Dryden served his Stuart masters well, despite a brief spell under Cromwell. On Charles II's death, Dryden also served James II faithfully, even converting to his Catholic faith. When James was ousted by his Protestant rival, William of Orange, Dryden stuck to his guns and his new-found faith, refusing to swear the oath of allegiance. For standing by his principles, rather than his monarch, Dryden was stripped of office, which passed to his Protestant rival, Thomas Shadwell. The new Laureate did not rest on his laurels, but set to task with industry, if not always ability, setting in motion the onerous custom of royal birthday odes. Shadwell has the dubious honour of being the first in a long run of poets who seemed picked for political loyalty rather than poetic flair, and whose lack of literary success gave the office a very bad name. Other political choices followed in quick succession: Colley Cibber, derided by his peers; William Whitehead, denounced as even worse than Cibber; Henry Pye, described by Walter Scott as a man respectable in everything but his poetry.

Pye drew contempt for a series of glowing birthday odes to ill-respected Hanoverian princes, which made the practice risible. He was also responsible for requesting that the gift of wine be suspended in lieu of cash. However, Sir John Betjeman requested that this be reinstated, when he was appointed in 1972; feeling that there was nothing to be lost in the pleasure of a drink and it might even free up the muse.

The honour is now freely given to one selected from all, on the recommendation of the Prime Minister, and the Crown makes no formal expectations. New appointments still trigger debate, just as they always have done. After the titan Alfred Lord Tennyson died, no candidate was regarded as adequate. There are still some who deride the appointment but each holder carries the office in a unique direction while maintaining a tradition that reaches back through Dryden, Shakespeare and Chaucer to the Greek ideals and the God Apollo.

Opposite: One of the attractions for visitors to Westminster Abbey, in London, is Poets' Corner. This church was founded by Edward the Confessor in 1065, and rebuilt by Henry III in the 13th century as a coronation church to rival that of Reims in France. It is regarded as the nation's pantheon and part of the south transept has been given over to monuments commemorating the great names of English literature and verse. Here Chaucer was buried and Shakespeare is honoured, in a busy clutter of lettered stones bearing poets' names that capture the momentary recognition of passers-by. Among the names are those of Poets Laureate, such as the first official titleholder, Dryden, and Tennyson. Here, standing among the casual tourists, is the current POET LAUREATE – *pen and paper in hand – observing the world, its people and its time.*

Poet Laureate

'The king's right hand at the pen, the issuer of the royal

manuscript authority, whether for the ends of state policy,

for transactions of law, or for private purposes.'

HISTORIAN OF THE SOCIETY OF WRITERS TO HM SIGNET, 1890

THE OLDEST SURVIVING OFFICE of State in Scotland is the Lord Clerk Register. The Act of Union in 1707 made many other appointments redundant because they no longer had a legislative or executive function once the Parliament at Westminster had taken over. However, the post of Lord Clerk Register survives as a link with Scotland's independent past, although most of its remaining functions were removed by Act of Parliament in 1879. He still retains a strong symbolic role as one of the guardian commissioners for keeping Scotland's ancient crown jewels, the Honours Three.

Combined with his primary role, the Lord Clerk is also Keeper of the Signet. This more junior appointment dates from the time when the King's authority was communicated through the land by writs or warrants, written and read by barely literate people. In order to authenticate these documents, a system of seals was developed, and those matters that related specifically to the monarch, or were private to him, were sealed with the King's own Signet ring. The oldest surviving impression of the monarch's private Signet dates from 1342, but Robert the Bruce is known to have used one even earlier.

As the volume of paperwork increased, the King appointed a Secretary to deal with it, and when the burden of work became greater still, the Secretary hired clerks to assist in the preparation of writs. These new clerks were first described as Writaries to the Signet, and their influence increased as fast as the workload. As the King did not have the time to seal everything that needed his Signet, he placed the ring in the care of his Secretary, who became known as Keeper of the Signet.

In 1532, James V overhauled his legal administration and established the College of Justice. The Writaries to the Signet were established as part of the new court system, advising applicants for justice on how to proceed. Further legislation that year established regulations by which the growing number of Writaries were to be bound. In 1594, Sir Robert Cockburn of Clerkington, who was Lord Secretary to the King and Keeper of the Signet, commissioned John Layng to be Deputy Keeper of the Signet. In this role he had authority over 18 Writaries, but Cockburn retained responsibility for the Signet.

The nature of civil writs in Scotland was such that, to achieve validity in law, they had to be seen by the monarch, and his sight of them was evidenced by the impression of his Signet on the writ. By the end of James V's reign, legal documents needed to be sealed with four Signets. Today only one is required. Among the documentation needing to be sealed by the Signet are those involving the Supreme Court, summonses from the Lords of Council and Session, letters of diligence and execution, and letters staying or prohibiting diligence. Each document is scrutinized by the Signet Officer to ensure it is 'right and proper' to go before the courts. Then it will 'pass the Signet', when the press is wound down and the document is impressed with the seal of the Signet.

The ancient appointment of King's Secretary, which evolved into Lord Secretary, was abolished in 1746, following a shake-up of Scottish institutions after the Battle of Culloden, which concluded the Jacobite Rebellion. However, the office of Keeper of the Signet survived, and in 1817 it was given to the Lord Clerk Register. The combined titles have historic significance: that of the Lord Clerk Register retains ancient links with the original Great Officers of Scotland before Union in 1707, while the Keeper of the Signet reminds us of the evolution of royal law from the 14th century to the present day.

The Sovereign's seal or Signet is held within an elaborate screw press that is kept in Edinburgh's Petition Office. The bulk and weight of this device convey something of the seal's authority, not least to initiate an action in the Court of Session. The LORD CLERK REGISTER AND KEEPER OF THE SIGNET is a symbolic guardian of an object that still proves vital.

Lord Clerk Register and Keeper of the Signet

Legend has it that a 16th-century king of Scotland was saved from death by a yeoman farmer, unaware of the rescued man's identity. The rescue and the farmer's reward were described by Sir Walter Scott in *Tales of a Grandfather* and resulted in a custom unrivalled for its symbolism and charm.

Cramond Bridge, between Edinburgh and the Forth Road Bridge, is an unremarkable place today, but it was here, in the reign of King James V of Scotland, that a farmer named John Howieson came upon a group of ruffians mugging a well-dressed gentleman. Fearing that they might murder the man, the farmer, with flail in hand, went to his aid. Unknown to him, the man was James V, who regularly travelled in disguise in order to learn what was happening in his kingdom.

After a short struggle, the muggers fled and John Howieson took the injured man back to his cottage and washed his wounds. He then accompanied him back towards Edinburgh in case the muggers struck again. The gentleman had introduced himself as the Goodman (tenant) of Ballengiech and holder of a lowly court appointment. Howieson told him that he was working on the King's farm at Braehead. The gentleman asked what was the one thing he would most like to own and, in the words of Scott's story, 'honest John confessed he should think himself the happiest man in Scotland were he but proprietor of the farm on which he wrought as a labourer'. When they parted, the gentleman invited Howieson to look over the royal apartments at Holyrood Palace the following Sunday.

The farmer kept the appointment in his best clothes and the Goodman of Ballengiech showed him around, 'amused with his wonder and his remarks'. When asked if he would like to see the King, Howieson excitedly agreed and was told that when they came into the royal presence, the King would be the only one wearing a hat. On entering a hall packed with courtiers, Howieson nervously searched for his hatted monarch. After looking everywhere, he turned to his escort and said, 'It must be either you or me, for all but us two are bareheaded.' The truth of this remark suddenly struck home, and the farmer knelt before James V, who gave Howieson the farm at Braehead that he wanted, but gave it away on condition that Howieson and his successors should be ready to present a ewer and basin for the monarch to wash his hands, either at Holyrood Palace or when passing by Cramond Bridge.

In 1822 George IV set out on the 'King's Jaunt' to Scotland. It was a significant visit, the first since the 1745 rebellion when much of Scotland's culture had been outlawed. For the first time in nearly 100 years the King (wearing a kilt) gave permission for bagpipes to be played. The rebirth of Scottish culture was helped along by Walter Scott's romantic retellings of history, including the rediscovery of the Honours Three (the country's crown, sceptre and sword), which were found wrapped in sheets behind the panelling of Edinburgh Castle's throne room.

To make the monarchy relevant to Scotland once again, the hitherto 'absentee' Hanoverians plunged themselves into all things Scottish. It was George IV who revived the service that his Stuart ancestor had instigated. William Howieson Crawford presented his ewer and basin to George IV, and the King broke the habit of a lifetime by washing his hands.

Whenever called upon since to perform the service, three members of the family (now called Houison Craufurd) come from Craufurland Castle with the silver basin and ewer made for George IV. The senior one holds the basin, while the other two pour the water and offer a linen towel from a salver.

Mr Houison Craufurd who washes the Sovereign's Hands

The ewer, basin and salver holding fresh linen have been used to wash royal hands by the HOUISON CRAUFURD family since George IV revived the ritual in the early 19th century. This bridge across the River Cramond, near Edinburgh, may have been where the family's kind ancestor saved a king from murderous thugs in an act of courage that was well rewarded. Mr Craufurd washed George VI's hands when he was 10 years old and Elizabeth II's soon after her coronation.

Just as John Howieson was presented with an honour from James V in gratitude for the service he had provided at a time of great danger (see page 126), there were many others who received similar gifts from the Royal House of Stuart for services rendered. It was then customary for monarchs to give posts within the wider royal court, as these provided the recipient with a useful income and valuable access to the monarch. When power lay with the King, his court was the place to be, and no matter what task was required, it allowed the recipient to have the ear of those who counted. For this reason, the history of many royal courts is awash with utilitarian roles granted as hereditary offices to deserving nobles. However, it is doubtful whether many were actually fulfilled in anything more than a ceremonial way, the actual task probably being left to paid servants.

Some of these appointments were given in such informal terms that no written evidence of them exists. In some cases, a change in family fortunes, particularly a lack of heirs, saw the appointments fade into obscurity. One such situation faced the Borthwick family, who claim to be hereditary Falconers to the Scottish monarch. No charter exists to prove the appointment, although there are references to their special role before the union of the crowns. In 1672, the 9th Lord Borthwick died leaving no heir, so the title and its honours fell into abeyance. It was not until 1986 that the Lord Lyon (see page 58) recognized a junior branch of the family and allowed both title and honours to be revived.

The Borthwicks claim that, in return for services to the Stuart kings, they received the privilege of acting as hereditary royal Falconers. This was a service associated with leisure, and therefore a sign of the King's particular esteem and friendship. When James I of Scotland was imprisoned by the English, the head of the Borthwick family offered himself instead, and his self-imposed sentence dragged on for three years. When he was finally returned to Scotland in 1430, the grateful monarch allowed Borthwick to build his own castle and gave him a peerage 20 years later. Over the centuries, the Borthwicks continued to give valuable service to the Scottish kings; in fact, the 3rd Lord Borthwick lost his life fighting beside James IV at the Battle of Flodden.

Falconry remained a very popular pastime until about the time that the Borthwick title fell into abeyance. According to the strict rules that governed what birds of prey could be owned by various ranks, eagles were restricted to emperors and kings; gerfalcons to other members of royalty; peregrines to earls; goshawks to yeomen; and sparrowhawks to priests. The 'hopeless' kestrel was for knaves and servants.

In England, the appointment of Hereditary Master Falconer was given to the 1st Duke of St Albans, the 14-year-old son of Charles II by his mistress Nell Gwynn, in the 1680s. He was also given permission to ride in a coach along Rotten Row, the sandy track that runs through London's Hyde Park, a privilege usually restricted to the Sovereign. The eccentric Duke's descendant was invited to The Queen's coronation in 1953, but having said that he would arrive as Hereditary Master Falconer, with a live falcon, he was dissuaded and consequently did not attend.

'O! for a falconer's voice,

To lure this tassel-gentle back again.'

William Shakespeare, *Romeo and Juliet*

The ancestors of the Hereditary Falconer hunted across this land near Heriot, Midlothian, in the southern uplands of Scotland, with falcons. Lord Borthwick, the 24th peer and current bearer of the title, is holding a female peregrine falcon into the wind. This species is still the most popular bird of prey to work these hills.

Hereditary Falconer

THE CHANNEL ISLANDS are all that remain of the once-powerful Duchy of Normandy, most of which was lost by King John to the French, along with most of his Angevin inheritance, in the early 13th century. (Not for nothing was he nicknamed 'Lackland'.) Sark remains a self-governing Crown protectorate within the bailiwick of Guernsey but, as a matter of administrative convenience, the current Duke (HM Queen Elizabeth II) asks her government in Britain to keep an avuncular eye on its business, provide defence and attend to the diplomatic interests of all her Channel Islands, while recognizing that they are not, nor ever have been, part of the United Kingdom. Nonetheless, the Seigneur of Sark knelt before her in 1978 and, in time-honoured tradition, pledged the loyalty of the last feudal constitution in the world: 'Souveraine dame, je demeure votre homme lige à vous porter foi et hommage contre tous.' (Sovereign lady, I remain your liegeman to render you faith and homage against all.)

In the 16th century Sark was deserted: raids from the French coast and a short period of occupation had left it derelict. Helier de Carteret, who already held the premier fief of St Ouen in Jersey, petitioned the Crown for Sark as well. However, the Royal Charter of 1565 granted it to him as a separate fief, the first time that Sark had been recognized as such. The Charter also formally defined the way this new Seigneur and his island's government would work.

The current Seigneur's family have enjoyed tenure since 1852, when, with the Crown's approbation, they accepted it in part payment of a debt. They can hold it in perpetuity, as long as the *rente* is paid to Her Majesty's Receiver General on Guernsey each Michaelmas. As this amounts to only 'one twentieth part of a knight's fee' (£1.79 in modern money), it is not onerous. The amount has not altered since it was set, although it was once a considerable sum of money. The Seigneur must also undertake to provide 40 armed men, who will stand and defend the island from attack, a task achieved by requiring each tenant to supply him with at least one man armed with a 'musket' when required.

The Seigneur is, in his own words, 'like a managing director or the captain of a ship. There's no one else to look after the community: people come to see me if they have any political or civil problems which they can't solve, and I am a representative for Sark in the outside world.' His predecessor and grandmother, the Dame of Sark, proved this in her handling of German invaders during the Second World War. By sheer force of personality, she insisted that the occupiers respect her feudal rights and issue no edicts until she had seen them first. In that way she helped prevent too many ill-conceived restrictions on rural life. The Seigneur explains: 'She'd kick up hell if the German officers were rude or intimidating, and say, "Don't you speak to me like that." Also, because they knew nothing about the islanders' lives, she often managed to ameliorate the invaders' absurd instructions.'

The Seigneur must appoint the Officers of the Island, who include the Prévôt, Greffier and Treasurer. A Seneschal was introduced by an Order in Council of 1675 to replace the old judge and jurat system, and this too is within his appointment. In a manner similar to The Queen in Britain, the Seigneur, with the Seneschal, summons the parliament, which is called the Court of Chief Pleas. Originally, this assembly contained just the 40 Tenants settled by the first Seigneur. While this was democratically representative of those who owned the land, today the line-up has altered to reflect greater diversity: it now includes 12 Deputies, who

Opposite: The cliffs that surround the island of Sark, one of the Channel Islands, have always provided its main defence. The SEIGNEUR OF SARK *maintains his obligation to hold this outpost for the Duke of Normandy by summoning 40 armed men from the tenancies. Their muskets have only an agricultural purpose today, but as recently as the 1940s they were part of the island's resistance to Nazi Germany's invasion.*

Seigneur of Sark

are elected by other islanders every three years.

Lying off the French coast, Sark appears like a fortress: 500-foot cliffs rise to a plateau of just three miles by one and a half, which is covered by a patchwork of small fields. There are no cars and the rural uniqueness is underpinned by numerous historical quirks. For example, the Seigneur is the only person allowed to keep an unspayed bitch. (This is to control canine proliferation in an area full of sheep.) He also has *droit de colombier*, making him the sole keeper of pigeons, for which there is a small dovecote at his residence, La Seigneurie.

The outside world regards Sark with fascination, misunderstanding and reforming zeal. To many, it appears an anachronism bogged down in arcane practices. However, the people of Sark do not appear to be in a great hurry for change: they have their own assembly, a peaceful lifestyle and few restrictions. The Seigneur is conscious of his responsibilities and rejects any notion that his role demands deference from the islanders. For him there is a parliament to call, appointments to make and a yearly *rente* demand to attend to. There is also an ancient French oath to teach his son and heir.

ALTHOUGH NOW RENOWNED as a centre of academic excellence with superb facilities, Oxford University has known hard times. During the mid-16th century, for example, it had no central library. Its book collections, built upon those bequeathed by Thomas Cobham, Bishop of Worcester, in 1327, and housed in a room over the old convocation house in St Mary's Church, had been dispersed, the final blow coming from the Protestant reformers in 1550, who were said to have given them away or sold them 'to Mechanicks for servile uses'.

The first hints of organized learning at Oxford were the theological lectures given by Robert Pullen in 1133, though it is possible that Henry I's palace at Beaumont may have attracted scholars to Oxford's royal court before. The Bishop of Lincoln appointed a Chancellor there in 1214, and the colleges of Balliol, Merton and University appeared in the last decades of the 13th century. Cobham's library was therefore established fairly early in the University's life, though funds nearly fell short at the start. Help came from Henry IV, his son Henry V, and the princes Thomas, John and Humfrey, Duke of Gloucester. The last of these donated a collection of rare manuscripts, many of which were new to England. When building of the new Divinity School was completed in 1488, the library moved into an upper storey. It was this collection that was dispersed during the religious upheavals of the 16th century and which left a 'great empty room' for 50 years where Oxford's growing heart had been.

To this shell in 1598 came the Devonian Thomas Bodley, recently retired from court. He was a scholar of Hebrew, who had studied at Magdalen College and lectured in Greek at Merton. After a lifetime of service to Elizabeth I, he hoped now to serve his University. Twelve years earlier he had married a wealthy widow, and was now bent on benevolence: his ambition was to restore and restock the library. After just four years, the doors were opened to the scholars and they found shelves filled with books that Bodley had collected from all over Europe. The appointment of Thomas James as the first Librarian marked the fulfilment of Bodley's ambition. Although he had achieved all this within the last year of Elizabeth's reign, it was her successor, James I, who dubbed him a knight in recognition of his achievement.

Sir Thomas went on to enter into an agreement with the Stationers Company that would distinguish his library from all others at the time. He persuaded the Company to send a free copy of every book it licensed to his library. This privilege was forfeited with the collapse of the Star Chamber, Henry VII's civil and criminal court, during the Civil War. Re-established only fitfully in the half century after the Restoration, it was fully restored by the Copyright Act of 1710. The library continues to receive a free copy of every book published, so there is a never-ending demand for space. The Quadrangle built in front of the Divinity School between 1613 and 1619 was equipped by Bodley with a floor dedicated to book storage, but this was quickly filled, and it has been the responsibility of each succeeding Librarian to arrange further storage as required.

It is impossible to quantify the benefits of the Bodleian collection on the increase of wisdom, but it has undoubtedly enabled some of the greatest minds in the world to pursue their academic endeavours. Sir Thomas Bodley's decision to spend the final years of his life turning the remains of a neglected library into a renowned place of study and research is one that has benefited generations of students. More than a memorial to a remarkable man, the library is a symbol of England's civilization.

Bodley's Librarian

The 22nd Librarian sits
on Sir Thomas Bodley's
Chair in Duke Humfrey's
Library, above the Divinity
School. Through the
window can be seen the
Tower of the Five Orders of
Architecture, which rises
above the main gate to the
Library in the heart of
Oxford University.
BODLEY'S LIBRARIAN is
supported in his role of
maintaining this complete
collection of all published
books in Britain by four
others, known as 'keepers'.
They include the Keeper of
the Printed Books, who
supervises a constantly
growing resource.

FOR OVER THREE HUNDRED YEARS the Fellows of All Souls College, Oxford, have held revelries at which they sing their traditional Mallard Song. The festivities are presided over by one of their number bearing the title Lord Mallard. Chosen for his singing voice, he holds the office for several years. In the 17th century there were annual Mallard processions round the College, rather riotous and disorderly in character. Their traditional date was on 14 January.

In the first year of each century since 1801, the Mallard procession has continued to take place, as a celebration of the College, while the song is sung each year at gaudies, or revelries. The word gaudy is an adjective meaning vulgar and extravagant. The Mallard Song, which was first written down in the 17th century, may have been sung from a hundred years before, being passed orally from term to term.

Centennial Mallard Dinners are controlled by the College's authorities. Gowned Fellows parade at night all round the College, not omitting the rooftops. They hold blazing torches, carry the Lord Mallard in a chair, and sing the song over and over again. At the head of the procession a mallard duck (nowadays a model, but in former times a real one) is carried on a pole. The procession is notionally a hunt for the mallard of legend, which allegedly flew up from an old sewer when the foundations for All Souls College were dug in 1438. No substantiated proof of this story has been discovered, although there is a false document, claiming to be a record of the foundation, which describes how the founder, Henry Chichele, Archbishop of Canterbury, had a dream in which he was advised where to build his college, and told that the 'schwoppinge Mallarde' appearing would confirm it. He dug in the place shown in his dream, only for the duck to fly from the drain as predicted. What is known as fact is that a seal was discovered in the foundations, on which was engraved an heraldic griffin and the name of a Clerk, called William Malard. Such a story, when exposed to time, creativity and nonsense, can easily develop into a good myth: this, in turn, provided the Mallard Song. Whatever the true source of the song, the fable has been dignified from observance by generations of Fellows, and the mallard now appears as a decoration on much of the college's tableware and other property.

The College of All Souls of the Faithful Departed, to give its full name, was established by Henry VI, with Henry Chichele, who endowed it. In its patent of creation, the Warden and College are called to pray for 'the souls of all the faithful departed … who … in the service of [Henry V] … ended their lives in the wars of the kingdom of France'. Archbishop Chichele had been closely involved in the war and its diplomatic consequences, and had taken part in negotiating Henry V's marriage to Katherine de Valois, daughter of the French king; thereafter he crowned her at Westminster and baptised their son, the future Henry VI. Chichele died in 1443, just 10 days after sealing the completed statutes of his college, and was buried in a tomb he had taken trouble to prepare in Canterbury Cathedral.

At the time of the 1901 procession, Cosmo Lang was the appointed Lord Mallard. Like the college's founder, he later became Archbishop of Canterbury. Perhaps it is not surprising then that he ended the habit of slaughtering a mallard and pouring its fresh blood into cups for all to drink: instead, he donated a silver mallard, from which Madeira was poured. A telegram was sent from the same 12-course dinner preceding the procession, to Lord Curzon, a former Fellow of All Souls who was by then Viceroy of India, in Calcutta. It contained one word: 'Swapping'. The reply from the potentate was just as simple and said, 'It was.'

Lord Mallard of All Souls

The Griffine, Bustard, Turkey and Capon, Lett other hungry Mortalls gape on

And on theire bones with Stomacks fall hard, But lett Allsouls' Men have ye Mallard.

Hough the bloud of King Edward, By ye bloud of King Edward,

It was a swapping, swapping mallard!

'THE MALLARD SONG' (C.16TH CENTURY)

THE CROWN JEWELS ATTRACT millions of visitors each year. They are the most tangible symbols of Sovereignty in the land, vested with both romance and spiritual significance, and have been kept for the last 700 years in the ancient and mysterious surroundings of London's principal fortress, the Tower, in the care of Masters and Keepers of the Jewel House. It is only in recent times that they have been set with valuable gems, making them priceless objects in their own right; however, they have always held value principally from the emblematic function each object represents in the religious ceremony of coronation. The English Regalia is still venerated for this quasi-religious role and its care and protection is taken as seriously as it ever was. It has also been the target of plots and ridicule from thieves and republicans, which perhaps is but another of the important roles it performs for the nation's cultural story.

In medieval times, the regalia, or *jocalia* as it was then called, was divided between the ancient Saxon symbols used for coronation, which were kept by the Abbot of Westminster in the care of the Abbey Sacrist, and the personal jewels of the monarch that were used at the *coronamenta*, or crown-wearing religious festivals, which were kept close at hand. Henry III established the Tower as the repository of royal treasure, a decision that proved its worth in 1303 when the Great Burglary took place at Westminster. The king's treasure was the responsibility of the Lord Treasurer and the Privy Wardrobe until 1378, when John Bacon was appointed *Custos Jocalium Regis*, which was later translated as 'Keper of ye Kinges Jewells'. Thus began the tradition of a principal guardian. One Keeper pawned the crown in order to raise funds for the Agincourt campaign against the French in 1415, an action that was frequently repeated.

The Keepers, or Masters of the Jewel House, supervised not a single building but a department: they were often noblemen for whom the appointment was a sinecure, the work being carried out by clerks and warders; while the actual maintenance was vested in the King's Goldsmiths. During the Civil War the then Keeper, Sir Henry Mildmay, defected to the Parliamentarians and took Henry Martin, a Member of Parliament, to make inventory in the Abbey of St Edward's Regalia. Exposing the sacred objects to ridicule, Martin tried them on, calling them 'monuments to superstition and idolatry'; later they were broken up and sold.

At the Restoration a new Keeper, Sir Gilbert Talbot, engaged Robert Vyner as Royal Goldsmith to make a complete set of new regalia. Although, like most goldsmiths at the time, Vyner's principal business was lending money as banks do now, it was he who made many of the objects that are still used and kept in the Jewel House. Subsequently the Vyner family established a tradition for making regalia as required and for maintaining and cleaning the existing collection, a job which is done today by the Crown Jeweller.

Ladies were appointed Exhibitors of the Jewels in the 19th century, but this tradition ended in 1900. However, the Deputy Exhibitor, as Jewel House Supervisor, is responsible for a number of women employees among the Warders, who supervise the vast queues of visitors. The Keeper's role was combined with that of Resident Governor in 1967. As Keeper of the Jewel House, or Crown Jewels, he remains responsible, like all his predecessors, through the Lord Chamberlain directly to the monarch. Although there have been few attempts to steal the crown jewels, their value and significance keeps this guardian in a constant state of vigil.

Opposite: In the entrance of the Jewel House at the Tower of London, the RESIDENT GOVERNOR AND KEEPER OF THE JEWEL HOUSE *holds the Jewelled Sword of Offering, by tradition the Sovereign's personal sword, used at coronations since 1821. Keepers have carried regalia at coronations since the 13th century. The* CROWN JEWELLER *always wears gloves to handle the Regalia. The* JEWEL HOUSE SUPERVISOR *carries keys to the secure vault – for good reason. In 1671 the Deputy Keeper was knocked out by Colonel Blood, who almost escaped with crown, sceptre and orb, which he grabbed, stuffed into a bag and attempted to steal. They were recovered and given to the Royal Goldsmith to be repaired. Blood was pardoned and given a pension.*

Resident Governor and Keeper of the Jewel House

Opened by Her Majesty The Queen · 24th March 1994

DIEU ET MON DROIT

4 Uniting a Kingdom

1603–1750

A GENEALOGICAL COINCIDENCE began the unification of the kingdom from two old enemies. Elizabeth, the Virgin Queen, died in 1603, and left the throne to her cousin James VI of Scots. James I of England, as he became, had written: 'God gives not kings the style of Gods in vain, For on his throne his sceptre do they sway,' hinting at the absolutism that would make the Stuart dynasty one of Britain's most controversial. This unification of crowns was the first step to political unity, joining the two countries both for economic advantage and for the defence of their interests against ideological opponents in Catholic Europe.

For Scotland, an absentee monarchy posed constitutional problems. With its single-chambered parliament, the country was arguably easier to govern than its southern neighbour. But the growing power of the Kirk since 1560 proved a formidable opponent. To maintain his authority from London, James appointed Commissioners to represent him both at Scotland's Parliament and in the Kirk's General Assembly. The Union in 1707 removed any need for parliamentary Commissioners, but the Crown's relationship was maintained with an increasingly independent Kirk.

England offered negligible resistance to the new Scots dynasty of Stuarts. This was partly because James I was staunchly Protestant and sought to centralize power in the monarchy. However, in due course Charles I's disinclination to consult his Parliament, together with his wife's Catholicism, led to a fundamental breach between the king and the Commons. Charles was blind to the reality of the political situation, and civil war and the king's own execution followed. Succeeding Charles as ruler,

Cromwell revived the title of Lord Protector, but stopped short of accepting the Crown.

Scotland disagreed with England's regicide, crowned the late king's son Charles II, at Scone in 1651, and as a result suffered Cromwellian brutality and eventual unification with England under the Commonwealth, from 1652 to 1660. Autonomy returned with the Restoration of Charles II, who rewarded his supporters well. The army was thanked (or forgiven, depending on which side they had taken) with the establishment of the Royal Hospital at Chelsea, which provided shelter for elderly men at arms. In Ireland, too, Charles gave out honours, including one creating the Hill family Constables of a fort they had built in the town of Hillsborough. When Titus Oates whipped up anti-Catholic fear against Charles, the king's natural son, the Duke of Monmouth, persuaded his father to protect himself better: as a result Monmouth was made the first Gold Stick.

James II succeeded his brother in 1685, having been, as Duke of York, both High Commissioner in Scotland and Lord High Admiral. He fell quickly from favour, having failed to reassure Parliament that he was not seeking, in this Age of Reason, to establish a Catholic despotism. The Glorious Revolution of 1688 ended James's reign, and Parliament invited his daughter, Mary, and son-in-law, William of Orange, to take the throne, subject to terms that restricted royal powers.

Many in Scotland did not share the English wish to replace James II, and the imposition of the new regime was carried out brutally, culminating in the massacre of the Macdonalds at Glencoe in 1696. To prevent such a thing happening again, after Queen Anne succeeded William in 1702 Scotland's

Parliament passed the Act of Security, to ensure that Scots could choose their own successor to Anne. This filled England with concern that James II's son, the Old Pretender, might inherit, and the queen was advised to withhold Assent. However, she had to live with this legislation because she needed Scottish taxes for her army, fighting abroad under the leadership of the Duke of Marlborough. The English Parliament retaliated with the Aliens Act, by which Scots were treated as aliens unless they accepted Anne's Hanoverian heir. At around this time the queen granted a charter to the Royal Company of Archers, who became in due course the monarch's official Body Guard in Scotland.

The political and economic tensions between the two kingdoms reached a point that could only be followed by separation or outright union. In 1707, the Act of Union came into effect. With the words, 'It is full time to put an end to it', power passed from Edinburgh to Westminster. Trading arrangements were shared, but Scots Law was retained, under the head of Scotland's legal structure, the Lord President of the Court of Session.

On Anne's death in 1714, while the Crown of the United Kingdom of Great Britain was passed to George I, who was a distant Protestant cousin from Hanover, rebellion brewed in Scotland around the figure of James VIII, the Old Pretender. Many rallied to this cause in 1715, and again in 1745. The Jacobite rising was put down at the last battle on British soil, at Culloden in 1746. Thereafter, the Hanoverians undermined the ancient Scottish clan system. At around the same time, Freemasonry, a society of secrets, was becoming organized, and attracted members from the intelligentsia and aristocracy, first in Scotland, then in England; it thrived too in Ireland, among affluent Protestants. The Royal Family united the movement in the following century.

George I spoke few words of English; therefore business was conducted in his name by Privy Councillors, who formed a Cabinet of ministerial advisers. Meanwhile he revelled in his new kingdom's wealth, just as James I had done. The kingdoms of Scotland and England were one

(the union with Wales had taken place in 1536) and in 1801 Ireland would join the fold. Westminster was now the seat of Britain's government and the Thames was the capital's thoroughfare: the Worshipful Company of Watermen and Lightermen saw business boom. But as the century progressed the chill wind of revolution began to blow through Europe and the British colonies.

Opposite: *Always in close attendance, the Colonel, The Blues and Royals prepares to escort the Sovereign to the Queen's Birthday Parade from the freshly raked inner quadrangle of Buckingham Palace. The first lady to hold the appointment carries the ebony stick with its golden tip, which was laid down by Charles II to be the symbol of office for* GOLD STICK IN WAITING. *Since Charles's time, the need for security has altered and the role has become increasingly ceremonial. Now Gold Stick accompanies the monarch when riding, travelling by carriage or moving among the public at ceremonial occasions.*

ONE OF THE OLDEST AND CLOSEST of royal body guards, Gold Stick once served a vital role as the Sovereign's protection officer. The post emerged at a time of crisis, during the fictitious Popish Plot – a 'hellish' conspiracy to kill Charles II and to put his Catholic brother James on the throne and massacre all Protestants. The Popish Plot was a tissue of lies, fabricated by a mischief-maker, Titus Oates, who hoped to win fame by discovering, if not inventing, Catholic plots. In a country where Catholics were passionately hated and pathologically feared, Oates's elaborate plot threw London into panic, precipitating the judicial slaughter of 35 innocent Catholics. Religious tension escalated to fever pitch. Parliament passed an act excluding all Roman Catholics from sitting in either house.

When the Popish plot gathered momentum, the Duke of Monmouth, Charles's illegitimate son, implored his doubting father to take precautions. Combining his responsibilities as Colonel of the First Troop of Life Guards with his filial concern for Charles II, Monmouth recommended a new appointment that would be directly responsible for the Sovereign's safety. The king concurred and created the post of Gold Stick in Waiting, the holder of which would be in constant attendance on the king 'from his rising to his going to bed…carrying in his hand an ebony staff or truncheon with a gold head engraved with his majesty's cipher and crown'. The post was thereby attached to Colonels in the Household Cavalry and, if they were unable to be in attendance an officer immediately junior could step in and be called Silver Stick in Waiting.

The growing anti-Catholic sentiment led parliament to persuade Charles to exile his brother James and make the Protestant Monmouth his heir. Later he changed his mind, and Monmouth lost his appointment as Gold Stick and was exiled in turn.

When James II succeeded in 1685, Monmouth returned to challenge him for the throne. Monmouth's vainglorious hopes were dashed at the battle of Sedgemore, where he fled the field, leaving his wretched peasant followers to certain butchery. By a quirk of just desserts, he was captured by his old regiment, the Life Guards, led by the Earl of Faversham. For his part in saving the Sovereign, Faversham was chosen as the next Gold Stick. Colonels of the Life Guards have since served as Gold Stick, with their lieutenants ever ready to stand in as Silver Stick.

After the tumultuous times of the Stuarts, royal security relaxed for some centuries. Apart from occasional risings in Scotland, any domestic threat seemed minimal. The greatest potential threat came from abroad, during the Napoleonic wars with France, until the Duke of Wellington swept the French from the field at the decisive battle of Waterloo in 1815. For his part in the action, Wellington was made Colonel of a regiment called the Blues by George IV, and the regiment was raised to the status of Household Cavalry in 1820. Ever since, Colonels of the Blues (now merged with the Royals) have shared the duties of Gold Stick with Colonels of the Life Guards.

The duties now are mainly ceremonial, accompanying the Sovereign on all state occasions and passing the Sovereign's orders to the Household Cavalry. Today the job of round-the-clock, front-line royal protection is carried out by a hand-picked squad of policemen, who field ever-present threats to the monarchy. Gold Stick still shadows the Sovereign on occasion, but purely ceremonial capacity, accompanies, the monarch when riding, travelling by carriage or walking through London. As cavalry officers, all Gold Sticks have been excellent horsemen.

Gold Stick in Waiting

Opposite: *For the duration of the Queen's Commission, which covers the sitting of the Church of Scotland's General Assembly, the* LORD HIGH COMMISSIONER *lives like a king. He stays here at the Palace of Holyroodhouse, from which he flies the Royal Lion Rampant flag, and keeps a retinue of staff. This is headed by the* PURSEBEARER, *who carries a purse embroidered with the Queen of Scot's arms, which once contained money to pay for any expenses. The fountain in the background plays only for The Queen or during the Commission.*

After 1603, when James VI left his court in Edinburgh to take possession of his English kingdom as James I, he relied on a Lord High Commissioner to represent his sovereign authority in Scotland's Parliament. Subsequent monarchs followed this practice until the Act of Union in 1707 ended the separate Scottish legislature. However, the Lord High Commissioner continued to represent the king at the assemblies of Scotland's established church, and in this viceregal role enjoyed many of the privileges that would otherwise be accorded to the Sovereign. Nowadays, for the week or so of the appointment, the Lord High Commissioner is driven in cars without number plates, uses the standard of the Scots Sovereign, is addressed as 'Your Grace' and resides in the Palace of Holyroodhouse. He or she also has a Pursebearer, who once carried money granted by the king to cover the Commissioner's expenses while in office: today the Pursebearer is the principal administrator of the Commissioner's suite and programme.

When Queen Elizabeth II acceded to the throne, she was required to sign a document promising to 'preserve the settlement of the true Protestant religion as established by laws made in Scotland'. This formality is a reminder of the struggle and broken promises between Stuart kings and Church of Scotland reformers in the 16th and 17th centuries. Principal among those reformers was the forthright Scot John Knox, a follower of the French Protestant John Calvin, who himself had been influenced by the radical ideas of Martin Luther, the founder of Protestantism in the 16th century. Knox was an outspoken cleric, who helped introduce reform to Scotland's Roman Catholic Church, historically a maverick institution. Protestantism, with its practice of non-episcopal (bishop-less) self-government, posed a very real political threat to the established Church, which had hitherto recognized royal authority in a more hierarchical fashion. Chief among the royal prerogatives was the power to appoint bishops, a power that monarchs were unwilling to relinquish.

The Confession of Faith (1560) established the Crown's obligation to protect Scotland's reformed church. It also gave rise to a regular Assembly to which, in 1578, James VI appointed two commissioners as observers. However, his unwillingness to lose power over the appointment of bishops, a policy enforced variously by his two successors, led to a running conflict between Crown and the growing Presbyterian church structure, which advocated leadership by church elders, all of equal rank. Charles I did not allow the Assembly to meet, and then provoked protest by forcing the 1637 Service Book on Scottish Presbyterians, who united against him in the National Covenant. In a final act of betrayal, Charles II, who had relied upon support from Covenanters to regain his throne, demanded the reimposition of episcopal leadership, anathema to the Scottish reformed church, whose interests he was committed to protect.

For the Covenanters, the Glorious Revolution could not have come soon enough. With William III and Mary II on the throne, Presbyterian Church Government was formally established in 1690 and a Commissioner has attended its General Assembly's annual deliberations ever since. Occasional interference continued, when Commissioners dissolved the meetings if things disfavoured the Crown but, in 1703, powers were curbed to operate as they do now. At the end of each General Assembly, the elected Moderator dissolves the meeting, ending the appointment of the Lord High Commissioner, who returns home without the trappings of royal authority that have been his for the duration.

Lord High Commissioner of the General Assembly of the Church of Scotland with Pursebearer

DEBATE DOES NOT SLACKEN about the advantages or otherwise of the Act of Union between Scotland and England. On 25 March 1707 there was an outbreak of mob violence in Edinburgh, as Scotland's ancient Parliament debated voting away its sovereignty. The document enshrining this decision, which was later delivered to Queen Anne, had to be signed in a secret location by terrified Scottish MPs, while the crowd cried for their blood outside the Parliament buildings. At a stroke, the United Kingdom was formed and an impending calamity between two historically quarrelsome neighbours was avoided. Scotland, however, maintained her identity in many ways, the most important of which was the continuance of its own legal system.

In 1425 the Scots Parliament had called a commission to review the 14th-century legal codes, *Regiam Majestatem*, and to incorporate aspects of the French legal system – an acknowledgement of Scotland's 'auld alliance' with France. Nearly three centuries of union have integrated many laws within the United Kingdom, but the procedure in Scotland remains very different. Since 1532, the supreme court in civil cases for Scotland has been the Court of Session, which was based upon the model of the Parlement de Paris. It has two parts: the Outer House is where cases are initially heard, and the Inner House is a court of appeal with two divisions. Three judges sit at any one time in the Inner House, whereas only one sits at hearings of the Outer House. Appeals against judgements of the Outer House are heard by a quorum of judges from the Inner House. The whole system is presided over by the senior judge, the Lord President of the Court.

When the Lord President is sitting with two of his colleagues from the Inner House, the hearing takes place in the First Division Courtroom. The Lord President is also the Lord Justice-General, and in that role he presides over Scotland's criminal court, the High Court of Justiciary. (It was this court that was responsible for the last public execution in Scotland – in 1865.) Its decisions are universal and binding: there is no appeal from here to the House of Lords. All judges of the Court of Session are, by definition, qualified to try criminal cases as Senators of the College of Justice and Lords Commissioners of Justiciary.

At a regional level, Scotland is divided into six sheriffdoms, with a Sheriff Principal presiding over the administration of justice in each one. The office of sheriff can be traced back to the reign of Alexander I at the beginning of the 12th century, when Scotland was divided into 25 sheriffdoms, each of which had a Sheriff Depute. The monarch's principal law officer is now the Lord Advocate, who, along with his assistant, the Solicitor General, is a political appointee. The creation of the Scottish Parliament in 1999 led to the new office of Advocate-General for Scotland. The lawyer who holds this post advises the government of the United Kingdom on matters of Scottish law.

Unfortunately, there were many bitter pills for Scotland to swallow in the Treaty of Union. One of them was Article XIX, which guaranteed Scots Law only on condition that Scotland's courts were subject to changes 'for the better administration of justice as shall be made by the parliament of Great Britain'. Soon enough, this guarantee was tested by an appeal to the House of Lords by a certain Reverend Greenshields. He was dissatisfied with a decision of the Court of Session in 1711, and his appeal was heard and upheld by the House of Lords. By this precedent, all decisions of the Court are now subject to appeal in London.

From his judicial seat in the First Division Courtroom of Old Parliament House, Edinburgh, the LORD PRESIDENT OF THE COURT OF SESSION, *wearing his robes as* LORD JUSTICE-GENERAL, *is symbolically empowered by the mace that stands behind him when he sits in court.*

Lord Justice-General of Scotland and Lord President of the Court of Session

To the men and women who have the task of leading a clan, no honours or titles can compete with the privilege of heading a great family. Scotland's history, geography and economy gave life to and sustained a large familial system in the wild and often inhospitable countryside of the Highlands. Battles and hardships distinguished the early life of the Clans, but conflict has long since given way to a sense of shared history.

In essence, the Clan system operated like this: wherever life was sustainable, a group gathered to work the land and live on the food they grew. From among their number, one would emerge as leader. All would give him their allegiance, and in return they would receive his protection. As the unit grew, increased resources were needed, and if they could not be sourced from within, a raiding party would be sent out to find what was required. As neighbours seldom had food to spare, these raids became skirmishes. Many died and, human nature being what it is, the desire for revenge took root. This pattern of existence was common to all parts of the Highlands, but certain Clans dominated. The greatest were those who wrested large tracts of land from their rivals and attracted the loyalty of sufficient clansmen to survive attacks from others. Tranquillity, like good weather, seldom dominated in the Highlands, and even today each clan jealously guards its identity.

One of the great families is Clan Cameron, the family name deriving from *Cam shron*, the Gaelic for 'wry nose', the name of an early Chief. But the 15th-century leader from whom the family can trace a continuous line of descent was Donald Duibh (Donald the Dark-haired). All his chiefly successors bear the name MacDhomnuill Duibh (Son of Donald the Swarthy). The Clan's beginnings are obscure. It probably arrived in Lochaber from the islands after leaving the Lord of the Isles' protection to seek security and fortune elsewhere. Over the centuries, the Clan and its Chiefs gained a reputation for tenacity and heroism, but this was became enduringly established because of its support for the Jacobite cause. Lochiel, as today's Chief is affectionately known, still supervises the lands his family has held since the 14th century.

Sir Ewen, the 17th Chief, known as the Great Lochiel, much admired James Montrose, a noted Scottish general who had fought the English with an army of Highlanders in 1645. At about the age of 25, determined to follow his hero's example, the Great Lochiel fought the English at Lochaber, now known as Fort William, and in a fierce encounter had to protect his life by using his teeth to tear out an Englishman's throat. Not surprisingly, he was said to have a 'look so fierce might fright the boldest foe'. Later, in the steep pass of Killiecrankie, Cameron's men fell on the English army and inflicted a heavy defeat, albeit at great cost to the Clan's numbers.

Some 27 years later, infirmity prevented the Great Lochiel from fighting in the 1715 Jacobite Rebellion, but he told his son John to lead the Clan into battle anyway. The result was disastrous: John was forced into exile, leaving his son, Donald, to take the helm as 19th Chief. The young man, less aggressive than his grandfather, became known as the 'Gentle Lochiel'. When news of Bonnie Prince Charlie's arrival in Scotland reached him, he was horrified to hear that the Prince had landed with only seven men and no French support. The Gentle Lochiel tried to dissuade the Young Pretender from marching south to claim the English throne, but royal enthusiasm prevailed, and the Chief was persuaded to call out the Clan in support of him. Of the 800 men he led from Lochaber in 1746, more than 300 were killed in the Battle of Culloden – the

Chief of Clan Cameron

last battle to be fought on British soil. This defeat sounded the death knell for the ancient Clan system, although, as ever, the Camerons performed heroically to the very end.

Following that decisive battle, Clan Chiefs, along with despised English noblemen, became owners of land rather than stewards of it, and were compelled to apply hard-headed economic criteria to their land management. A collapse in the rural economy towards the end of the 18th century led to the Highland Clearances, in which tens of thousands of men, women and children were evicted from their homes to make way for large-scale sheep farming.

This policy was enforced with great brutality, even by some of the Chiefs themselves – a betrayal of their original role as protectors, which has left an enduring sense of bitterness in some of the areas that were worst affected. People already on subsistence level were forced into a life of hunger and destitution, and many ultimately had no option but to migrate from Scotland to the United States of America and elsewhere.

The Clan system, now peaceful and once again benign, is overseen by a Standing Council of Chiefs, which aims to maintain the fundamental principle of the Clans – kinship.

The 26th CHIEF *stands near Loch Arkaig in Inverness-shire, looking across land on which Camerons have lived for centuries. Three eagle feathers in his cap mark him out as Chief, as does his shoulder-borne 'plaid' of the chiefly tartan and his cromach (shepherd's crook). His kilt is made of Clan Cameron tartan.*

THE BATTLE OF FLODDEN, in 1513, tied Scots monarchs close to their archers. It is said that James IV, who died along with most of the 'flowers of Scottish Chivalry' on that day, fell among a close escort of French archers. His great-grandson, James VI, respected the skills of archery so much that he passed an edict banning football in favour of bowmanship. When James rode south to claim his English throne in 1603, he found two English Body Guards waiting to protect him in the palaces he inherited. His grandson, Charles II, could have done with a Scottish body guard when he sailed to Scotland in 1650. He could not be sure what reception would be given him, under a year since his father, Charles I, had been executed.

The Royal Company of Archers started out as a private club in 1676. The Constitution they drew up still governs the Company today. The Scottish Privy Council not only granted a request for recognition, but also established the Queen's Prize for shooting. In addition they granted the title The King's Company of Archers, which Queen Anne confirmed with a Royal Charter in 1704. In return, the Archers are expected, if asked, to provide the Sovereign with a Reddendo, comprising three arrows. Since then, too, a vast roll has been kept which every Archer signs on appointment.

George IV's visit to Edinburgh in 1822, known since as 'The King's Jaunt', provided the Royal Company with a chance to bid for the vacant position of Scotland's King's Body Guard. Walter Scott dressed them in a fanciful uniform based on his own whimsical imagination; the Duke of Montrose swore them in and the Earl of Elgin marched them to the quay at Leith to await the arrival of the Royal Barge. Throughout the visit they escorted the king in state, and a grateful monarch made the Duke the first Gold Stick for Scotland.

William IV was so glad to inherit his brother's throne, in 1830, that he busied himself signing documents 'William R' to the point of having to ease his painful hand in a bowl of warm water. Among these papers was one granting a new Gold Stick, with a Silver Stick and ivory ones for the Royal Company's council members; also the first set of Colours. There were more replacement sticks in 1837, when William's 18-year-old niece – Victoria – inherited the throne.

Royal visits to Scotland had been rare and for this reason Victoria's first state visit went badly. Rehearsals had not been made and a change of plan meant that, when the young queen climbed into her carriage, the Royal Company was still shaking itself into formation. They were left in a cloud of dust as the queen's cavalcade sped off, and despite a valiant attempt the Archers failed to catch up. This was soon put right by the queen, who ensured that she was properly escorted the next day when she claimed the keys of Edinburgh Castle.

Traditionally only a Scot may join the Company, and many famous people have served in its ranks. Its senior officers and a good number of its members are noblemen, many of whom have also served as distinguished military officers. Each of its 400 or so members is still encouraged to be proficient with bow and arrow.

Each year, the Queen's Body Guard parades at events during The Queen's stay at Edinburgh. Most ceremonies take place around Holyrood Palace. Here, across the wall and dominating the city's remarkable skyline, is the craggy feature called 'Arthur's Seat'. Its name reputedly evolves from Archer's Seat because the predecessors of the Royal Company were supposed to have rested there after practising in the valley beneath.

Captain General of the Queen's Body Guard for Scotland, Royal Company of Archers and Gold Stick with Officers and Members of the Royal Company of Archers

The archers, commanded by the CAPTAIN GENERAL as Gold Stick for Scotland, all carry longbows with a 'graith' of three arrows tucked into their belts. The Captain General carries a symbolic gold-topped stick and, like Clan Chiefs, wears three eagle feathers in his cap. Archer's Hall is where the Royal Company meets and practises the skills of toxopholy before shooting matches, where each archer tests the accuracy of his bowmanship on targets called 'clouts'. Every summer, the Royal Company of Archers shoots for the Musselburgh Arrow. Started in 1603, this is the oldest continual sporting event in the world.

THE FORT AT HILLSBOROUGH in Ireland was erected in 1630 by Peter Hill to monitor the chief road through Hillsborough, a small village named after Peter's family. Originally, the Fort was commanded by the Hereditary Constable, a member of the Hill family. Although the Constable no longer lives at the Fort, his former home remains a well-known site in Northern Ireland.

The story of the Hills of Hillsborough started in the late 16th century, when the Earl of Tyrone raised an insurrection in Ulster against Elizabeth I in 1597. The Earl of Essex was sent to Ireland to put down the rebellion, and among his officers was Moyses Hill. The expedition was not a success. Instead of defeating Tyrone, Essex made a truce and returned to Court, incurring the queen's wrath – a mistake that led ultimately to his execution.

Moyses Hill, on the other hand, was rewarded for his part in the campaign. He was appointed Governor of Oldfleet Castle, which protected the mouth of Lorne Harbour from the Scots. Later Moyses was knighted and served as Provost Marshal of the Province of Ulster. In 1611, he gained some land close to the ruins of St. Malachy's Chapel in County Down: it was called Cromlyn, which means 'crooked glen' in Gaelic. There he built a large family house that he named Hill Hall. In time, a small village grew up around this home, which was called Hillsborough. Moyses's son, Peter, went on to build a fort in 1630 to protect the road that led from Carrickfergus to Dublin.

During the Civil Wars (1639–60), Moyses's grandson, Arthur, managed to remain friendly with both the Cromwellians and the Royalists. He completed the construction of Hillsborough Fort and, after the Restoration of the monarchy in 1660, Charles II rewarded him for his loyalty by appointing him Constable of the Fort. This title was to be hereditary for the Hill family and implied that Hillsborough was in future to be a royal fort. The Hereditary Constable of Hillsborough Fort was expected to recruit and train a garrison of 20 men in order to ensure that the Fort remained a viable and effective military asset for the Sovereign's army. This number is no longer maintained. However, the Constable still appoints a bugler, and this lone guard turns out on special occasions, adding local colour to the picturesque village.

During the 18th and 19th centuries, the wealth and influence of Arthur Hill's descendants grew as a result of managing the estate well and marrying into families with resources. The Hills also gained in importance, becoming part of the aristocracy. Trevor Hill was made Viscount Hillsborough in 1717 and his son, Wills, became the first Marquess of Downshire (a derivation of County Down) in 1789.

The family invested much of their time, energy and resources in the village of Hillsborough and its community. It was Wills Hill who, in 1760, built a market house – today's Court House –a new church where St. Malachy's Chapel had stood, and Hillsborough Castle. He also converted a gatehouse in the north-west rampart of Hillsborough Fort, where large-scale entertainments were once held on the first floor.

When Ireland was divided in the early 1920s into two separate states – the Republic of Ireland in the south and Northern Ireland, formed from the Province of Ulster, in the north – the Hill family sold Hillsborough Castle to the British government. Today, Moyses Hill's family home has become Northern Ireland's royal residence, where the Secretary of State for Northern Ireland stays when in the country on government business. However, a descendant of Moyses remains Hereditary Constable of the royal fort.

Opposite: The Royal Fort of Hillsborough has undergone considerable changes since it was erected to protect the road. The HEREDITARY CONSTABLE OF HILLSBOROUGH FORT, *whose family built the village that bears their name, no longer lives here. However, with the government's affirmation he still appoints a bugler.*

Hereditary Constable of Hillsborough Fort

Opposite: *A new* Sister *takes the oath watched by her sorority in the Hospital's hall. All the Sisters wear conical hats and scarlet capes embroidered with the Howard of Northampton family crest, apart from the Warden, who has a three-tiered cape. The Secretary records the event, which is witnessed by a member of the Howard family, whose ancestor was the founder of the Hospital.*

WHILE THE DISSOLUTION of the monasteries made Henry VIII a wealthy man, its adverse effects were many and various. The 16th century closed on ruins where great abbeys had stood, and while there may have been little sympathy for the religious orders they dispossessed, the work they had done in caring for the elderly was sorely missed. As the old and destitute wandered around in search of food and shelter, they fell victim to a law that branded them idle beggars and imposed a fine on those who failed to apprehend them. Into this welfare vacuum stepped patrons of varying wealth, responding to the moral imperative that successful men should fulfil their Christian obligations by helping those in need.

One such beneficiary was Henry Howard, the Earl of Northampton, whose family had garnered wealth through ownership and development of land in Norfolk, particularly at Kings Lynn, where a thriving port attracted good revenue. Born at the beginning of the Dissolution, the Earl lived through the worst of the Reformation and saw his brother Thomas, 4th Duke of Norfolk, lose his head after plotting against Elizabeth I. Like most Howards, the Duke held proudly to Roman Catholicism and died in the faith.

The Earl himself was a powerful man, being Lord Privy Seal for James I, as well as Constable of Dover Castle and Warden of the Cinque Ports. Having established charitable institutions at Clun and Greenwich, in 1616 he went on to found the Hospital of the Most Holy and Undivided Trinity at Castle Rising. He stipulated that 12 local ladies were to be cared for in the new Hospital, but they had to meet strict criteria for admittance as the Earl was determined that his money should support only the most reputable of the less fortunate: 'They must

be of honest life and conversation, religious, grave and discreet, able to read, if such a one be had, a single woman, her place to be void on marriage, to be 56 years of age at least, no common beggar, harlot, scold, drunkard, haunter of taverns, inns and alehouses.'

Having satisfied this range of requirements and gained admittance, the ladies, who were known as Sisters, were to pray for the lives and souls of Howard's noble family. (Their benefactor might have been influenced by a pre-Reformation practice whereby wealthy people built chantry chapels and funded priests to say masses eternally for their soul – a sort of spiritual life insurance.) In return, the Hospital provided a welcome refuge for those admitted to its secure environment at a time of religious upheaval.

Qualifications for membership and the rules to be observed by the Hospital inmates have changed considerably since the 17th century, in line with evolving compassion and growing respect. In 1959 the building was completely renovated and reorganized to the Charity Commission's approval, but its primary function – to look after 12 needy women – remains its *raison d'être*.

The Sisters wear a uniform based upon that approved by their historic benefactor. The high-crowned hats, originally worn over white, coif-like headpieces, were considered highly fashionable when first adopted. Their cloaks, originally made from dark blue and brown fustian, were changed to red during the 20th century at the request of the Sisters themselves. Full uniform is now worn only on special occasions, such as the swearing in of a new Sister. Such events are supervised by the Warden and attended by a member of the Howard family because the Hospital remains a Howard family concern.

Sisters of the Hospital of the Most Holy and Undivided Trinity

FOLLOWING HIS DEFEAT by Oliver Cromwell at the Battle of Worcester in 1650, Charles II became a fugitive and spent several years trying to evade capture by Cromwell's men. During his years in the wilderness, he found many protectors, but none so sturdy and silent as the Boscobel Oak in Shropshire. The future king hid in this tree to avoid capture, and thereafter celebrated the part it had played in his return by wearing a sprig of oak on 29 May, the date of his Restoration in 1660.

In days that followed his resumption of the throne, Charles II searched for ways to show his gratitude to the people who had fought for and supported him. Some say that it was his mistress – the infamous Nell Gwyn – who gave him the idea to build 'an hospitall for maimed soldiers at Chelsey'. However, it seems more likely that he took the idea from the Hôtel des Invalides in Paris, which had been established some years earlier and was widely admired.

Sir Christopher Wren was commissioned to design the Royal Hospital, as it was to be known, and the king laid the foundation stone in 1682. Ten years later it was ready to admit 476 retired military men. The In Pensioners, as the residents are known (to differentiate them from Out Pensioners, who include most retired soldiers), are looked after by five retired officers, known as Captains of Invalids, who are answerable to the Governor of the Hospital.

It is the Governor's duty to ensure that the In Pensioners are looked after according to the highest military traditions while also imposing a gentle discipline. This, of course, must be done with sensitivity, as the old soldiers represent thousands of years' service between them. Above all, the Governor must ensure that the Pensioners' lives are dignified,

as they follow in the footsteps of the Roundhead and Cavalier veterans, who first occupied Wren's large and elegant building.

The Hospital is one of the great landmarks in London and was designed to command an uninterrupted view of the Thames and the boggy ground of Battersea beyond. Unfortunately, that vista has altered over the years. Now traffic thunders alongside the river, while trees struggle to blot out the un-Wren-like structure of Battersea Power Station. Internally, however, the Hospital has lost none of its appeal. In a dining room hung with regimental colours and paintings the red-coated Chelsea Pensioners take their meals, surveyed by a vast allegorical portrait of Charles II. In return for being housed, fed and clothed, the veterans surrender their army pensions. Across the hall, the chapel is almost always open, and the Governor's stall beside the door is set at a slight angle so that he can survey his congregation.

The open quadrangle of the Hospital is colonnaded and lined with memorials to previous Pensioners and Governors. Along its length, benches provide rest for the residents and, as the Hospital is open to the public, visitors converse with the old comrades. In the centre of the grassy quadrangle stands a statue of Charles II by Grinling Gibbons. Rather oddly, the king is depicted as a conquering Roman emperor, with laurels at his temples.

To commemorate the founder's birthday the Chelsea Pensioners parade around the statue on 29 May (Oak Apple Day) every year and each participant wears a spray of oak leaves to recall the king's lucky escape from Cromwell in 1651. In similar time-honoured fashion, the Governor ensures that the statue keeps the lion's share of the leaves for camouflage.

On Founder's Day at the Royal Hospital, beside the River Thames at Chelsea, the Romanesque statue of Charles II is surrounded by oak branches, and all the In Pensioners and officers wear sprigs of oak. The GOVERNOR OF THE ROYAL HOSPITAL stands in the centre of Wren's riverside 'barracks' on a grassy parade ground. Uniquely, when the elderly soldiers return a salute here, they do so with the hand furthest away from the saluting officer – a custom derived from medieval knights, who identified themselves by raising their helmet visors with the hand that would not hide their face.

Governor of the Royal Hospital

Painters have served in Scotland's court since pigment first became available to decorate the chill fortresses in this northern climate. These painters, who had been listed in the records since 1300, might have illuminated documents, painted holy icons within the Chapel Royal or, in later times, recorded the monarch's likeness. The first King's Painter was appointed in 1434, when the poet king, James I, developed a manor house into his most splendid residence, the palace at Linlithgow.

The Reformation in the 16th century seriously affected artists living north of the Alps. Lucrative work to decorate great churches dried up as sober Lutheran Protestantism took the place of Catholic splendour. England's court benefited from this when a painter from the Swiss city of Basel, called Hans Holbein the Younger, travelled to London, with a letter of introduction from the scholar Erasmus, to his friend, Thomas More. It was to change his life. After painting More, he was asked to make likenesses of others in the Tudor Court, then one of the most influential in Europe. Henry VIII appointed Holbein Court Painter in 1535 and later the artist painted Henry symbolically in the company of his father and family for Whitehall Palace.

Henry's sister Margaret Tudor married James IV of Scots in a bid to unite the old enemies but this was not achieved until their great-grandson James VI was crowned James I of England in 1603. The Scottish court became increasingly influenced by the culture of the Continent and with the fashion for portrait painters. Arnold Bronckorst was appointed the first King's Painter by the 15-year-old King James VI: the young monarch lived under the tutelage of Protestant teachers, while his mother, Mary Queen of Scots languished in an English prison. Bronckorst's successor served until his master left Edinburgh for London.

After the execution of Charles I, his son Charles, later Charles II, escaped to Scotland where it was safer to be crowned King of Scots. He appointed David des Granges, who had recently come north from London, as the first official Limner. In 1703 Queen Anne appointed George Ogilvie to be the first Painter and Limner in Ordinary. His first responsibility was 'drawing pictures of our person or of our successors'. In total, Anne suffered 17 pregnancies, all but one resulting in stillbirth; the one child who survived, a boy, died the year before Ogilvie's appointment.

Ogilvie, who suffered an 'inteire loss of his hearing' was succeeded in 1723 by a succession of Abercrombies: a family that lacked any ability to paint but knew a sinecure when they saw one. The reputation of the post was restored in 1823, when perhaps Scotland's greatest portrait painter, Sir Henry Raeburn, was appointed a few months before his death. George IV, who admired a portrait of his historic arrival at Edinburgh's Holyrood Palace by David Wilkie appointed the artist to be his new Limner. Wilkie set about painting the king in the kilt, an outfit that included flesh-coloured tights, which cost £1,354 in 1822. Later, Wilkie painted Queen Victoria receiving her first council in 1837 and to make her youth more pronounced by comparison with the politicians, he replaced her black dress with one in white.

Since 1933 the appointment has been unpaid and has been made with no expectations on the holder to produce images for either the monarch or the state. When Dr David Donaldson died in 1997, the position of Painter and Limner fell into abeyance. With the establishment of a new Scottish Parliament the power to recommend an appointment to The Queen was vested in the First Minister, who advised its revival in 2001.

Opposite: The new Scottish Parliament recently revived the appointment Queen Anne formalized almost exactly 300 years ago, when the original Parliament still sat in Edinburgh. At her studio, in that city, the Painter and Limner in Ordinary *works on paintings that no longer have to meet the vain expectations of the Scots monarch. The symbols of this utilitarian office remain what they always were, the canvas, brushes and paint of the artist.*

Painter and Limner in Ordinary

Opposite: *Chequered
flooring symbolizes the light
and shade Freemasons
experience in life, and
represents the floor of
Solomon's Temple – the
building of which is the
allegory around which Craft
rituals are constructed. The
GRAND MASTER FOR THE
UNITED GRAND LODGE OF
ENGLAND stands by his
throne in the Grand Temple
at Freemason's Hall, in
London's Holborn, where he
holds the gavel first used by
his great grandfather,
Edward VII. The stylized
Mason's apron and a gilt
collar carry emblems of his
rank. As First Grand
Principal of the Grand
Chapter of Royal Arch
Masons he wears a neck
badge. The flags are the
Grand Master's personal
standard (left) and the
standard of Grand Lodge
(right). The Bible sits on
the pedestal, with the
Square and Compasses,
representing virtue and
morality, placed on top.
Beside them is the State
Sword of United Grand
Lodge.*

Ten centuries before Jesus Christ walked the banks of the River Galilee, King Solomon ruled the kingdom of Israel. One of the symbols best associated with the wise king was the temple he built in Jerusalem. Legend has it that the building was perfect in every way – an achievement, we are led to believe, that resulted from the quality and character of the masons and their leader. The historical links with the reign of King Solomon may be doubtful, but the existence in the British Isles of free and accepted Freemasons can be argued from documents that survive from around 1390, which record rituals that are still in use now. The Royalist antiquarian, Elias Ashmole, was made a mason in Warrington in 1646 and records in his diary visiting other Lodges (places where masons meet).

The first Grand Master was chosen in 1717, when four London Lodges came together at the Goose and Gridiron tavern near London's St.. Paul's Cathedral. (Most Lodge meetings were held in pubs, as the ceremony was also a sociable event with food and drink.) On this historic occasion, the four Lodges established a central authority, known as a Grand Lodge, and elected from their number their first Grand Master, called Anthony Sayer. A few years later, Dr John Desaguliers followed into the Grand Master's Chair and brought direction to the Grand Lodge. Amongst other innovations, he introduced the aristocracy to the Craft, as Freemasonry was called, thus providing a major fillip to the movement.

The advantages of incorporating the aristocracy into Freemasonry were to be seen almost a century later. The movement by then had developed into a number of separate and independent factions, with a central and ongoing conflict existing between the two main groups, the Premier Grand Lodge and the Antients Grand Lodge (started by Irish Masons in 1752). In 1813, this all changed when Prince Augustus, then the Duke of Sussex, became Grand Master of the Premier Grand Lodge, and his brother Prince Edward, then the Duke of Kent, became Grand Master of the Antients Grand Lodge. The bickering that had existed between both Grand Lodges, and which looked set to continue for years to come, was almost instantly resolved by a fraternal pact. By the end of the year, the Princes had solved the remaining problems and the United Grand Lodge of England was formed with the elder of the two Princes in the Chair.

The creation of the role of Grand Master provided the leadership and direction that the movement needed, while the union of the principal Masonic groups consolidated the strength of the Craft. By the 19th century the fraternity's appeal stretched across the Empire, to countries as far flung as Australia, New Zealand, Canada and India. In 1901, the Duke of Connaught became Grand Master, a post he held for longer than any other, until 1939 – a period of office that enabled him to oversee the construction of Freemason's Hall in London's Covent Garden, built as a memorial to the thousands of masons from all over the Empire who died in the First World War.

The United Grand Lodge of England is made up of 8,500 Lodges with some 350,000 members. Much ritual in Masonry, based on customs and masons tools, is misunderstood by outsiders. The main challenge of the leadership today is to explain the Craft's purpose and recruit new masons, while also reassuring a public that remains sceptical and suspicious of any institution that appears to operate through hidden signs. Meanwhile, the Royal links continue, and the charity goes on, with hospitals, schools and other support organizations funded by the generosity of masons throughout the world.

Grand Master for the United Grand Lodge of England

Above: The QUEEN'S
BARGEMASTER *leads the*
ROYAL WATERMEN
*whenever they serve the
monarch, either on barges or
carriages. This study was
photographed at a London
studio. The Bargemaster
can be seen with the Royal
Watermen at Hampton
Court Palace, on the banks
of the River Thames, on
page 5.*

GEORGE I, THE FIRST OF THE Hanoverians to
rule England, decided to hold a great water
pageant on the River Thames on 15 July 1717.
George Fredrick Handel, the composer and sometime
Master of the King's Musick, wrote the Water Music
especially for the occasion. The king liked it so much
that he commanded that it be played three times, and
it is still among Handel's best-loved works. George I
had been on the throne for just three years, spoke
little English, and, frankly, was not much interested
in Britain. But he loved his music, and his vivacious,
if ageing, mistress, Madam Kilmanseck (popularly
nick-named 'Elephant and Castle'), loved a party.
Another guest – the cuckolded husband – was left
holding the £150 bill for the musicians alone.

At his musical concert on the river, George I was
attended by Royal Watermen, led by the King's
Bargemaster. Gathered around his retinue the
attendant grand families and merchants were
tended upon their barges by bargemasters and
watermen of their own. Watermen had ferried
British monarchs up and down the Thames since
medieval times, when the river was London's most
used highway. When King John signed Magna Carta
in 1215, for instance, his barge was in attendance at
Runnymede. In the Tudor period especially, with
Hampton Court, Greenwich and Westminster
spaced out along the Thames's winding banks, the
royal barges frequently bore the monarch, his family
and courtiers from one palace to another.

The formal royal appointment of Watermen dates
from the 14th century. From then until the middle of
the 19th century, Royal Watermen ferried the Royal
Family up and down England's waterways. When
roads improved, carriages took over as the most
popular means of transport, and today, Watermen
are used as royal coachmen on duties that were
originally carried out by Royal Barge, especially

when the Sovereign opens parliament. On this
occasion, the Watermen act as Footmen on the
carriages bearing the Symbols of Sovereignty – the
crown, Sword of State, maces and Cap of
Maintenance – which in earlier times had been
ferried along the river to Westminster. Even today,
when the carriage arrives at Westminster, The
Queen's Bargemaster formally hands the crown over
before it is borne into Parliament. Royal Watermen
still take part in the State Ride during State Visits,
originally a river duty for the Royal Barge.

The Queen's Bargemaster and the Royal
Watermen accompany the Royal Family when they
travel ceremonially along the Thames. When The
Queen is embarked, the Queen's Bargemaster takes
eight Watermen. This is because the fastest of the
old Shallop barges used eight oarsmen. Other
members of the Royal Family warrant six or four
oarsmen. Plans are well advanced for a new Royal
Shallop Barge for the River Thames. Designed for
training able-bodied and disabled men and women in
the skills of fixed-seat rowing, it will be available for
The Queen's use, when the vessel will be 'pulled', or
rowed, by the Royal Watermen. The Royal
Watermen have taken part in the 'Tudor Pull' each
year since 1995. Starting at Hampton Court Palace
and changing crews at Richmond, they complete the
25-mile charity pull down to the City of London in
about four hours.

All Royal Watermen belong to the City of
London's Company of Watermen and Lightermen,
which was established by an act of Parliament in
1514 and provided a reliable taxi service for the City
of London's merchants and regulated the waterway
and the fares charged by Watermen. The
Watermen's comrades, the Lightermen, essentially
moved cargo around, thus lightening the ships, but
they also shared some skills with the Watermen,

Queen's Bargemaster and the Royal Watermen, Bargemaster of the Company of Watermen and Lightermen, and Winners of Doggett's Coat and Badge

whose licence is for carrying passengers. Together, they worked the merchants' grand city barges, each of which was run by a Bargemaster.

Another thread connecting Watermen, Lightermen and George I's water concert is Doggett's Coat and Badge Race, an annual event initiated by Thomas Doggett to mark George I's accession on August 1 1715. Doggett, an enterprising Irish actor, Whig and comedian, decided to mark the occasion by setting the Watermen a wager: something commonplace among the plentiful Watermen who plied their fares across and along the Thames. The

prize, which included money, a red livery and silver badge, was hotly contested each year by six Watermen. Doggett faithfully set the wager every year until his death in 1721, at which he left funds for the race to continue. The responsibility for running the race was taken up by the Fishmongers' Company, who still stage the annual event today (now the oldest annual sporting event). Every August opens with this unique competition to mark the anniversary of the music-loving Hanoverian's arrival. Most Watermen compete, and the liveried coats and badges are highly prized.

Until 1760 London Bridge was the only crossing point on the River Thames other than by boats crewed by members of the Company of Watermen and Lightermen, who waited for hire on the river bank. Here, the BARGEMASTER OF THE COMPANY OF WATERMEN AND LIGHTERMEN *waits with two* WINNERS OF DOGGETT'S COAT AND BADGE *under Blackfriars Bridge in London.*

THE POST OF LORD GREAT CHAMBERLAIN dates from the time of the Norman Conquest, when William the Conqueror appointed his compatriot Robert Malet to the office. In this role, Malet supervised the improvements at the Palace of Westminster while the Tower of London and other fortifications were being built under the watchful eye of the new king.

The Chamberlaincy is one of the Great Offices of State and was made hereditary by Henry I in 1133, when Aubery de Vere was granted the appointment. De Veres continued in the post until 1526, when the last male of that line died. Mary and Elizabeth Tudor then appointed a distant male heir, and his descendants inherited the post until the same problem occurred again in 1626. The final beneficiary was Lord Willoughby d'Eresby, and yet again his line ended without male issue. As a result, several families disputed the right to the post, so the House of Lords reached a decision in 1902 to let them share the privilege, according to a complicated arrangement whereby one claimant shares the duty with two others, who take it in turns to fulfil the privilege. The appointment survives, but nowadays it is largely ceremonial and without much power.

The Palace of Westminster, which was once entirely the Lord Great Chamberlain's domain, is now his responsibility only as far as ceremonial matters are concerned: he plans the domestic arrangements whenever The Queen visits her Parliament, such as for the State Opening. When her carriage draws to a halt under Victoria Tower, the Lord Great Chamberlain greets her and leads her inside. He carries a white stave, which is a little over six feet long, and on the back of his uniform he wears a golden key, an entirely symbolic emblem of his office.

In former times monarchs always stayed the night at Westminster prior to their coronation, and a custom arose whereby the Lord Great Chamberlain had the privilege of handing the monarch his shirt, stockings and drawers on the morning of the coronation and helping him to dress. In return for this service, the Lord Great Chamberlain was entitled to claim the bed, bedding and nightgown used by the king on the eve of his coronation, plus all the furniture, valances and curtains used in the royal chamber.

In addition, the Lord Great Chamberlain was entitled to demand the clothes worn by the king at the coronation, which included his underclothes, socks and other personal belongings. Quite what was done with these items is not known, and some monarchs objected to the claim anyway, even though there was little room for negotiation as the terms were framed in law. James I, who had just arrived from chilly Edinburgh to claim his English crown, would not part with any of his clothes or belongings, and paid a fee of £200 in lieu. Queen Anne was similarly disconcerted by the demand and sent £300 to keep her 'bottom drawer intact'. Things are different now, as monarchs prefer to spend a quiet night at Buckingham Palace before their coronation. Since 1821 the complex processions from the Hall at Westminster to the Abbey are no longer necessary, so the job of the Lord Great Chamberlain has been reduced still further.

As the Palace of Westminster is now a royal residence in name only, the Lord Great Chamberlain's remit no longer extends very far, and others now carry out his ancient responsibilities. The Lord Chamberlain, for example, is the full-time Managing Director of the Royal Household, while Black Rod (see page 109) keeps order in and around the House of Lords.

Opposite: *By 'antient…just and lawful right' the* LORD GREAT CHAMBERLAIN *keeps the Consort's Throne and the Prince of Wales's Chair in the Stone Hall at Houghton, his home in Norfolk: when needed, he takes them to Parliament. The symbolic ceremonial key on his back shows that he once had responsibility for domestic arrangements at the Palace of Westminster. The white stave of office is held throughout a reign and broken at the monarch's graveside. When leading the Sovereign to the Lords the Great Lord Chamberlain walks backwards.*

Lord Great Chamberlain

WHEN LOOKING FOR THE REAL POWER in Britain, a good place to start is the Privy Council, the source of the present-day Cabinet's legal powers. Its structure derives from the Normans' *Commune Concilium*, which in turn was based on the Anglo-Saxons' Witenagemot, a council of nobles and clergy who advised the king. This advisory body has had several titles during its evolution, but the current name, Privy Council, emerged in the 13th century because its members met in private.

Apart from acting in an advisory capacity, the Council saw that justice was done, that the royal will was exercised and that the monarch's executive power was kept in check, thereby guiding the royal prerogative. The relationship between monarch and Council changed with each incumbent. The Council would exert greater influence over a weak king, just as a capable monarch could swing the pendulum in the other direction. Early Norman Councils consisted of the Chancellor, Chief Justiciary, Treasurer, Steward, Constable, Marshal, the Archbishops of Canterbury and York, and others the king selected. Many of these titles still exist, though most play their part only at the Accession Councils and coronations of new monarchs.

In Plantagenet times the *Curia Regis* (King's Court), as the Council was then known, grew fairly large and often misused its power to draft legislation from petitions submitted by the relatively impotent House of Commons. The Tudors believed that a small council was vital to good government, and it suited Henry VIII to limit it to any but the most essential Councillors. The Civil War led to the Council's temporary disbandment, and the Restoration saw its return, but not immediately. Charles II's experiment of appointing 30 new Privy Councillors was not a success: he felt there were too many to keep business confidential, so he

returned to having a small inner clique, which helped set the pattern for how the Council is organized today. While the Glorious Revolution of 1688 saw constitutional supremacy move from the Crown to Parliament, the Privy Council continued to help monarchs exercise their remaining powers, carry out any judicial obligations and fulfil any other responsibilities.

It was the arrival of George I, who spoke no English, that passed greater executive power to the Privy Council. A gathering similar to Charles II's cabal, known as the Cabinet, incorporated the king's ministers.

The progression from the Hanoverian Cabinet to the parliamentary executive of today has come about largely through the emergence of an increasingly representative democracy and the decline of royal influence. As a result, the Privy Council has waned in importance and membership of it has evolved into little more than part of the honours system. Nonetheless, every member must take an oath of confidentiality to facilitate cross-party briefing by the executive, which means that party-political differences are set aside. They also swear 'to give good advice, to protect the king's interests, to do justice honestly, (and) to take no gifts'.

Nowadays, every member of the Cabinet is a Privy Councillor, but the Council's total membership of nearly 400 also includes other Parliamentary figures, judges, bishops and members of the Royal Household. All the appointments are for life.

Once a month, or whenever necessary, The Queen meets in Council with just four Counsellors from the government to give formal approval to legislation drawn up in advance by government departments. In return, Privy Councillors are available to provide advice on constitutional matters at any time to The Queen and her Ministers.

A PRIVY COUNCILLOR in the National Liberal Club, close to Parliament and London's Whitehall. Once a select band of trusted advisers close to the king, the Privy Council now has around 400 members, some of whom are drawn from the Commonwealth. Court dress is seldom worn these days, but it was once the ceremonial wear of imperial potentates who drew on the status conferred by their Privy Council membership to exercise power in various parts of the world.

Member of the Most Honourable the Privy Council

Opposite: *To achieve spiritual purification, medieval candidates to become Knights of the Bath kept vigil with their swords overnight in a holy place – sometimes here in William the Conqueror's private chapel in the White Tower at the Tower of London. They also achieved bodily purification during this ritual of preparation by taking a bath. The 1725 Order of the Bath has no formal links with its medieval predecessor but the robe of a* KNIGHT GRAND CROSS OF THE BATH *retains the double cordon of white silk worn on the left shoulder in 1399.*

BY COMPARISON WITH OTHER ORDERS of chivalry, the Most Honourable Order of the Bath, founded in 1725 by George I, is relatively modern. Its inspiration, however, is more ancient, as it derives its name and many of its symbols from the rituals associated with the creation of knights in the Middle Ages. For instance, to repeat the sacramental immersion in water of Christian baptism, a symbolic bath was taken, and allegorical robes symbolizing purity put on. When the order was revived, mulberry-coloured satin, lined with white taffeta, was selected for the robes, these colours symbolizing the blood of Christ and the purity of the Virgin Mary.

It was deemed necessary for a warrior preparing for the accolade of knighthood to undergo certain rituals that would purify his body and soul so that his commitment could be worthy of God, in whose name the honour was conferred. First the candidate fasted, spending time in religious contemplation and confession to prepare his soul for the obligation ahead of him. Then he had to have a bath – a rare act of cleanliness in those days – to ensure that his bodily purity was on a par with his spiritual state. When the washing was complete, the dripping candidate was led by his squires to a bed, where the covers absorbed the wetness and symbolically drew any remaining impurities from his body. After this, the knight was believed to be 'of a pure mind and of honest intentions, willing to conflict with any dangers or difficulties in the cause of virtue; to take care both in his words and actions to follow the maxims of prudence; and religiously to observe the rules of fidelity and honour'.

Before the Norman invasion of England, it was the tradition for Anglo-Saxon knights to visit a cleric in some place of worship and spend a night in contemplation before being dubbed with a special sword by the priest at dawn. The medieval knights of the Bath also symbolically offered their own shield and sword at the altar as instruments of God's will. The only part of this ritual to be retained in modern times is the use of a sword for the dubbing ceremony.

Another link to the history of knighthood and to the spiritual lives of Norman and Plantagenet kings can be found in the upper floors of the Tower of London's White Tower. Here, at the Chapel Royal of St. John the Evangelist, knights of old observed many of their rituals. Kings also did vigil here before their coronations, and it was here, before his crowning in 1399, that Henry IV founded the original order. Forty-six knights of the Bath were initiated, having 'watched all that night, each with his own chamber and bath, and the next day the Duke of Lancaster made them knights at the celebration of Mass…and the said knights had on their left shoulder a double cordon of white silk, with tassels hanging down'. This last detail was incorporated into the robes currently worn.

The old Order of the Bath fell into disuse under James II, but, according to the writer Horace Walpole, was revived in 1725 on the suggestion of his father, Sir Robert Walpole. Although intended to be a military order of knighthood, it also included many civil members. The new order's statutes still required knights to bathe before doing vigil in Henry VII's chapel at the east end of Westminster Abbey, where the stalls are decorated with the plates of knights and festooned with the heraldic banners of the most senior living Knights Grand Cross. The order burgeoned in classes and membership after the defeat of Napoleon at Waterloo in 1815. While bathing is no longer mandatory, it is hoped that all those honoured do so anyway.

Knight Grand Cross of the Most Honourable Order of the Bath

Opposite: *Four* VERDURERS
OF THE WOODMEN OF
ARDEN *on Forest Ground,
near Meriden in the West
Midlands – land that was
owned by the founding Earl
of Aylesford. On the left is
the* MASTER FORESTER, *a
senior appointment given to
the Woodman who gets the
first Gold, or bull's eye, in
Grand Week. They wear the
forest green uniform
designed in 1785 and carry
bows made of yew with a
pulling weight of between
50 and 60 pounds. The
personal medals that they
wear have bars recording
Society honours for
shooting. In the background
is the clout, or target.*

AT THE CENTRE of what was once a wooded wilderness in the Midlands, which encompassed the forests of Sherwood, Hatfield, Cannock Chase, Charnwood and Wye, is the ancient forest of Arden. It was one of the wild areas that provided a buffer between the Saxon settlements that formed the kingdom of Mercia. At its heart is the town of Meriden, where, on 15 November 1785, Heneage Finch, the 4th Earl of Aylesford, and five enthusiastic friends gathered at the Bulls Head. In one of England's most traditional settings, they laid the foundations for the Woodmen of Arden. It would become the country's most exclusive society of archers – one that maintained and celebrated the longbow's story.

From the Saxons to the Tudors, the longbow's military effectiveness earned it a significant place in England's history. It was developed from a rough and cumbersome implement into a mass-produced and inexpensive military weapon. In particular, Edward I recognized the longbow's possibilities and ensured that, by his grandson's reign, the improved properties of tensile strength and performance combined to provide English kings with an armament that was almost to win the crown of France in the Hundred Years War.

Among the victories it gave to Edward III, Edward the Black Prince and Henry V were the battlefields of Crécy, Poitiers and Agincourt. A position overlooking the battlefield added both height and the force of gravity to the longbow's effectiveness, and the records of the Woodmen of Arden describe how longbowmen were deployed to strategic effect: 'On word of command they shot rhythmic volleys of arrows into the ranks of their charging opponents, shifting their targets successively until every living one of them was killed,

or maimed or routed.' Edward III, like his successors until Edward VI, made practising this military skill mandatory after Sunday Mass.

When saltpetre and guns propelled the efficiency of war a further macabre step along the path of barbarity, archery became more of a noble pastime than a vital military skill. The Tudors developed the sport, with Henry VIII proving a formidable shot. London became a venue for matches, led by the Society of St.. George. By the middle of the next century small archery societies proliferated as far as Warwickshire.

The 4th Earl of Aylesford had been loosing off arrows at his Meriden estate for years before founding the Woodmen. Since then, succeeding earls have presided, first by the traditional toxophilite title of Captain of the Grand Target, which was changed in 1786 to Warden of the Forest. And, before the year was out, the prefix 'perpetual' had been added. The Lieutenant of the Grand Target was also renamed by the Woodmen as Senior Verdurer. Membership of the Woodmen has always been limited to 80, though in 1835 it was increased by one to include the police reformer Sir Robert Peel. The society remains a fairly closed shop, with preference given to applicants related to or descended from former members. Each new member is given a number and must record his cresting, a unique mark, on the shaftment of all his arrows and on the aschams, or bow lockers. There is both a Captain and a Lieutenant of Numbers, and the first to score a Gold, or bull's eye, in Grand Week becomes Master Forester for the year. The uniform was established in 1786, with the hat following a hundred years later. Forest ground was bought and, according to the records for 1788, 'after a long interval, a Wardmote was first held by the Woodmen'.

Master Forester and Verdurers of the Woodmen of the Ancient Forest of Arden

'When the Saxons came first into this realm in King Vortiger's days, when they had been here a while, and at last began to fall out...they troubled and subdued the Britons...with their bow and shaft, which weapon being strange...was wonderful terrible unto them.'

ROGER ASCHAM, TOXOPHILUS, 1544

5 Growing an Empire

1750–1901

AFTER THE KINGDOMS OF England, Scotland and Wales were united there followed a gradual rationalization of national offices of state, particularly in Scotland. Those with specific historical provenance survived, especially if they belonged with a single family or if they embodied moments in history, as did the Royal Banner Bearer of Scotland, whose rights carried the hallmark of the Scottish wars of independence. Many English appointments, however, were elevated to encompass the whole of the newly named United Kingdom of Great Britain and Ireland: the Earl Marshal, for example, took responsibility for Britain's state ceremonial because it was mostly in London.

Britain had united to protect itself politically and from the continuing threat of Roman Catholicism. It also sought to increase its wealth through trade by establishing favourable trading links with distant corners of the world, in an ongoing quest for raw materials and markets. Conflicts of interest in these new places often led to the use of arms, either in defence or aggression, and so markets and plantations usually became colonies. More by accident than design, a colonial structure developed that encircled the globe. It was expensive to maintain these colonies and, although they offered economic opportunity, they were resented. The British Museum helped to change this, by alerting the public to discoveries from the far corners of this new world. Also the Colonial Reform Movement in the 1830s persuaded people that there was a moral imperative to invest in the colonies as well as exploit them. Colonial service became popular.

To head these colonial structures, Britain sent governors provided with blueprints for administration. Communication between Westminster and the governors of the colonies was maintained through the Corps of King's Messengers. Britain had established colonies first in America; but in 1776, rejecting the burden of taxation without representation, these declared themselves independent. It was India that became the focus of imperial effort. Traders became executive Governors, Clive of India advanced British interests and, after the Indian Mutiny of 1858, Governor Generals became Viceroys. Disraeli formalized the empire's existence by the Royal Titles Act of 1876, under which Queen Victoria proclaimed herself Empress of India. Orders of chivalry were created, including the Order of the Crown of India for ladies. The empire became the largest the world has ever seen.

Hanoverian rule was secure, following the defeat of the Jacobites in 1746, and for the first time the United Kingdom could confidently celebrate itself. As a result, the pageantry today recognized as a British heritage was largely invented in the 18th century. This new ceremonial echoed historical patterns, revived history and quickly became tradition: it met the requirements of a growing Empire, hungry for symbolic expressions of splendour.

The French Revolution in 1789 changed Europe. Its secular and republican ideology and its territorial ambitions set France against most of the Continent and, when Napoleon Bonaparte's military successes had earned him enough power, his army and navy challenged Britain. Nelson's victory at Trafalgar in 1805, as Commander-in-Chief of the Mediterranean Fleet, thwarted invasion and earned the Royal Navy unchallenged supremacy. Wellington's victory in 1815 against Napoleon at Waterloo gained him a reputation to match the Field Marshal's baton recently presented to him by the Prince Regent, the future George IV.

George IV succeeded to the throne in 1820 and in the euphoria still felt in Britain after Napoleon's defeat, Parliament indulged the profligate king's desire for a splendid coronation - not just to please him, but to celebrate the nation. This was perhaps the most magnificent coronation ever, including the appointment of the king's old friend as Herb Strewer. Later, to heal the wounds from Culloden, the king visited Scotland to celebrate its Highland revival. Quashed practices, such as playing the bagpipes and wearing tartan, were resurrected, and eventually George's niece, Victoria was to make a home in Scotland and appoint her own Piper. It was to Balmoral, in the Highlands, that the queen fled when her husband died. Republicanism grew, but the Crown was saved by her reluctant return to public duty. Her popularity grew with old age.

As the 19th century progressed, people became increasingly interested in local and indigenous customs. In Wales and Cornwall druidism was re-established, no longer as a cult religion but as a means to celebrate cultural inheritance. The royal court, too, appointed Welsh harpists.

Feudal responsibilities that had lingered as a way of administering the land died away. Cities mushroomed as industry grew to meet the demands of the burgeoning empire, and with these new urban centres came challenges to law and order. Sir Robert Peel's police force was established from the roots of existing constabularies, such as the force responsible for order among the undergraduates at Oxford. The Great Reform Act in 1832, which enlarged the franchise and altered Parliament's make-up, was a further step towards democracy. The Lords, however, maintained the significant connection between land and power.

Britain's empire allowed the Church of England's missionaries access across the world. Funding for the splendour of Anglican cathedrals was scrutinized by Parliament but administered by Commissioners, while the tidal wave of Victorian morality carried bishops and their doctrines to greater authority. Since Wesley's conversion,

Methodism had grown to challenge orthodoxy, and its adherents reflected the shift towards personal empowerment that reform engendered.

Victoria's Diamond Jubilee in 1897 was the ceremonial apogee of the western empires. As her carriage approached the steps of St Paul's she was surrounded by an establishment preening itself in splendour: from Indian princes, ministers, ambassadors and governors to flag-waving children, this was a great display of confidence. Beneath the display, however, this establishment was also to prove vulnerable.

IN CENTURIES PAST, two Scottish families – the Scrymgeours and the Maitlands – claimed the right to carry the Royal Banner of Scotland, and both had a strong legal argument for doing so. Their dispute was eventually resolved in the 20th century when it was decided to use the two flags that have represented the nation's identity since before the 14th-century wars of independence.

The Scrymgeours (a Gaelic word meaning 'skirmishers') gained their name and their position of Bannermen when an ancestor called Carron led a Scottish army to victory during the 12th century. In gratitude, the king asked Carron to carry his standard.

Little more evidence of the honour exists until William Wallace's charter of 1298, which confirms that Alexander 'called Skirmischur' carried the Royal Banner. He supported Robert Bruce's bid for the crown in 1306 and paid for it with his life. A further charter after Bannockburn in 1317 confirmed the privilege on his son, along with the Constabulary of the Castle at Dundee.

Having served as Royal Bannermen of Scotland through the 13th- and 14th- century wars of independence, the family turned out for subsequent battles against the English, including the tragic Battle of Flodden in 1513, when John Scrymgeour fell with banner in hand beside his King. The banner was again aloft for Charles II at the Battle of Worcester in 1650, and after the Restoration Scrymgeour was rewarded with the earldom of Dundee. Following his death in 1668, the terms of the inheritance were not adequately clear, and this prompted the powerful Duke of Lauderdale, head

Opposite: *Victory on the field of Bannockburn in 1314 earned Scotland its independence, and the Standard that Robert Bruce flew as King of the Scots has been carried by Banner Bearers ever since. A 20th-century ruling returned the right to be* HEREDITARY BANNER BEARER FOR SCOTLAND *to the Scrymgeour family, whose ancestors stood beside the King in 1314. The lion rampant design can be seen in the caparison covering Bruce's charger in the statue on the left.*

Hereditary Banner Bearer and
Hereditary Bearer of the National Flag

of the Maitland family and Secretary of State for Scotland, to take possession of the Scrymgeour estates. In fact, the story goes that he sent a troop of dragoons to the Scrymgeours' home, Dudhope Castle, in order to carry off all the family's deeds of ownership. Without written evidence, it was impossible for the Scrymgeour claimants to regain their lands. In 1790 the Royal Banner and Saltire were added to the Lauderdale arms, confirming their role as Royal Bannermen.

In 1910, however, the Scrymgeours went to the Court of Claims and once again asserted their right to carry the Royal Banner – this time for George V's coronation. After hearing the evidence, the House of Lords gently strictured the Lauderdales for treachery in 1668. The stolen lands were no longer available for return, but the Lauderdale successors were required to pay all the costs of the hearing. Consequently, in 1911 George V was the first monarch since Charles II to have a Scrymgeour as his Royal Bannerman.

Following Elizabeth II's coronation in 1953, the year when the earldom of Dundee was restored to the Scrymgeour family, a meeting was held between the Earls of Dundee and Lauderdale, the heads of the feuding families. At their request Sir Thomas Innes of Learney officiated in his capacity as the Lord Lyon King of Arms (see page 58), and the meeting produced a solution to the ancient rivalry, which was subsequently confirmed by the Queen.

The agreement drawn up recognized that both families held legitimate and long-standing claims to be Royal Bannermen and laid down that Scotland's two flags should thereafter be included in national ceremonies so that both families would have a role to play. However, it reaffirmed the 1603 ruling that the Royal Banner took precedence over all other flags. Thus, from 1954 onwards, the

Scrymgeours of Dundee have been Hereditary Banner Bearers for Scotland and carry the Royal Banner, showing the lion rampant within a double treasure (two frames), surrounded with red fleurs-de-lis on a gold ground. This flag represents the chiefly status of the monarch's leadership, which once drove the Scots who fought alongside William Wallace and Robert Bruce against the English. Meanwhile, the Maitlands of Lauderdale, as Hereditary Bearers of the National Flag of Scotland, carry the Saltire. This flag, part of the Union flag of Great Britain, shows a white diagonal cross on a blue background and symbolizes the crucifixion of St Andrew, Scotland's patron saint.

The conclusion has been an amicable one for both families, but the history of their dispute is rather like that between Scotland and England, and this is borne out by the design of the English Royal Banner. Two years after Wallace was defeated by Edward I, the 'Hammer of the Scots', at Falkirk in 1298, a chronicler described how the English banner reflected Edward's political agenda for the subjugation of Scotland. The King, however, reckoned without his son's failures and without the success of the Scottish army under Robert Bruce. The description goes as follows:

'On his banner were three leopards courant [running], of fine gold set on red; fierce were they, haughty and cruel, to signify that, like them, the King is dreadful to his enemies. For his bite is slight to none who inflame his anger; and yet, towards such as seek his friendship or submit to his power, his kindness is soon rekindled.'

CHRONICLER OF CAEVERLOCK, 1300

Opposite: The HEREDITARY BEARER OF THE NATIONAL FLAG OF SCOTLAND, *a member of the Maitland family, is standing on the lower part of Salisbury Crags, close to Arthur's Seat, which dominates Edinburgh's skyline. This spot overlooks the Palace of Holyroodhouse and the site of Scotland's new Parliament building.*

IT WAS THE GREEKS who gave the Celts their name. They called them *celtoi* (hidden people) because their languages, myths and culture, transmitted through the druidic class by oral tradition only, left no trace. As a result, a distinct Celtic identity is appreciable mainly in areas of Celtic settlement where oral memory is preserved, such as Brittany, Wales, Ireland, the Isle of Man, Scotland and Cornwall. In fact, during the last century, enthusiasts have revived the Bardic Orders to keep this tradition alive.

Celtic migrants arrived from the Continent in the course of the 1st millennium BC, initially in Ireland and then on mainland Britain. They introduced two Celtic languages: one, Irish or Gaelic, was the only language spoken in Ireland until the 5th century; the other, often called Brythonic – from the Welsh *Brython*, for Briton – influenced the island of Britain, including Wales, the Isle of Man and some parts of Cornwall.

In 926, King Athelstan fixed the boundary of the 'West Welsh' as the River Tamar, and this remains the boundary of Cornwall. Use of Brythonic Cornish gradually dwindled, until it died out during the Reformation because no effort was made to translate the new prayer book into the language. In Cornwall, the Celtic language has not been spoken since the 18th century. In Wales, on the other hand, it is very much alive.

Since the 12th century, the Welsh bards have formed part of the traditional Celtic hierarchy, or Bardic Order, which included druids, or priests, and bards (from the Celtic word for poet, 'he who gives voice', referring to the oral performance of poetry). The Gorsedd is a meeting of the Bardic Order closely associated with the eisteddfod, and more especially the annual Royal National Eisteddfod of Wales, in which competitions are held in music, poetry, drama and the fine arts. Everything is presented in the Welsh language.

In Cornwall there had been no Bardic Order since the 12th century. But in 1928, with support from the 'Mother Gorsedd' of Wales, the Gorsedd of the Bards of Cornwall was revived at the traditional site of Boscawen in Un, near Land's End. Since then, meetings have been held every year, on the first Saturday in September, on sites throughout Cornwall. Their intention is to 'maintain the national Celtic spirit of Cornwall; to encourage the study of literature, art, music and history in Cornwall; to encourage the study and use of the Cornish language; to link Cornwall with the other Celtic countries; and to promote cooperation amongst those who work for the honour of Cornwall'.

The Gorsedd ceremonies begin with the sounding of the symbolic horn, the *Corn Gwlas* (Horn of the Nation), which calls to the four points of the compass. The Bards wear simple blue robes, the Grand Bard additionally adorned with a crown and plastron (breastplate). Invited guests then compete in rhyme and performance for awards of both literary and musical merit. A specially selected Lady of Cornwall makes an offering of Fruits of the Earth, and children dance to harp music, before the Grand Bard receives new Bards into the Gorsedd.

Over the centuries, the Celts developed a great artistic identity. Their craftsmanship, ingenuity and adventurousness were matched by their literature – different humanities feeding from each other. It is a race that has always celebrated learning and wisdom through a ritual celebration of both. Unfortunately, the Anglo-Saxon and Norse invasions pushed the Celts to the far west of Britain, particularly to Wales – a country named by the invaders from a word that means 'foreign'. The Gorsedd today seeks to recover their lost culture for Britain.

Among more than 200 ancient stone circles and monuments in Cornwall, which are older than the Egyptian Pyramids, is the spiritual monument of Carn Brae, above Redruth. The Gorsedd's regalia is made from beaten copper with Celtic designs on a background of knotwork. As the GRAND BARD *stands with her followers to watch the sun set, Cornwall's flag is carried by a Past Grand Bard of the Gorsedd.*

Cornish Bards

THE BRITISH MUSEUM is generally acknowledged to house one of the finest collections of antiquities in the world. Here, treasures of ancient civilizations are admired by a general public, who regard accessibility to such works as a national right. Yet the notion of public ownership – and guardianship – of works of art is only relatively recent, as the story of the British Museum, and its Trusteeship, shows.

Up until the end of the 17th century, collections of art and science had been gathered by the wealthy in order to decorate their homes or, occasionally, to display cultural interests. But with the coming of the 18th century, disillusionment at the restrictive attitude of religion to the world and its creation, coupled with a reaction against the Church's power, led to the Age of Enlightenment. This reappraisal of man's secular, rather than spiritual, role on Earth gave birth to a new hunger for knowledge. At the same time, the world was opening up to discovery, and the Imperial Age was dawning. As a result, explorers and scientists were returning from journeys of discovery with boats filled with artistic and scientific treasures.

One such collector was the noted physician and scientist Sir Hans Sloane (1660-1753). Perhaps most widely remembered for the London square that bears his name and the Chelsea Physic Garden he created, Sloane had a long life during which he amassed one of the finest collections of plants, animals, coins and general antiquities of his time. Anxious that his work should survive, he bequeathed his collection to the British nation on his death – an act that forced Parliament to accelerate plans for a national museum. After protracted discussion, the government purchased the Sloane Collection and combined it with the library of Sir Robert Cotton to create the nucleus of the British Museum. On 7 June 1753, the British Museum was formally established by Act of Parliament and a site was selected at Montague Square in Bloomsbury. In honour of the fact that the collection belonged to the nation, the museum was held in trust by a Board of Trustees, whose main task was to ensure that the collection was preserved for the benefit of internal scholarship and the enjoyment of the general public.

In the years that followed, the museum's status was enhanced by several royal contributions, such as the addition of the Royal Library by George II in 1757, and Egypt's Rosetta Stone, offered by George III – himself a keen collector and patron – in 1802. The increasing size of the Museum led, in 1832, to changes in the make-up of the Board of Trustees. For the first time the Sovereign was given the right to make an appointment, and other families whose forebears had made significant donations to the Museum could also nominate a Trustee each. King William IV nominated his first cousin, Prince William Frederick, the Duke of Gloucester and Edinburgh, and a succession of royal Princes, Dukes, and two Deans of Windsor have been appointed as Royal Trustees ever since.

The present holder of the title Queen's Trustee of the British Museum is the Duke of Gloucester, appointed by Queen Elizabeth II soon after the introduction of the 1963 British Museum Act, which established a Board of 25 Trustees: one appointed by the Sovereign, 15 by the Prime Minister, four by learned societies, and five by the Trustees themselves. One of the Trustees' most important recent tasks has been the supervision of the radical Millennium Project, caused by the relocation of the world-famous British Library and the construction of the Museum's latest addition, the glass-roofed Great Court, said to be the largest covered public square in Europe.

Queen's Trustee of the British Museum

EW INSTITUTIONS FIND THEMSELVES more
challenged by the changing moods of this
century than the Established Church of England.
Its history is one of logical and inevitable
integration, making it now so much a part of the
constitution that while separation of Church and
State remains an option, it is not an easy one.
However, the Church has been acutely aware of its
own need to reform and respond to changing
circumstances that challenge its principal task of
making the ministry of Christ's gospel available in
every square mile of England.

One evolutionary step came in 1948 when two
traditional sources of funding, both vital to
underpinning the work of the Church, were united
under a board of 90 commissioners, to be
administered by the First, Second and Third
Church Estates Commissioners. Although their
task was new, the appointments had been created
nearly a century earlier.

Both sources of funding were themselves
pragmatic evolutions, established in response to the
changing situations and demographics that affected
the Church's ministry. The first was Queen
Anne's bounty. Established by Royal Charter in
1703, it was set up to relieve the plight of poor
clergy. Since Norman times, the local priest was
given a glebe – land to farm for income – and he
supplemented this with tithes, which were taxed
tenths of the parish's income from agriculture or
industry. Rome, however, insisted on receiving the
first year's income from each priest and a tenth of
what followed. This was called *Anales et Decimae*
(First fruits and tenths), which, after Henry VIII's
break with Rome, was paid to the Crown. Queen
Anne's bounty diverted this money back to the
Church as a resource from which to pay clergy who
ministered in places that had no adequate funding.

As this was State money, Parliament retained a keen
interest in its management and does so still.

Industrialization at the start of the 19th century
moved large numbers of people into cities, where the
Church's traditional funding was non-existent. The
1832 Reform Act produced a mood for change, and
the Church responded by redirecting excess diocesan
assets to fund both poor clergymen and the new
urban churches. Episcopal and cathedral riches were
given in trust in 1836 to a new body called the
Ecclesiastical and Church Estates Commissioners
for England. The commissioners of these historic
Church assets included several bishops and various
officers of State, as they do to this day. In 1850,
three joint treasurers were appointed to administer

*Opposite: The Church
Commissioners' building
is situated between
Westminster Abbey and the
Houses of Parliament. The
photograph naturally
divides, with the Church in
an unencumbered setting to
the left and Parliament
surrounded by cranes, cars
and offices to the right.
This represents the balance
between spiritual and
material needs that
the FIRST CHURCH
ESTATES COMMISSIONER
must maintain.*

First Church Estates Commissioner

the corporation of the Ecclesiastical Commissioners: they were the First Church Estates Commissioner, appointed by the Crown; the Second, selected now from the back benches of the governing party in the House of Commons; and the Third, nominated by the Archbishop of Canterbury.

As the work of both organizations overlapped, they were united in 1948 to form the Church Commissioners for England, with the three administrative commissioners continuing their work. Since then, they have managed the combined assets of Queen Anne's Bounty and the Ecclesiastical Commissioners in order to support the costs of funding the clergy, chiefly their stipends and pensions. The Church Commissioner also reviews

the Church's pastoral organization, acting as an impartial arbiter when there are no objections to local plans to reorganize parishes (and consequently patterns of ministry), and decides the future of redundant churches.

The task of the Commissioners was not made any easier by major investment errors in the 1980s, which reduced endowment values considerably. Dramatic management changes have since endeavoured to ensure that remaining resources continue to provide approximately one quarter of the Church's annual running costs. In doing so, the First Commissioner must maintain the balance between a financially strapped Church and a rightly inquisitive Parliament.

'It's a job of balance: on the one hand there are the needs and requirements of

the Church, and on the other the expectations and scrutiny of Parliament.

The Commissioners are accountable to both for making these assets work wisely.'

FIRST CHURCH ESTATES COMMISSIONER, 1998

When Cardinal John Henry Newman preached in St Mary's College, Oscott, near Birmingham, in 1852, it was to celebrate the restoration two years previously of a metropolitan see at Westminster and 12 Roman Catholic bishoprics in Protestant England. In this famous sermon Newman referred to this 'restoration of the hierarchy' as a 'second Spring': indeed, these events signalled a new start after nearly three centuries of English intolerance towards Catholicism.

Roman Catholics had been seen as potential rebels since the accession of Queen Elizabeth in 1558. This heralded the separation of the English Church from Rome, and in 1559 the Act of Supremacy committed all office bearers to acknowledge the monarch as supreme 'as well in spiritual things or causes as temporal'. Catholics who made it clear they disagreed with this often ended by being burnt at the stake.

Succeeding Stuart monarchs showed varying degrees of tolerance towards Catholicism, until in 1687 James II made the Declaration of Indulgence, which suspended the existing laws against Catholics. This was enough to convince Parliament that he would soon 'subvert and extirpate the Protestant religion', and in 1689 he was replaced by William III and Mary II. Anti-Catholic legislation was quickly passed to prevent a Catholic from sitting on the throne, from holding public office or from inheriting land. The Jacobite rebellions furthered the view that Catholics could not be relied upon to be loyal to the Crown, though by 1778 attempts to re-integrate them into public life were starting to be made. Then William Pitt the Younger and Sir Robert Peel pushed for legislative reconciliation between Catholic and Protestant, as changing circumstances made religious prejudice seem increasingly unnecessary. The Catholic Relief Act of 1829 overturned most anti-Catholic legislation. However, this was seen by diehards as 'Papal aggression', and, although it was never enforced, the Ecclesiastical Titles Act was passed to stop new Roman Catholic bishops from taking territorial designations.

The first Archbishop of Westminster was Nicholas Wiseman, who received his Cardinal's hat in 1850. Catholic ritual was gradually reintroduced, and a sword bearer became part of the Cardinal's retinue because he could not carry arms himself. The task was given to a Gentiluomo, a well-born swordsman, who stood nearby ready to defend his master if necessary. The second close attendant was the Cardinal's Secretary, who was a priest. As one Gentiluomo described it: 'I am supposed to defend him from brigands, while the Secretary protects him from the Devil. We are the temporal and spiritual protectors of our master.'

The former Cardinal Archbishop of Westminster, Basil Hume, was the last Roman Catholic Metropolitan to retain a Gentiluomo. His predecessor, Cardinal Heenan, had appealed against one of the Vatican's instructions that sought to reduce Cardinals' retinues, rituals and crimson wardrobes. While the Cardinal embraced the need to evolve the symbolism of the Church, he did not wish to do so at the expense of a loyal servant whose family had served his predecessors since 1932. Special permission to retain the post temporarily was received from the Vatican in January 1968. The reprieve lasted until the Requiem Mass conducted for Cardinal Hume in 1999, when the last Gentiluomo carried his master's insignia of the Order of Merit. His comment, 'I am a sort of Dodo. I am officially extinct,' reflected his humorous understanding of the unique survival of his role. Soon after this final duty he too passed away. The appointment has now gone for ever.

Opposite: The Cardinal Archbishop of Westminster discusses Church business with the Master of Ceremonies in the Throne Room of Archbishop's House beside Westminster Cathedral. The Gentiluomo of the Cardinal Archbishop of Westminster, *a sort of body guard who can bear arms when his religious master may not, keeps watch. He wears Court dress with full lace cuffs and jabot. This appointment is now in desuetude, following the demise of the last Gentiluomo, soon after his last Cardinal died.*

Gentiluomo of the Cardinal Archbishop of Westminster

In 1813 the Prince Regent wrote to the 1st Duke of Wellington: 'You have sent me, among the trophies of your unrivalled fame, the staff of a French Marshal, and I send you in return that of England.' By these words the campaigning general learnt of his promotion to the rank of Field Marshal following his victory at Vitoria against Joseph Bonaparte. However, the communication brought no baton, as is proved by a letter sent to him from the Commander-in-Chief's office 18 days later: '…It does not appear that there ever has been an English Baton; and no better occasion can ever occur of establishing one than the present…and if I am not interfered with from the Fountain of Taste [a satirical reference to George IV], I trust it will be found an appropriate badge of command…you must have the "baton of England".' Since then, Sovereigns have presented all Field Marshals with a red velvet baton scattered with crowned lions and topped with a golden St George killing the dragon. The recipient's name is engraved on the base.

The roots of the appointment and its symbol can be traced back to Richard III, who gave the-then Earl Marshal of England a baton of office in the 15th century. The inspiration for the creation of the post is unknown, but it may be connected with the Roman *Marescalcus Campi* (literally 'marshal of the field') who carried out certain executive responsibilities on behalf of the Marshal, who was the monarch's military leader immediately beneath the Constable. In England the Marshal, while also technically inferior to the Constable, took command of the King's troops in battle.

George II appointed the 1st Earl of Orkney a Field Marshal on 12 January 1736. Two days later the honour was extended to the Duke of Argyll, who had defeated the Old Pretender's army at Sheriffmuir in 1715 and had served with the 1st Duke of Marlborough, who received the earlier honour of Captain-General.

For Wellington, the appointment to Field Marshal must have come as a surprise. At 44 he was much younger than any previous recipients, most of whom had received their rank more as a mark of longevity than military prowess. Lord Drogheda was 91 when George IV celebrated his coronation by handing out his baton, and until the end of the 19th century it was rare to find any Field Marshals younger than 70. Excluding members of royal families, there has never been a younger appointee than Wellington. Following his appointment, he went on to command an army in the field – at Waterloo – something that few others have achieved. Among the notable exceptions are Lord Raglan in the Crimea, Lord Roberts in South Africa, Earl Haig in the First World War, and Lords Montgomery and Alexander in the Second World War. Similarly, no other British appointee since Wellington has also become Prime Minister.

It must also be noted that three Field Marshals ruled countries that declared war against Britain: Kaiser William II of Germany, Emperor Franz Joseph of Austria-Hungary and Emperor Hirohito of Japan.

The rank of Field Marshal is described as 'five star' and is seldom granted in the United States; Dwight D. Eisenhower and Omar Bradley, as Five-Star Generals in the Army, were the nearest equivalent. Through its membership of NATO, Britain became aware of a growing imbalance in the ratio of its highest ranks to its military power. After the Cold War ended and the size of the army was much reduced, it was recommended in February 1996 that further five-star appointments should cease. Field Marshal batons have not been abolished but, other than giving them to monarchs in an honorary capacity, no new appointments to the rank are likely unless Britain goes to war.

Field Marshal

The FIELD MARSHAL'S
baton of office is also shown
on his uniform. Crossed
batons within laurel wreaths
appear on his shoulders and
cap badge, and his five-star
rank is indicated on his

vehicle. Although largely
ceremonial, batons are
sometimes used to direct
troops in the field – as with
the Royal Green Jackets on
this training ground near
Aldershot, southern England.

Vice Admiral Horatio Nelson considered his responsibilities when preparing for the day when he would face the decisive encounter with Napoleon's fleet. 'The business of an English Commander-in-Chief', he said, was 'being first to bring an Enemy's Fleet to Battle, on the most advantageous terms to himself ... and secondly to continue them there, without separating, until the business is decided.' On the eve of the Battle of Trafalgar, which would cost his life but earn him immortality in the annals of naval history, he summoned all his captains and deployed what he called the 'Nelson touch' as he explained his tactics. He wrote afterwards to Lady Hamilton that 'some wept' and 'all approved'. On that day, high on Victory's fore-mast flew Nelson's flag as Flag Officer and Commander-in-Chief and, ever since she was berthed in Portsmouth, the longest-serving commissioned warship in the world (commissioned 1778) has worn the flag of the senior officer based at the Royal Navy's principle dockyard.

Distinctive flags were used to divide the fleet into three squadrons in 1625: each formation was given the colour red or blue or white. They flew distinguishing flags and ensigns of that colour and were commanded by a Flag Officer, or 'Flag man', called Admiral of the Red, Vice Admiral of the Blue and Rear Admiral of the White. However, in 1653 this order of seniority was altered to Red, White and then Blue, which remained in force until the squadron colours were abolished in 1864. These squadrons grew so large during the Dutch wars that they were each subdivided into Centre, Van and Rear Divisions, needing three Flag Officers for command: the senior division was commanded by the Admiral of the Red, while the Van and Rear Divisions had the Vice Admiral and Rear Admiral of the Red. The Admiral of the Red, as senior officer of the senior squadron, was called the Admiral of the Fleet: a post

that became the most senior rank in the Royal Navy.

Nelson achieved Captain's rank when he was just twenty years old, but it was another eighteen-and-a-half-years before he was further promoted, taking the lowest of 'flag-rungs', Rear Admiral of the Blue, in which he won the Battle of the Nile. By the time he was forty-two he had become Vice Admiral of the White. This rank hardly reflected the importance of the command he was then given as Commander-in-Chief Mediterranean.

The navy's role had grown. It no longer merely protected domestic shores (see Lord Warden and Admiralty Judge of the Cinque Ports, pages 24–7) but it maintained growing imperial interests across the globe. The admirals who commanded these fleets needed status, and this was provided by appointment as Commanders-in-Chief.

As the Royal Navy's power and influence grew with that of the British Empire, Commanders-in-Chief were established as shore-based appointments as well as sea-going. During the Second World War there were three sea-going Commanders-in-Chief: they commanded the Home Fleet, Far East Fleet and Mediterranean Fleet. These were strategic formations in no way descended from the coloured squadrons but which continued a triumvirate structure, each commanded by an Admiral.

From the start of the century the Commanders-in-Chief at Portsmouth have surveyed a dockyard that was once packed with naval power. Gradually masts gave way to funnel and nuclear-powered submarines. Now there are many empty berths, but despite fewer ships, the strategic power of the modern navy far exceeds the great battleships of the past. In naval reorganisations of the 1980s Victory became the flagship of a new appointment, the Commander-in-Chief Naval Home Command, who is also Second Sea Lord.

Opposite: HMS Victory is still the spiritual symbol of the Royal Navy and, as Lord Nelson flew his flag here as a Commander-in-Chief during the Battle of Trafalgar, so the Commander-in-Chief Naval Home Command, *who is also* Second Sea Lord, *does today. The ship is still commissioned, and therefore flies the White Ensign from this Upper Deck while looking forward, across the Quarter deck where Nelson fell, the Union Flag, which was first used in 1801, just before the famous victory, can be seen flying from the Jack mast: hence, 'Union Jack'.*

Commander-in-Chief Naval Home Command and Second Sea Lord

The state dining room in the Governor's official residence, which is called The Convent, in the centre of Gibraltar, awaits his guests. The walls are hung with portraits of previous Governors, dating back to the Moors of the 8th century. The Port Sergeant hands the GOVERNOR AND COMMANDER-IN-CHIEF the Keys to the Fortress of Gibraltar, proof that the Rock – so strategic in building an empire and fighting two world wars – is a secure dependent territory of Britain for another night.

Britain's Empire was the largest the world has ever seen: it once included much of the United States, Africa, India, Australia, New Zealand and the Caribbean. It was built through trade and the exploitation of opportunity, and was distinguished by a sense of duty and purpose. Started by accident in the 17th century, it was seen as a mixed blessing during the 18th, became a valued asset in the 19th but finally proved to be untenable in the 20th.

The spread of territories it encompassed presented a major administrative challenge, and it became necessary to improve communication and strategic support from the mother country. In 1704, one such opportunity arose during the War of Spanish Succession. English troops, under the command of Prince George of Hesse Darmstadt, attacked the Rock of Gibraltar as part of their plan to put Archduke Charles of Austria on the Spanish throne. The job was finished by Admiral Sir George Rooke, who took possession in the name of Queen Anne – a step ratified by Westminster and confirmed in the 1713 Treaty of Utrecht, but which Spain has never accepted. Possession of the Rock did three things: it gave the growing Empire a strategic hold on the Mediterranean's entrance, started a long-running feud with Spain over sovereignty and produced another outpost to be governed.

Britain thought it governed colonies well, but it took time to get the attitude and balance right. Mirroring Britain's constitution, representatives of royal authority were needed. They were called Governors and graded according to the size of the territory they governed – Lieutenant Governors for the smallest, through Governors up to Governor-Generals for the largest. In both Ireland and India they were given the title Viceroy for additional status.

Power went to the head of some early governors, who became as despotic and absolutist as medieval monarchs. Over time, however, checks and balances were introduced and each colony followed its individual path to democracy and independence, while Governors became constitutionally aloof. In the case of the few remaining dependent territories, of which Gibraltar is one, this aloofness retains diplomatic clout.

The British troops who secured the Rock had to defend it from a succession of Franco-Spanish counterattacks, notably during the Great Siege of 1779–83, when a Captain Fisher and 17 men defended the Round Tower from 500 French grenadiers. Following the small band's remarkable success, it became the custom to demonstrate that the Rock was secure by the Port Sergeant delivering the Keys of Gibraltar to the Governor at his official residence. In memory of both events, the colony's coat of arms depicts a fortress and keys.

Gibraltar's strategic importance meant that, until the late 1990s, the Governor was always a senior officer from the armed forces. This continued a line of military governance dating back to 711, when Al Walid Ibn Abdulmalic became Caliph on the Rock. That military significance is now marked only on special ceremonial occasions.

The Governor's diplomatic role has increased to reflect a broader European outlook and to address Spain's continued claim to the Rock: recently non-military diplomats have filled the post. Gibraltar's House of Assembly, which opted for membership of the European Union, must leave responsibility for external affairs, defence and internal security to the Governor, and therefore indirectly to the government of the United Kingdom. Gibraltar may choose to end its governance by Britain at any time, but sovereignty would then revert to Spain. Recent surveys indicate that Gibraltarians wish to continue with things as they stand, but the British Government is discussing the province's future with Spain for the first time.

Governor and Commander-in-Chief of Gibraltar

POOR DRAINS AND NOXIOUS GASES were a fact of life in Britain until the 19th century as nobody had found a clean and efficient way of dealing with human waste. James I remarked on the problem when he arrived in London from Holyrood in 1603, but little could be done to rid the Court, or anywhere else, of unpleasant smells. The most common solution was to try to disguise them with other, more fragrant, aromas, such as strewn herbs.

Following the Restoration, Herb Strewers were employed to wander through the royal apartments, distributing rue, mint, sage and camomile along with roses and lavender. Theirs was a vital role as it brought relief to everyone. The herbs scattered about were probably gathered from the King's Herb House in the grounds of the old Palace of Whitehall. Herb Strewers spread their fragrant items wherever the monarch went, but were especially valued when the route led out among the 'great unwashed' for ceremonies such as the Royal Maundy or for meeting scrofula victims, believed to be cured by royal touch.

The first recorded Herb Strewer was Bridget Rumny, who served from 1660 until 1671. She received £24 per annum, as did all her successors, until the appointment fell into abeyance the year before Victoria came to the throne. To this generous income was added an annual grant of two yards of superfine scarlet cloth for livery.

Many Herb Strewers served for considerable periods, while successors waited in the wings. One such hopeful, Anne Edwards, died waiting for Elizabeth Jux to expire. The longest-serving, full-time Herb Strewer was the last, Mary Rayner, who spent 43 years in the post and served George III and two of his sons.

When George IV finally inherited the throne from his father in 1820, he celebrated by planning the most flamboyant coronation Britain had ever witnessed. Improved hygiene meant that a Herb Strewer was no longer needed to keep the air sweet, but the new King decided to use the role to inject another note of fashion and display into the proceedings. He had already promised the post to an old friend, 56-year-old Anne Fellowes, who had supported his brother, the Duke of Sussex, by witnessing his secret (and illegal) marriage to Lady Augusta Murray in Rome. Some thought Miss Fellowes too old to add lustre to the show, but the King kept his word and provided her with a gleaming badge of office.

Perhaps to offset Anne's fading charms, it was decided that six maidens of gentle birth would attend her. This excited much competition, but Anne had the final say and, unsurprisingly, two of her nieces were chosen. They carried silver-gilt baskets and scattered flowers along the rich blue carpet from Westminster Hall to the Abbey, and it was reported that 'a more interesting or lovely group never was exhibited on any occasion'. Anne was reported to have 'scattered exotic flowers and aromatic herbs, from time to time filling a small hand basket from the large baskets of her attendants, who always made a profound obeisance as they presented their fragrant burthen to the mistress'.

Anne Fellowes applied again for the post of Herb Strewer at William IV's coronation and was granted the job; however, cutbacks in the ceremony left no role for her to perform. Queen Victoria eschewed any extravagance, so did not have a Herb Strewer at her coronation, and Edward VII followed suit. However, this did not deter the Fellowes from petitioning for the position as of right. They still defend the claim in the name of the senior unmarried daughter of the family, who waits for the chance to sweeten the air at Westminster Abbey once again.

Opposite: The HERB STREWER *sits at the West Door of Westminster Abbey in London – the coronation church of England's monarchs since 1066, when William the Conqueror was crowned. Her predecessor led the procession of the most flamboyant coronation Britain has ever seen when George IV was crowned in 1821. Then, as depicted here, she and her ladies strewed herbs and petals across the royal path.*

Herb Strewer

DISCRETION AND LOYALTY are valuable qualities at any time, but they become particularly important during periods of intrigue and war. Monarchs have always known this and have taken great pains to find people who can be trusted with delicate, often confidential information.

The first record of royal Messengers occurs in clothing accounts of 1199. Those chosen for the task were noblemen or trusted courtiers, and they performed a range of services from collecting taxes to escorting felons accused of High Treason.

Medieval heralds later acted as royal Messengers and were sometimes entrusted with basic tasks of diplomacy. The first record of a person with the title of King's Messenger dates from 1454, when Henry VI appointed Robert Asshewell. It was not until the reign of Henry VII that an emblem was chosen for the Messengers. The King selected the silver greyhound of Richmond as one of the heraldic beasts to support his royal arms, and, perhaps to speed them on, it was embroidered across the tunics of the Tudor Messengers. When the future Charles II was in exile during the Civil War, he is supposed to have broken off silver greyhounds decorating the edge of his dish and given one to each of his English and Dutch couriers to enable them to be recognized. Then, it is said, he decreed that his Messengers should wear silver greyhounds on Garter-blue ribbon around their necks. Many of these were stolen and not a few were lost when Messengers fell from their horses. Today these emblems are worn only on special occasions.

Henry VIII formed the first Corps of Messengers in 1547, when they were known as the Gentlemen of the Great Chamber in Ordinary or Extraordinary and were members of the Royal Household. During the mid-17th century the Corps gave invaluable service to Charles I when he and his troops were fighting against the New Model Army of Oliver Cromwell. But, as executive power was transferred from kings to their ministers, so the Messengers began to serve the government rather than the monarch. On 6 May 1722, a group of 16 were transferred into the King's Foreign Service Messengers, and the Corps left the palace for the Foreign Office.

During both world wars, King's Messengers played a vital role in carrying secret communiqués to and from Germany, thus helping Britain to defeat first Kaiser Wilhelm and then Adolf Hitler. The Messengers also worked as encoders and decoders, which helped safeguard the contents of the messages they carried.

As international correspondence increased, so did the need for permanent ambassadors abroad, and they in turn needed a secure and reliable means of passing information back and forth with their government. Under the terms of the Vienna Convention for Diplomatic Relations, bags containing official government communications can be carried by appointed people without fear of interference. In Britain the Corps of Messengers still undertakes this task, and each Messenger travels about 250,000 miles a year, the diplomatic bags he carries never leaving his or her sight.

The Corps, led by the Superintendent, whose title is now Head of Classified Bag Services, undergoes continuous financial review, and ways of improving the service are under constant scrutiny. Even though the security of electronic communication is improving, hand carriers remain the safest way of exchanging confidential messages. As a result, the Queen's Messengers will probably continue to be needed to carry sensitive and sometimes bulky items of Her Britannic Majesty's diplomatic business around the world safely and discreetly.

Superintendent of the Corps of Queen's Messengers

LAW AND ORDER are important parts of any civilized society, and leaders have attempted to impose both since the earliest times. In England in 1285, Edward I passed a statute of Watch and Ward, which established formal surveillance of the streets of London. However, the Constables of Oxford University claim to be the oldest police force in the world, their Proctors who patrolled the city predating Edward's initiative by 70 years.

Until the 19th century saw the national introduction of officers and courts to keep the peace, civil order outside London was maintained by lords of the manor. Serious offences were referred to higher courts and ultimately to the King's mercy. Within the early manor courts the office of Constable was an influential one, inspired by the dignitaries that emperors employed to look after their horses. These 'counts of the stable' often commanded large and powerful armies for the emperor, but the title is now the lowest rank held by policemen in Britain.

In the same year that Proctors first patrolled Oxford, the barons forced King John to sign Magna Carta, which curtailed royal power in favour of justice for the individual. Justice can only be exercised when the law is enforced, but despite this, British culture consistently rejected an organized force of law. People regarded such an institution with distrust and feared it would curtail their freedom. By the 19th century, however, as the industrial revolution brought urbanization and the power of religion declined, civil order deteriorated and people began to favour stricter law enforcement.

Britain's earliest organized police force (based in London) was the Bow Street Runners, founded about 1745 by the writer Henry Fielding, who was a Justice of the Peace. In 1829, this force was reorganized by the Home Secretary, Robert Peel,

but many people objected to the State assuming control of law and order. Over time, the blue-uniformed officers became familiar figures on the London streets and were nicknamed 'Peelers' or 'Bobbies' after their founder. In 1835 police forces were established in the London boroughs, and four years later they spread to the counties.

In the same year that Peel's legislation was passed, the Vice Chancellor of Oxford signed the 'Plan for the Establishment of an Efficient University Police', in which the duties and powers of the Oxford Constables were formalized. University Constables, and the Proctors before them, were principally responsible for the supervision of scholars. They retained the power to issue avuncular reprimands, but the new plan also allowed them to act as quasi-policemen within the University precincts.

Until the end of the Second World War, the Constables operated *in loco parentis*, which allowed them to remove students from pubs and get them back into College before the gates were locked. Misdemeanours, such as being out after curfew or being found with the opposite sex, were punished by either the College or the University on evidence presented by the Constables, nicknamed 'Chief Sniffers of University Bulldogs'. The punishments for minor transgressions have varied with the passage of time, but cheating has always been treated with the utmost severity. Formal hearings are now conducted into allegations of cheating, but Proctors were originally allowed to send down a student suspected of dishonesty without referring the matter any further.

The Oxford Constables are now trained by Thames Valley Police Force, as the nature of modern misdemeanours – and the students who perpetrate them – requires a different approach.

Opposite: *Standing in front of the Clarendon Building in Oxford, designed by Nicholas Hawksmoor, the* SENIOR CONSTABLE *is surrounded by the* CONSTABLES OF OXFORD UNIVERSITY. *They have worn bowler hats since 1946, when the uniform of top hat and cape were dropped. The University Police are now the last private police force in Britain, and carry warrant cards with the power of arrest within Oxford City or on University property.*

Senior Constable and Constables of Oxford University

AFTER NAPOLEON'S DEFEAT in 1815 Britain was able to concentrate once again on its overseas interests and, as the Empire continued to grow, so did the need for medical support for all races and creeds in its colonies. What better than to dust down the traditions of the Knights Hospitaller of St John, who had held sway in many places? Britain's largest voluntary first-aid service was created, first unofficially and then formally by a Royal Charter granted by Queen Victoria in 1888. The Most Venerable Order of the Hospital of St John of Jerusalem was established in the remnants of the knights' priory at Clerkenwell in London, and had branches in New Zealand, Australia, South Africa and Canada. Victoria became its first Sovereign Head.

The history of the order stretches back to the First Crusade, called by Pope Urban II in 1095. He urged the faithful to recapture the Holy Land from the Muslims and, in return, offered blanket forgiveness for their sins. Knights and their servants were mobilized under the authority of the Church and, on 15 July 1099, an international army led by Geoffrey de Bouillon retook Jerusalem with pious hearts but bloodstained hands.

A hospital run by Blessed Gerard, the Custodian of the Poor in Christ of the Hospital of Saint John, had been established in the city for half a century at least, caring for all who were wounded, and many crusaders were inspired to offer themselves to 'serve Our Lords the Sick'. They formed an order of military monks, the Knights Hospitaller, which was recognized by the King of Jerusalem in 1104 and by Pope Pascal II in 1113. The English Hospitallers formed one of the order's eight langues, or tongues, and a domestic headquarters was established just north of the City of London where, between 1130 and

1145, Prior Walter of England built the Church of St John. Its crypt still survives.

The Second and Third Crusades saw the Hospitallers fighting beside their brother orders, the Knights Templar and the Knights of the Holy Sepulchre. But the Crusaders lost their hold on Jerusalem and withdrew first to Acre, which fell in 1291, then to Cyprus and, finally, to Rhodes in the early 14th century. The Knights Hospitaller became one of the most powerful naval forces in the Mediterranean. They were finally driven from Rhodes in 1522 by Suleiman the Magnificent and eight years later an English knight, William Weston, sailed into Malta's Grand Harbour to take possession of the island for St John.

Philip IV of France had charged the Knights Templar with heresy in 1307 and when Pope Clement V confirmed this in 1312 the order was stripped of its European possessions in favour of the Hospitallers. Egle, an estate near Lincoln, was included in the booty that fell into their hands – its bailiff was one of the order's principal officers until 1999, an appointment that has since been revived by the new Priory of England and the Isles. Henry VIII dissolved the Knights Hospitaller along with the monasteries, and although Mary I revived the order it was soon suppressed again. However, it lived on in Malta until the French Revolution cut off vital resources. Napoleon subsequently took the island and ousted the knights.

The order, which was reorganized in 1999, is responsible for many voluntary associations that provide first-aid support and training in the United Kingdom and abroad. It also retains a link with its origins: it runs the St John Ophthalmic Hospital in Jerusalem, which provides help close to the religious strife that is still a feature of the city.

Prelate, Bailiff of Egle, Chancellor and Lord Prior of the Most Venerable Order of the Hospital of St John of Jerusalem

The PRELATE OF THE VENERABLE ORDER OF ST JOHN OF JERUSALEM kneels in prayer at the crypt altar of the Order's 12th-century church in Clerkenwell, which is close to one of the City of London's gates. In the foreground are (from left to right) the BAILIFF OF EGLE, the CHANCELLOR and the senior non-royal appointment, the LORD PRIOR. All three wear the sopravest (cassock) and mantle of Bailiffs Grand Cross. They coordinate the work of an army of volunteers throughout the United Kingdom, the Commonwealth and in the United States, who all wear, like them, the eight-pointed cross of St John. This symbolizes the four Christian virtues – prudence, justice, temperance and fortitude – and the eight beatitudes that spring from their practice.

METHODISM CAN BE SAID to have begun when a 15th child was born to the Reverend Samuel Wesley in 1703. The infant John, steeped in clerical tradition, was to found a religious movement that would have far-reaching consequences.

When Wesley senior's Rectory was burnt to the ground, the Duke of Buckingham provided money for John's education at Charterhouse, which eventually led to his studying at Oxford. At the age of 26, John was appointed Father of the Holy Club, a small society that met every Sunday to study the Greek Testament, and that fasted each Wednesday and Friday. The club followed a simple 'rule', the Greek word for which is 'method', and in time this became the foundation of the Methodist Church.

The evangelical pursuit of Jesus Christ amongst the precepts and rituals of the Established Church of England has often caused tension within the Anglican communion. This was particularly true when John Wesley became an ordained member of England's dominant church. He did not find fault with the 39 Articles, which form the foundations of Anglican faith, or with Archbishop Cranmer's *Book of Common Prayer*. However, this was the Age of Reason, and his egalitarian belief that the word of God should reach beyond the church door, out into the kingdom's roughest communities, was one that contradicted established practice. He led a revival that 'spread Scriptural holiness over the land'. Methodism was to become another strand of factionalism, which was identified more by the zeal of its adherents than by the nature of their faith. They believed that the Gospel was for everyone.

The doors of Anglican churches were closed to Wesley and his adherents, so they made street corners their pulpits and travelled widely in search of souls. They found people hungry for ministry, many of then having been cast out of churches when they could no longer pay the rent demanded for pew space. Travelling preachers visited communities and established Methodist Societies with their own local preachers. Each was dedicated to worship, fellowship, service, prayer, Bible study and responsible giving. Shunned by Anglicanism, Wesley had to ordain his own preachers: thus Methodism took independent root.

All human institutions developed for the worship of God seldom match the demands placed upon them by individual members: this was true of Methodism, which could not contain the aspirations of its fast-growing Societies. Many of these splintered off into different groupings, among them America's Episcopal Methodists, the Calvinistic Methodists and even the Salvation Army.

Wesley understood mavericks, having been one himself. Perhaps he also anticipated the fallout that followed his call in 1784 for a 'Yearly conference of people called Methodists'. While many initially rebelled against the idea, it subsequently provided a means for uniting them all.

Wesley died leaving no nomination for his Church's leadership, so by default responsibility fell to the Methodist Conference. During the period of disunity, the appointment of President was held by Wesleyan Methodists, often for long periods. However, by the time all the Methodist factions were reunited into the present-day structure, this system had been changed and it is now the practice to select a new President every year. Unchanged, however, is the tradition of pulpit evangelism. Few Methodists are unaware that during Wesley's first sermon at his purpose-built Chapel in the City of London on All Saints' Day, 1778, he launched into a tirade against the sea of expensive hats that filled the building. To him they symbolized wealth and privilege, which were at odds with Gospel simplicity.

John Wesley's pulpit stands at the centre of his Chapel in London's Old Street. Methodist symbolism surrounds the PRESIDENT OF THE METHODIST CONFERENCE, *who holds aloft a copy of the Gospel, which Wesley believed was for everyone.*

President of the Methodist Conference

THE APPOINTMENT, IN 2000, of a young Welsh musician as harpist to the Prince of Wales reinforced a link between court and music that stretches back to at least the 12th century when Rahere, an itinerant minstrel, was musician to Henry I. It also revived a connection first made 400 years ago when Robert ap Huw, a poet and musician from Wales, became harpist to James I of England. He was the first of many Welsh musicians who held the post of harpist in the royal court.

Queen Victoria broke with this tradition when she appointed an English harp-player, John Chatterton, to her Private Band. However, on his death in 1871, she immediately appointed a replacement from Wales, the traditional source of royal harpists. She chose John Thomas, a native of Bridgend, who had studied under Chatterton. Thomas was a composer and an expert on old Welsh melodies. He retired from the Queen's State Band in 1899, but when Victoria died, in 1901, Thomas asked her successor Edward VII for the entirely new post of Honorary Harpist to the King, which he held until his death in 1913. John Thomas was probably the last recorded harpist in a string that stretched back to the 15th century.

In 1969, there were plans to mark the Investiture at Caernarfon Castle of a new Prince of Wales by reviving the appointment of royal harpist; by way of precedent George, Prince of Wales, had been served by the harpist Edward Jones between 1794 and 1796. Osian Ellis was selected as a suitable candidate but the Royal Household and Whitehall viewed the appointment as arcane and unwise. In 2000 these hesitations were set aside, enabling the appointment of a young Welsh harpist for a period of two years. The Harpist to the Prince of Wales is called upon to play for the Prince, particularly when he is in the Principality.

Queen Victoria enjoyed the soothing harp but is perhaps better known for introducing another musical tradition into the court. In 1842, when she and Albert travelled to Scotland and saw the wild scenery of the Highlands for the first time, the Marquess of Breadalbane and his Highlanders, dressed in Campbell kilts, greeted them at Taymouth Castle, at the head of Loch Tay. 'It seemed as if a great chieftain in olden times was receiving his sovereign,' Victoria wrote in her diary on Wednesday 7 September, and later, to her mother, she wrote, 'We have heard nothing but bagpipes since we have been in the beautiful Highlands & I have become so fond of it that I mean to have a piper.' The playing of Breadalbane's piper had so impressed her that soon afterwards she wrote and asked the Marquess for his help in recruiting her own bagpipe-player. A year later, on 25 July 1843, Angus Mackay was sworn in as Piper to Her Majesty.

In 1847 Prince Albert took the lease of the estate of Balmoral, in Aberdeenshire; negotiations were finally settled in 1852. To celebrate, a cairn, or pile of stones, was built on a nearby peak called Craigowan while Angus Mackay played his pipes. Beside the old castle a new one was built, where Victoria and the Prince Consort sought to live the life of Highland lairds. Each morning the Queen's Piper played under their windows, and on expeditions into the hills they were attended by staff including a growing number of pipers. Most of these wore the Balmoral tartan, designed by Victoria and Albert in grey and red and quite different from the majority of red and green setts proliferating in the romantic revival of clan symbols which had begun with George VI's visit to Scotland in 1821.

When Mackay retired in 1854 the army provided his replacement, a custom that has been followed ever since. Pipe-Major William Ross, of the Black

Harpist to the Prince of Wales
(Overleaf) Queen's Piper and Page of the Presence

The HARPIST TO THE
PRINCE OF WALES, *standing
within Caernarfon Castle,
was appointed in 2000 for
a period of two years,
marking the revival of a
previously long-standing*

*tradition that has seen
many Welsh harpists at the
Royal Court. Edward I
proclaimed his son, the
future Edward II, the first
Prince of Wales from the
castle's battlements in 1301.*

*In the 20th century, two
princes of Wales have been
invested here. The castle was
constructed in coloured
layers to echo Emperor
Constantine's fortress
in Constantinople.*

Watch, was the Queen's Piper during the period of Victoria's domestic happiness at Balmoral with Albert. It was also Ross who played laments when Albert died. With the death of the Prince Consort the atmosphere at Balmoral immediately changed, as did the uniform, to black. Another Highlander on the staff, John Brown, encouraged the Queen to resume excursions into the hills. On one of these she decided to build a new house in a remote place called the Glassalt, or 'grey burn'. It was located on the shore of Loch Muick, surrounded by steep craggy hills and below the mountain Lochnagar. Here she felt safe, at peace and close to Albert. As at Balmoral Castle, the Queen's Piper played each morning outside her window. It was the Scottish idyll she first imagined possible at Taymouth in 1842.

William Ross's successor, James Campbell, led Victoria's coffin from Osborne House in 1901. Edward VII retained his services, and each of the king's successors has loved Balmoral and appointed pipers. When The Queen is at Buckingham Palace, Holyroodhouse or Balmoral her piper plays under her window every morning. She wears the Balmoral tartan when on the estate; elsewhere he wears the green Hunting Stewart in the morning and the red Royal Stewart for his evening duties.

Today the Queen's Piper is also one of three Pages of the Presence whose responsibilities include attending royal visitors and supervising the arrival and departure of ambassadors and other guests at the Grand Entrance to Buckingham Palace. This dual role requires tact and discretion as much as it does musical ability.

The QUEEN'S PIPER *wears the Balmoral tartan whenever he is on the estate. The house behind him, in a small wood at the far end of remote Loch Muick, is called the Glassalt Shiel. Queen Victoria built it, in 1868, on* *land she didn't own, but where she and Albert had found solitude. Here she lived for long periods. Later, in 1950, George VI bought the land. For some, it retains a haunting atmosphere, for others it is a romantic idyll.*

IN 1871, FLUSHED WITH HIS triumph over Napoleon III of France, King Wilhelm I of Prussia sought to humiliate the French by holding his victory celebrations at Versailles. The German Chancellor, Otto von Bismarck, declared Wilhelm *Kaiser*, or Emperor, of Germany. Shortly afterwards, Kaiser Wilhelm infuriated Queen Victoria by claiming that his heir, the Crown Prince of Germany, as an emperor's son, should take precedence above the Prince of Wales. The queen curtly responded to this imperial snobbery by ignoring it point blank.

Victoria may have held the technically less grand title of 'queen', but the British had never felt the need for her to claim more than this. The Russian Tsar also weighed in to slight Victoria's 'lesser' status, requiring that his daughter, Marie, who had married her son, Prince Affie, should be described as 'Imperial' rather than 'Royal' Highness, 'as in all civilised countries'. Victoria's crisp response was that 'Royal' came first.

Irritated and at times infuriated by these wearing rounds of imperial rivalry, the queen asked Parliament to grant her formally the imperial title over India. The task proved almost impossible, as there was little appetite for it in the Liberal administration. An opportunity arose when the Conservatives returned to power in 1874, but still it took all Prime Minister Benjamin Disraeli's skill to oil the Royal Titles Bill through. However, on May Day in 1876, Victoria was proclaimed Empress of India. The title made her the focus of cohesion for a vast and growing empire that was, in size and population, more than a match for the strutting European emperors.

To celebrate her title, in 1877 the new Empress created an exclusive order of chivalry designed for British and Indian women above the age of 18. It was called the Imperial Order of the Crown of India

and was given to British royalty, the wives of viceroys, some governors' wives and ruling Indian princesses, as well as wives of Indian princes. It bonded the top echelons of the imperial administration with the Indian nobility. Britain's imperial involvement in India was controversial, however, and comparatively brief.

The Second World War stripped Britain's resources and it was no longer possible for the United Kingdom to administrate its vast empire. Attitudes too had changed and, in the new world order, the moral argument tended against colonial power. In particular, Britain's Labour government, elected in 1945, and the new Prime Minister, Clement Attlee, were anxious to divest the crippled national Exchequer of an empire it could no longer afford. But progress towards independence was slow, as Indian Nationalists were divided on the question of partition – on whether to create separate states for Muslims and Hindus. In the ensuing deadlock, savage riots broke out.

The Prime Minister sent for the Emperor's cousin Lord Mountbatten of Burma, an ambitious admiral and a war leader, and appointed him to be the last Viceroy and Governor General to oversee the transfer of power. Within months of his arrival in Delhi, an earlier date for independence was agreed, on 15 August 1947. On that day the British Raj was formally dissolved, starting a trend that would dismantle the largest empire the world has ever seen. It also brought Victoria's hard-won title to an end. In a touch of paternal affection, just before independence George VI altered the statutes of the Order of the Crown of India. This enabled him to give the honour to both his daughters, the younger of whom was under 18. It was the first honour that Princesses Elizabeth and Margaret received; it was also nearly the last act of their father as Emperor of India.

Opposite: The youngest recipient of the honour, as a LADY OF THE IMPERIAL ORDER OF THE CROWN OF INDIA, *pictured here at Kensington Palace where Queen Victoria was born, wears the insignia given by the last King-Emperor, shortly before the British Raj ended. It consists of Victoria's cipher 'VRI': V for Victoria is picked out in diamonds, R for Regina (Queen) in pearls and I for Imperatrix (Empress) in turquoises. It is surrounded by pearls, surmounted by a jewelled crown and suspended from sky-blue watered silk ribbon edged in white.*

Lady of the Imperial Order of the Crown of India

Opposite: *The* MARSHAL
OF THE DIPLOMATIC
CORPS *escorts all newly
appointed foreign
ambassadors and most High
Commissioners to present
their contributions to The
Queen. Here, he escorts the
High Commissioner from
the Zambian High
Commission, located in
Kensington, London, in a
Semi-State landau drawn
by four horses. The* HIGH
COMMISSIONER *carries
Letters of Credence for The
Queen from the President of
Zambia. There is a special
purpose to the Marshal's
badge of office, which is
suspended from a chain
around his neck. The side
visible here shows the dove of
peace but on the reverse is a
sword of war; according to
the situation between
Britain and the relevant
country, the badge can be
turned around.*

THE MARSHAL OF THE DIPLOMATIC CORPS acts as a link between the Sovereign and foreign diplomats. He is a member of the Royal Household and has an office in Ambassadors' Court at St James's Palace, which is still the official residence of the Sovereign. The Marshal supervises the attendance of diplomats at ceremonies.

The present-day position of Marshal of the Diplomatic Corps originated in the first years of James I's reign (1603-1625), in order to ensure that all meetings between the Sovereign and ambassadors were conducted properly. The new Master of Ceremonies – as the Marshal was then called – and his Assistant were responsible for conducting court ritual, including the visits of diplomats. An abundance of different ranks then formed diplomatic missions, depending on the size of a territory. An empire would field an Ambassador, either 'ordinary', meaning permanent, or 'extraordinary', being appointed for a specific purpose; smaller states would send either Residents or Agents. All sought access to the king's court, though some had achieved their status by paying for the privilege in their own country and were therefore effectively fraudulent. The Master of Ceremonies had to establish a form of precedence that would satisfy all. In the end, this was done by giving seniority according to time served at the Court of St James's, with the senior diplomat becoming head of the corps, or Doyen.

The Master also became responsible for the Levee, a ceremonial reception within the court. The name comes from the French word *lever*, to rise, and from the bizarre court practice in the *ancien regime* at Versailles, whereby Louis XIV's rising from bed was witnessed at its various intimate stages by different grades of the nobility and ambassadors. The British equivalent was less eccentric, being more of a stylised gathering to which diplomats were given special access: Buckingham Palace was constructed with a Levee Entrance, through which ambassadors still technically have special access to the monarch, which is regulated by the Master's successor.

In 1714, the appointment became the sinecure of the Cotterell family but this practice proved unsatisfactory. Later it was vested in a retiring senior military officer. Constitutional changes in the 19th century led to the end of the monarch's direct influence over foreign policy. In 1930, George V changed the title of Master to Marshal of the Diplomatic Corps, which better described the function as the king's link with visiting diplomatic missions. By this date, the monarch's role in directly influencing foreign policy had ceased, though the Royal Prerogative remained intact and was vested in the hands of the Foreign Secretary. With the establishment of the Dominions within the Empire it was not appropriate for territories over which the monarch was Head of State to send ambassadors to their own king's court, and a new appointment of High Commissioner was established. Later, when some of these nations not only gained independence but also became republics within the new Commonwealth of Nations, the need for them to present Credentials was re-established. To mark their special status, the Marshal was instructed to escort High Commissioners of Republics in landaus drawn by four, rather than two, horses.

The number of diplomats in London soared in the second half of the 20th century. As recently as 1938 there were just 16 ambassadors and 7 high commissioners accredited to the Court of St James. Now, as a result of both the break-up of empires and the growth of new nations, these numbers have risen to 122 and 50 respectively. The Marshal still escorts those with Credentials to The Queen and organises the annual Diplomatic Reception.

Marshal of the Diplomatic Corps

6 Change of Emphasis
The 20th Century

THE REFORM ACTS of the 19th century precipitated fundamental changes in the shape of British society. Britain's Government became increasingly democratic, and the Queen Empress evolved into more of a figurehead than an influential participant in government. Her passing heralded a new century, and new voices made the case for change.

In 1909 the Chancellor of the Exchequer delivered a finance bill that included a 'super tax' on wealth and land, to pay for the modest social measures expected by voters. The House of Lords threw it out, and the Liberal government reacted to this with outrage, firmly returning the bill to the Lords to be accepted. It was the Lords' rebellion that eventually precipitated the Parliament Bill, which began a steady erosion of the old powers vested in the landed peerage since the beginnings of feudalism.

Both 'people' and 'land' have always been represented in the English parliament, a situation that enabled balance between urban and rural interests to survive, even after universal suffrage gave increasing power to densely populated places. When the hereditary peerage finally disappears from the legislature, it is to be hoped that whatever system takes its place will equally reflect this need for balance. In any case, the old hereditary titles will survive. They will remain as living clues, alongside others in this book, that enable Britain to trace its history and the development of its hard-won freedoms.

The Great War of 1914-18 claimed a generation of young men, and the hideous bloodshed involved in trench warfare raised many questions in the minds of ordinary soldiers, as well as in those of their youthful, Sandhurst-trained, commanders. The war was fought in the air, too, a new development that required new skills and a new command structure: the Royal Air Force and its Air Staff were the result. One dead soldier was selected, from the multitude that died on the battlefields of France, and entombed to represent the millions that had been killed in the war. He came to be known as the Unknown Warrior: a title that caught the imagination of a grieving nation then and since.

Survivors from the battlefields returned home to the same working conditions they had left behind and, despite high expectations, change for the better was slow. Communism erupted in Russia, and in Britain the trade union movement and the Labour party embodied the aspirations of the working class. The years of the financial Depression, and then the Second World War, left the British Empire bankrupt, but when the Labour Party came to power in 1945 their manifesto promised healthcare and education for all. Soon several new universities were built, each with a new Royal Charter, another chancellor and another university court.

The imperatives that originally united the kingdoms of England, Ireland, Scotland and the principality of Wales lost relevance as the 20th century progressed. First, the philosophy of imperialism died, and the colonies, beginning with India, gained their independence. Second, the tensions between Protestants and Roman Catholics seemed irrelevant in a society where few people went to church regularly. Third, nationalists in different parts of the United Kingdom campaigned for independence. As a result of this, Westminster granted limited devolution and, in 1999, a parliament was re-established in Edinburgh.

The development of former colonies into a Commonwealth of Nations included some countries that chose to keep the British monarch as their head of state. As a consequence, the role of Counsellors of State, had to change. Counsellors before had been selected from the British political establishment, but within the new Commonwealth this could have led to a British politician influencing the affairs of a former colony. To avoid this, Counsellors are now only drawn from the Royal family.

Millions gathered around television sets to watch the coronation of Elizabeth II, in 1953. During the ceremony, according to an ancient practice, the Lord of the Manor of Worksop's glove was presented to The Queen, although since then the title has been put up for sale. It was around this time that the Church approved the removal of the prefix 'Lord' before the title of High Almoner, and began to invite office bearers of other religions to take part in national ceremonies.

The Queen appointed her son, Prince Charles, to be Prince of Wales and Earl of Chester when he was nine, and invested him formally later, in 1969, at Caernarfon Castle: this raised fears of terror attacks from Welsh nationalists in a period of increasing terrorism. In Northern Ireland's city of Armagh, where two denominations claim the same Episcopal titles, terrorism took a grip and since then the path to establish peace in Ireland has been a rocky one, despite the best efforts of some religious leaders.

One of the oldest appointments in the United Kingdom is that of Sheriff. In order to maintain the relevance of this ancient Saxon post, the Shrievalty Association is responding to encouragement from Government by making every effort to alter its selection, in order to ensure that holders represent society's mix of race and gender more fully.

It is interesting that the largest creation of new appointments ever in Britain has come about within the last few years. The Labour landslide in 1997 brought forward legislation that considerably altered the constitutional form of the United Kingdom, and the creation of a Parliament in Scotland, and Assemblies in Wales and Northern Ireland, will have long term effects - just as the Reform Acts of the 19th century did long after they were enacted. Further devolution is planned in the regions of England. This will lead to the creation of still more positions with official titles that it will be the responsibility of someone to fill and to pass on. The creation of the Greater London Assembly in 2000 brought about a directly elected post, called Mayor of London. There will be many more appointments made that will continue this story, each born of need and each with a story to tell in the future.

Chosen to represent the ultimate sacrifice, THE UNKNOWN WARRIOR *lies in Westminster Abbey surrounded by poppies under earth brought from Flanders in Belgium. The inscription begins: 'Beneath this stone rests the body of a British Warrior, unknown by name or rank…'*

THE TYBURN NUNS, a cloistered community close to the bustling commercialism of London's Oxford Street, have their roots in Paris where Mother Marie Adele Garnier, their first Superior General, founded the Adorers of the Sacred Heart of Jesus of Montmartre, Order of St Benedict, in 1898. Within three years, however, the anticlerical French government passed the Laws of Association. These ordered the dissolution of all religious communities that were not authorized by the state and in 1901 the congregation was forced to leave France. In a reversal of the journey that had been made centuries earlier by English Roman Catholics, who fled to the Continent in order to keep both their faith and their lives, the French nuns crossed the Channel and came to England. After two years their foundress settled the community close to Tyburn, famous as a site of martyrdom during the English Reformation. By popular acclaim its members were instantly known as the 'Tyburn Nuns'.

Tyburn was London's public place of execution for more than six centuries, from 1196 to 1793, and during this period more than 50,000 criminals were hanged on its 'King's gallows'. The first martyr of the English Reformation to die there was John Houghton, a Carthusian prior, who was hung, drawn and quartered on 4 May 1535. It was less than a year after Henry VIII had created the Church of England with himself, and not the Pope, at its head and Houghton's crime was that he had refused to acknowledge Henry's supremacy. Such a refusal was considered to be treason, as was, later, being a Catholic priest or associating with Catholic priests. In the 150 years that followed, more than 350

people died for their faith. At Tyburn alone, where a triangular gallows – the Tyburn Tree – was in use from the reign of Elizabeth I, 105 men and women were martyred. The last of these was Oliver Plunket, Archbishop of Armagh, whom Titus Oates, an anti-Catholic agitator, implicated in a fictitious plot to murder Charles II and re-establish the Catholic Church in England. Plunket was executed on 1 July 1681 and canonized nearly 300 years later, in 1976.

Close to the monastery a stone marks the site of the gallows, and within Tyburn Convent itself there is a shrine to the martyrs of the English Reformation. Visited by people from all over the world, its altar is surmounted by the three crossbeams of the Tyburn Tree, transformed into a religious symbol. The monastery is now the senior of six convents, in the British Isles, Australia, New Zealand and Peru, and in all of them the nuns – Mothers who have dedicated their lives to the order and Sisters who have yet to make this final commitment – live according to the Rule of St Benedict. This was established in the 6th century, at Monte Cassino in Italy, and although Benedict described it as 'a little rule for beginners' it became the basis of Western monasticism. Benedictine orders are disciplined communities within which the emphasis is on contemplation and prayer, and the Tyburn Nuns meet seven times a day to chant the offices stipulated by the Rule, led by the Superior General. Sisters also take it in turns, two at a time, to pray in an unending vigil at the martyrs' shrine for the many thousands who died on the Tyburn Tree, for mankind as a whole – and for the Pope, the head of the Roman Catholic Church, and The Queen.

Superior General of the Tyburn Nuns

*Flanked by nuns at prayer,
the SUPERIOR GENERAL OF
THE TYBURN NUNS (centre
right) kneels before two
candles inscribed 'For the
Pope and the Church' and
'For the Queen and*

*England'. The Tyburn
convent was established by
Mother Marie Adèle
Garnier, foundress of an
order called the Adorers of
the Sacred Heart of Jesus of
Montmartre, on Bayswater*

*Road in London. This was
the site where 105 Catholics
were martyred during the
English Reformation, at a
permanent gallows,
called the Tyburn Tree.*

In 1919 THE POLITICIAN ERNEST BEVIN won a minimum wage of 16 shillings a day for dock workers. Despite that, these veterans of the trenches in northern France felt undervalued and exploited. Having won a war, they were now ready to fight for themselves. A few years later, with Bevin's help, a group of unions amalgamated into the Transport and General Workers' Union. It was democratic in structure and led by an Executive, Chairman and Secretary. Through the Depression of the 1930s and the years of modernization that followed, this union defended millions of workers against exploitation.

Worker exploitation has a long history, but the events that gave rise to trade unionism can be traced back to the 18th century when England's industry and infrastructure went through massive changes. The Industrial Revolution brought mechanization and mass-production, creating thousands of jobs in the process. People and goods had to get from one place to another, so there was a phenomenal increase in the number of roads being built. Added to this was a new system of canals. These long, straight waterways offered direct links between inland and coastal towns, and provided a fast and cost-effective means of transporting large quantities of goods. As the home market grew, so colonial and European trade increased. It was a time of change and opportunity, but many of those who helped to create the country's wealth benefited little themselves.

The age-old human values and mutual dependence between servant and master that had operated in rural communities did not survive the transition to cities. Those who moved into industrial work found no philanthropic masters to protect them. Hundreds of thousands of families were exposed to hideous exploitation and dreadful living conditions, and their lack of political power meant that they could do nothing about it.

Britain became the first industrialized society, an achievement that ill-rewarded those whose backs were broken to bring it about. Workers' movements were formed but had no power. Robert Owen, one of the few philanthropic industrialists, did his best to set up a general Trades Union in the 1830s, and the 1833 Factory Act, which protected children from the worst excesses of exploitation, was one constructive result. That year George Loveless, a Methodist preacher, organized six agricultural workers in Dorset into a Trades Union. They were subsequently convicted under a law forbidding 'unlawful oaths' and transported to Australia, becoming known as the Tolpuddle Martyrs in the process. In a rare example of people power, public opposition to their treatment eventually won them a pardon.

Here was the key: power lay in organizing a united response to bad management. To achieve this the growing union movement relied on persuasive orators who could take on the boardroom but also encourage workers to rebel against the deferential habits of a lifetime.

The union movement tries to ensure that working conditions and pay are fair and protected. It also takes up cases of unfair dismissal. At the forefront of the Union's campaigns is the General Secretary, who acts as national spokesperson for the workers. At a local level, their interests are represented by Shop Stewards.

Legislation passed during the last 20 years has made it more difficult to deploy the strategic power of the Transport and General Workers' Union, both on its own and as part of the greater union movement. The nature of politics has also changed, as have the expectations and conditions of the workforce. Many improvements have been achieved since the union movement began, and the General Secretary exists to continue that vital work.

Opposite: The GENERAL SECRETARY OF THE TRANSPORT AND GENERAL WORKERS UNION, *flanked by busts of Ernest Bevin (left) and the Socialist innovator Keir Hardie (right) at Transport House, the Union's headquarters in London, continues to work according to the principle that they established: a fair day's work for a fair day's pay. Worker solidarity is depicted in the banners that have led marches over the years, and the philosophy of strength in numbers remains a cornerstone of the union movement.*

General Secretary of the Transport and General Workers Union

Four-and-Twenty Unions in the days of yore

Played a silly sort of game and all were very poor;

Amalgamation came along, The men began to sing,

'We've been divided long enough, Unity's the Thing!'

HOLLAND (POLITICAL CARTOONIST)

TODAY, THE OFFICE OF British Prime Minister, who, as head of the government holds the lion's share of executive power, has never been more presidential in style. In the information age, where personalities catch the popular attention and celebrity sells, it is a truism that approval ratings are a key to acquiring and maintaining power. A power base has always been important.

Robert Walpole, Britain's first Prime Minister held office as 'first among equals' from 1721–42, having been appointed First Lord of the Treasury in 1715. When offered a place in the House of Lords, he declined – the better to consolidate power in the Commons.

It is typical of the way that the British Constitution operates that the principal post of Prime Minister, despite having existed in practice since Walpole took office in 1721, was in fact only formally recognised by statute in 1937. Previously, the leading minister of the day had always been the First Lord of the Treasury, because it has always been the case that whoever holds the purse strings controls the power. The office dates from 1066 when William the Conqueror created Odo, Earl of Kent, first Lord of the Treasury.

Sir Robert Walpole, who served under Queen Anne, is generally regarded as the first Prime Minister, not only because he managed to exercise the concept of collective responsibility, by which Cabinet government still operates, but also because he needed the support of Parliament to stay in office. What is now known as the 'Cabinet' refers to the select number of Privy Counsellors who hold ministerial appointments. Cabinet Government developed during the reign of William III, when the 1689 Bill of Rights was passed, restricting the Sovereign's powers and making the Parliament sovereign.

The next step in the diminution of royal power stemmed from the succession of the Hanoverians, starting with George I in 1714, who could not speak much English. As a result, the new king could not chair Cabinet sessions. Instead, the First Lord of the Treasury became 'first among equals' – taking the chair and running government. Inevitably, responsibility for administering the country in the king's name fell increasingly upon the Cabinet. Since the late 17th century, the Cabinet system has largely worked, and contributed to Westminster's self-image as 'Mother of Parliaments' – an example to democracies everywhere. Backbenchers challenge Cabinet directives and frequently scupper them. Ultimate power devolves downwards and no Prime Minister, however enveloped in international affairs, forgets that the electorate hold all the democratic cards.

The first formal reference to the appointment of Prime Minister occurs in the Congress of Berlin Treaty, 1878, where Benjamin Disraeli, who had described becoming premier as like reaching the top of a greasy pole, is called 'First Lord of Her Majesty's Treasury, Prime Minister of England'. In Edward VII's reign, a new Order of Precedence approved by Royal Warrant in 1905, set the Prime Minister immediately after the Archbishop of York.

Appointing the first minister of the Crown always was and technically still is the monarch's prerogative. In a constitutional monarchy, such as Britain's, the monarch's right is to be consulted, to advise, encourage and warn. Premiers visiting Buckingham Palace will have valued conversations there. The monarch can speak freely and the PM will probably return to Downing Street wiser.

When a new Prime Minister arrives at the door of Number 10 Downing Street, he or she is reminded of the much more ancient title they bear. The inscription on the letterbox reads, 'First Lord of the Treasury' and still makes no reference to 'Prime Minister'.

Opposite: At his Party Conference, in the Brighton Conference Centre, the Head of Government in the United Kingdom must keep the support and votes of his party, their supporters and sufficient Members of Parliament to keep the Executive administration of the realm. Watched by Ministers of the Crown, which he nominates but the monarch appoints, the PRIME MINISTER AND FIRST LORD OF THE TREASURY projects his message into the media for instant distribution and analysis. The democratic process follows in due course.

First Lord of the Treasury and Prime Minister

THE BRITISH ARMY'S MILITARY ACADEMY, formed in 1741 at Woolwich, London, was among the first European institutions created to provide future officers for the highly specialized branches of an army. Until then, military officers learnt their duties mainly through following the advice and example of their seniors. Following his experience of the War and Revolution in France, John Gaspard le Marchant, a brilliant British cavalry officer of French Huguenot descent, dreamt of an army commanded by professionally educated officers. It is to his determination that the Royal Military College (as it was then called) owes its existence, and was established, originally at Marlow, but later at Sandhurst, in 1799.

King George III regarded Sandhurst as 'an object of the deepest national importance'. In 1813, two years before Wellington achieved his victory over Napoleon at Waterloo, Queen Charlotte presented the Royal Military College with its first set of colours. The Sovereign's Parade took place, as it still does, in front of the Grand Entrance, with its eight large Doric columns supporting a pediment, showing the figures of Mars and Minerva, the god and goddess of war. Amongst the officers looking on would have been the Adjutant, whose title derives from the Latin *adjutare* (to aid), and every military formation has one. His duties are to support a superior officer, to see to general administration and to oversee the training of recruits. At Sandhurst this came to include the disciplined drill of parade manoeuvres, the basis of all military teamwork.

The Royal Military College had originally been founded to train young gentlemen as potential cavalry and infantry officers. Today, the course includes general military education and training for commissions in all branches of the army, except artillery, engineering and signals. At the conclusion of their training, which lasts 18 months, officer cadets parade in front of Old College's impressive building at Sandhurst.

The climax of the 'Passing Out' or Sovereign's Parade comes when the graduates turn to march slowly up the 10 steps and into the Grand Entrance of Old College: the Adjutant follows them up the steps on his grey charger, thereby symbolizing their passage from trainees to commissioned officers.

Major Frederick 'Boy' Browning, Adjutant at Sandhurst from 1924 to 1928, is credited with initiating this curious custom. The story goes that during the Sovereign's Parade of 1927, a storm cloud burst overhead, and 'Boy' Browning – some say fearing for his best uniform, others that he wished to display his horsemanship – trotted indoors behind the cadets.

Major 'Boy' Browning of the Grenadier Guards was one of the Royal Military College's most famous Adjutants. He was known as the best turned-out officer in the army and a steely disciplinarian. In 1944, he became commander of the Allied Airborne Corps as Lieutenant-General. After the war, his distinguished career led him to become Comptroller of the Household of the newly married Princess Elizabeth and the Duke of Edinburgh, setting up their establishment at Clarence House with great success and moving to Buckingham Palace when Elizabeth became Queen in 1952.

Both the Royal Military College at Sandhurst and the Royal Military Academy at Woolwich closed at the outbreak of the Second World War. They re-opened in 1947 as a single combined establishment, under the name of Royal Military Academy, Sandhurst. Since then, Major 'Boy' Browning's apparently impetuous act has become a Sandhurst tradition, which has been upheld by all successive Adjutants ever since.

Adjutant of the Royal Military Academy, Sandhurst

'Hard pounding this, gentlemen; let's see
who will pound longest.'

DUKE OF WELLINGTON AT WATERLOO, 1815

Marching through the Grand
Entrance of Old College at
the Royal Military
Academy, Sandhurst in
Surrey marks the start of
an army officer's career.
Recently the tradition has
come to include the
ADJUTANT on his charger
shepherding the cadets up
the steps. This is the climax
of a ritual that once
preceded immediate
dispatch to the front line.

THE ROYAL NAVAL RESERVE (RNR) comprises a corps of dedicated men and women who train in peacetime and stand by in readiness to support the Royal Navy in times of crisis or war. Of the 4,000 or so in the Reserve, about a quarter have previously served in the Royal Navy, but the majority include former merchant seamen and civilian, medical and nursing volunteers.

For more than a millennium, Britain has relied on the marine skills and seagoing vessels of local seamen to defend her coastline and trade routes. Alfred the Great was probably the first ruler to create a maritime force when, in c. 876, he launched a fleet of longships, manned by local seamen, that successfully repelled a Viking invasion.

As warfare grew more sophisticated during the Renaissance, merchant ships proved increasingly inadequate. Recognizing the need to create a specialized fighting force, Henry VIII created the Navy Board in 1546, and built a fleet of warships armed with large guns. Under Elizabeth I, the new naval force developed in size and stature. Up until the mid-19th century, however, the Royal Navy still relied on merchant mariners and fishermen to man her ships. Other less willing or less well-trained sailors were notoriously 'press-ganged' to serve aboard ships.

After the Napoleonic Wars (1803–15), and as Britain's empire expanded, her supremacy at sea became ever more necessary, and the old habits of the Press Gang were no longer adequate or tolerable. The Royal Navy became a professional force, in which a lifetime of service provided a career and a steady income. As the Royal Navy grew in strength an emergency reserve force of trained naval manpower remained essential, prompting the formation, in 1859, of the Royal Naval Reserve (RNR), drawn essentially from the Merchant Navy.

With Germany's rise as a naval power at the turn of the century, a further force, the Royal Naval Voluntary Reserve (RNVR), recruited from civilian volunteers, was formed in 1903 to supplement the RNR. After a slow start, thousands enlisted with enthusiasm. Both forces served with distinction in the two 20th-century World Wars – thousands as infantry in the great battles of Passchendaele, Gallipoli, Cambrai and during the Somme campaign. By 1945, three-quarter's of Britain's naval manpower (some 500,000 strong), on ships, submarines and in the Fleet Air Arm, comprised Reservists. The two Reserve forces merged in 1958 to form today's RNR: it included the former Women's Royal Naval Reserve (WRNR), as well as Queen Alexandra's Royal Naval Nursing Service (Reserve). A Combined Cadet Force (CCF) and Sea Cadet Corps (SCC) complemented the full Reserve force. At this time the Duke of Gloucester was appointed the first Honorary Commodore. The post of commodore, which had been adopted from the Dutch navy in the 17th century, was, until recently, an appointment not a rank held only for the duration when a Captain commanded a squadron of ships. During the forces review in 1994, called Options for Change, the RNR was reorganised again and another royal Honorary Commodore was appointed.

Today's Reservists undergo regular training, to equip the Navy with a skilled back-up force. The 'Senior Service' has been steadily reduced since the 1960s and today's Navy is far from the fearsome fleet with which Britannia once ruled the waves. Nonetheless, the Royal Navy still performs a vital defence role and maintains a fleet of nuclear-armed submarines and surface ships. In the event of an emergency, the RNR stands ready to do its duty and support the Royal Navy.

Opposite: THE HONORARY COMMODORE, ROYAL NAVAL RESERVE *stands beside the signal lamp in the starboard wing of HMS* Westminster's *bridge, from which the vessel's commander can command the ship. On his sleeves can be seen the thick gold stripes that denote 'Commodore', shared with the regular Royal Navy, but distinguished by a small gold R for 'Reserve' within the curl. His hand rests on the ship's compass as* Westminster *sails in the Solent, waiting to enter Portsmouth harbour. This is close to where, over a thousand years ago, Alfred the Great launched a fleet of longships, manned by native seamen – the forerunners of today's Reservists – to repel a Viking invasion.*

Honorary Commodore, Royal Naval Reserve

The MADNESS OF THE WESTERN FRONT, which was endured by millions during the Great War of 1914–18, was an engine of slaughter. Stalemate forced soldiers to fight inch by inch across land pockmarked by bombs, while enduring the nauseating decay of their fallen comrades. The Prussian strategist Karl von Clausewitz had written a century earlier about the importance of maintaining strategic momentum, and commanders of the opposing armies struggled to find it in order to mount the vital breakthrough. Every advantage was exploited, including offensive operations in the air.

The aeroplane was in its infancy at the outbreak of the First World War, but both the army and the navy recognized the advantages it offered, principally in reconnaissance, so it became the beneficiary of increased investment. The first military aeroplanes were unarmed, so the pilots flew with one hand on the controls, keeping the other free to wield a pistol.

The Royal Flying Corps was formed in 1912 as a naval and military air wing, but just before the war, the navy created its own separate formation, the Royal Naval Air Service. Inevitably, the two divisions competed for resources. Meanwhile, Germany had developed the revolutionary Fokker monoplane, which was faster than British planes and fitted with a machine-gun synchronized to fire through the propeller's blades. Commanders of air operations had to find a way of combatting these superior aircraft, so they relayed their concerns to Asquith's government, who, in turn, tried to ensure that the forces had the planes they needed and that they were efficiently administered.

In June 1916 and July 1917 German planes made two bombing runs on London. Public opinion demanded what many were coming to accept – that Britain needed a coherent air force run by its own ministry in order to defend national interests and mount offensive operations. Consequently, the Air Ministry was born in July 1917, and the Air Force (Constitution) Act came into force later that year. General Jan Smuts, a member of the imperial war cabinet, played a crucial role in achieving this. Under the terms of the Act, power rested with the Air Council. Gradually, however, the naval and military air components were brought together, and the Royal Air Force was created on 1 April 1918.

Brigadier General Hugh Trenchard, who had fought in the Boer War and subsequently served in South Africa and Nigeria, became the first Chief of the Air Staff and thereby discovered a new outlet for his energies. During the Fokker offensive he pressed for retaliation when losses were heavy, a costly strategy that ultimately proved successful. He became known as the 'Father of the Royal Air Force' and remained in charge until 1930. During that time, he built its infrastructure, despite strong pressure to dissolve the service back into the navy and army. Trenchard's successors inherited a force that defended the country through the darkest hours of the Battle of Britain. The young pilots who gave their lives in the skies against Germany's Luftwaffe more than earned their memorials in Westminster Abbey and at Runnymede – they ensured that Britain was free of Nazi tyranny.

The Chief of the Air Staff now leads an air force that is structured, equipped and trained for expeditionary operations. Today's precision weaponry is a far cry from the pistols of 1914, and enables Britain to wield strategic clout throughout the world. As the first Chief would have wished, this air power, which works in concert with the navy and army, enables the country to protect its legitimate interests while also contributing to the effectiveness of NATO, the EU and the United Nations.

Opposite: *Royal Air Force Cottesmore in Leicestershire was first surveyed as an airfield in 1935 and was used during the Second World War by British and American air forces. Soon it will be home to the Joint Force Harrier, bringing together Royal Air Force Harriers and Sea Harriers of the Royal Naval Air Service. The* CHIEF OF THE AIR STAFF, *wearing a flying suit, stands next to a Harrier GR7 of Number 1 (Fighter) Squadron, which he led during the Falklands conflict. In the background, armourers can be seen preparing Sidewinder missiles.*

Chief of the Air Staff

IN ORDER FOR THE Crown to fulfil its constitutional obligations, the Sovereign has to enact or approve certain elements of government business. However, in the event that the monarch is unable to perform this role, Counsellors of State are appointed from within the Royal Family to act on the Sovereign's behalf. It is perhaps the least known of the family's responsibilities, but this is the only occasion when members of the family, apart from the monarch, take on an entirely necessary function within the constitution.

The abdication crisis of 1936, when Edward VIII renounced the throne, brought the family of his younger brother, the Duke of York, into the limelight. Albert, Duke of York, had married Lady Elizabeth Bowes Lyon, known today as the Queen Mother, in 1923, and together they had had two daughters, Elizabeth and Margaret Rose. The abdication of Edward meant a change of destiny for them all, and one of their worries was the thought that King Edward's desertion could have made the monarchy unpopular. Therefore one of the main tasks for the first years of the reign of King George VI, as he became known, was to restore public confidence after the abdication. This was largely achieved by the time of the Second World War.

The constitutional implications for the new king were considerable, both for himself and for his eldest daughter, who was 10 years old and now only a heart's beat from the throne. The last 'minor' to succeed to the throne had been Edward VI, in 1547. With this in mind, George VI asked Parliament to make statutory provision to deal with four scenarios: the monarch being a minor; the monarch being permanently incapacitated; the monarch being temporarily incapacitated; and the monarch being temporarily out of the country.

The changing form of the Empire made the drawing up of these provisions quite complicated. The existing arrangements for Counsellors of State, drawn up at the start of the 20th century, allowed for Great Officers of State, such as the Prime Minister, as well as members of the Royal Family, to act on the Sovereign's behalf. This was acceptable within the United Kingdom, but George VI was also Head of State in many other countries. Some of these had once been colonies of Britain but were now self-governing dominions and they rejected the idea that members of the British government might, as Counsellors of State, exercise constitutional power over them.

King George's request was eventually dealt with by the Regency Act of 1937. This established that minority or the permanent incapacity of the monarch would be met by establishing a Regency, with the next adult heir in order of succession acting as Regent. Meanwhile the absence of the monarch abroad, or temporary incapacity, would necessitate a Council of State being established. Membership of this, however, was restricted to the Royal Family. The council would include the Sovereign's consort and the next four adult members in order of succession. Total incapacity of the monarch had to be confirmed by three of the following: the Sovereign's next of kin, the Lord High Chancellor, the Speaker of the House of Commons, the Lord Chief Justice and the Master of the Rolls. In 1953, the Regency Act was altered to allow the Queen Mother to continue serving and to provide for Prince Philip to act as Regent, if Prince Charles came to the throne prior to his 18th birthday.

Counsellors of State are restricted in what they can do: in particular they may not dissolve Parliament or sign acts that alter the order of succession. However, without them the process of constitutional government is unable to operate.

Opposite: The 1844 Room in Buckingham Palace is where The Queen receives her Privy Council. In the monarch's absence abroad or through ill health, two COUNSELLORS OF STATE *must take her place, when Government business dictates. They stand where the monarch does – before the fireplace and beside a table laid, according to long-established custom, with paper, pens and letter openers – to receive a quorum of Councillors. This generally consists of the President of the Council and three other Ministers, with the Clerk of the Council. All stand for the brief meeting. Candle and sealing wax are to hand, but seldom used.*

Counsellors of State

MANORIAL LORDSHIPS CAN PASS from one generation to another, and therefore, like other titles, appear to be inherited. However, they are actually property, so they can also be bought and sold. Therefore, the manorial lordship is held by whoever has legal possession of the title deeds.

During the reign of the present Queen, the title of Lord of the Manor of Worksop was sold, and, for the first time in centuries, the title is now owned by someone born, educated, working and living in Worksop, near Nottingham. With this appointment comes the responsibility of Grand Sergeanty, which involves the Lord of the Manor petitioning the Court of Claims to be allowed to present a special glove at the coronation of a new monarch. Behind this ceremony lies a story that starts with Edward the Confessor, the last of the Saxon kings.

As the Normans claimed the throne of England through a promise made by Edward the Confessor, their apologists worked hard to enhance the Saxon's reputation after his death. So successful were they at this, that centuries after his demise Edward was declared a saint.

One of the legends told about him concerns a dream he had that, wandering through his palace at Westminster, he heard a noise coming from his treasury. He opened the door and came face to face with the Devil, who was dancing on chests containing coins gathered under an unpopular tax, known as the Danegeld – money originally levied to bribe to Danish invaders to stay away from Britain's shores. When Edward woke from his dream, he decided to repeal the tax and resolved that nothing so punitive should ever be collected from his people again. It is thought that the glove presented during the coronation ceremony was designed to be a symbolic reminder of this lesson. Just before the Archbishop puts the Sceptre of Kingly Power in the monarch's right hand, a single glove is presented as a reminder that power should be exercised with gentleness.

In the time of Edward the Confessor a Saxon noble named Elsi held Worksop, but eventually, in 1542, the manor was granted to Francis Talbot, Earl of Shrewsbury, in Grand Sergeanty. This obliged the Lord of the Manor of Worksop, in the county of Nottingham, to attend the coronation of any new monarch. He was to step forward just before the sceptre was given to the monarch, to kneel and present 'a glove for the King's right hand' and then to remain available to support the sovereign's arm if necessary. The Lord of the Manor of Worksop or his nominee has performed this service at every coronation since that time. It is a silent but deeply symbolic moment in a ceremony full of significance.

At Queen Elizabeth II's coronation the undertaking of this ceremony became more complicated than previously because the Manor was then owned by a limited company, and allowing a commercial organization to take part in the coronation was deemed unacceptable. A compromise was negotiated, and the Chancellor of the Duchy of Lancaster presented the glove by proxy.

While much else may evolve in the coronations of British kings and queens, it would be a shame to lose this symbolic presentation of a single glove. Surely no person could be more suitable to present it than a man who is Worksop through and through, who is ready to play his part in reminding the Sovereign, on behalf of us all, to be gentle in taxation and power.

Worksop Abbey in Nottinghamshire is where the new LORD OF THE MANOR *was christened, schooled and married. Purchasing this feudal history, he hopes to continue Worksop's unique offering of a symbolic glove. On bended knee, his predecessors have presented a single embroidered glove to the new monarch moments before the symbol of Kingly Power is invested. It is supposed to remind the monarch to be gentle with royal power. The glove shown here is a copy of the one given in 1953.*

Lord of the Manor of Worksop

EVERY YEAR ON MAUNDY THURSDAY, in the week before Easter, The Queen continues a royal tradition by making a journey to a cathedral city and giving specially minted coins to a group of women and men equal in number to her age. The ceremony is the responsibility of the High Almoner and the Royal Almonry, which is administered by The Queen's Privy Purse.

The Royal Maundy is one of the duties and observances that Christian monarchs have carried out to show that they remember and follow Christ's example at the Last Supper, when he showed humility to his followers. The Christian calendar of high days illuminated important events in red, and these 'red letter days' required the monarch's attendance at Mass, sometimes a crown-wearing ceremony (*coronamenta*) and sometimes preparatory fasting. The most important period in the Christian calendar is Holy Week, the seven days leading up to Easter Sunday when Christ rose from the dead. On the eve of Good Friday it was usual to observe the *mandatum* (commandment) of Jesus, who said, 'I give you a new commandment: love one another as I have loved you.' (The word 'Maundy' is actually a corruption of *mandatum*.)

To observe this command, monarchs were expected to follow Christ's example of humility, which he displayed by washing his disciples' feet at the Last Supper. On the night before his crucifixion, Christ 'laid aside his garments and took a towel and girded himself. After that he poureth water into a basin, and began to wash the disciples' feet, and to wipe them with the towel wherewith he was girded.' Many early monarchs followed his example literally and washed the feet of the poor, but this practice had ended by 1730 because most could not stand the dreadful smell and were also worried about other health dangers associated with close contact with the poor.

Specially minted silver coins were always part of the monarch's charity, as Maundy Money is today. Other traditions of giving out food and cast-offs from the royal wardrobe were later replaced with more money, which was popular with paupers, who could do more with a full purse than clean feet or fine clothes.

Only since the late 19th century have monarchs started to take an active part again in the annual Maundy Service. For years preceding that time the Lord High Almoner (as he was then called) would distribute the purses on the monarch's behalf to a gathering of men and women who equalled the number of the monarch's age. When attending the service, the High Almoner now wears towels made in 1883, which symbolize those worn by Jesus. However, he was once charged with controlling much more.

In the Middle Ages the Lord High Almoner would strew the route with money from the King's Treasury in order to attract an enthusiastic crowd when his master passed through towns. He could give the fish dish from the King's table to 'whatever poor person he pleased'. Also, he received all 'deodand' – any moving thing that had caused the death of a person – which, by dint of its action, became forfeit to God, in the person of his representative, the Sovereign. So the Lord High Almoner received horses, carts and ladders, which he distributed to the needy after taking a small percentage. This practice was abolished in 1846.

The first Lord High Almoner was appointed in 1103 to assist in the religious service on Maundy Thursday and to administer the Sovereign's obligation to give alms to the poor. His status was emphasized by inclusion among the great officers of State. It has always been an ecclesiastical appointment filled mostly by bishops, but occasionally by archbishops. Now the High Almoner concentrates solely on planning The Queen's annual act of humility.

Opposite: *The* HIGH ALMONER, *in the sanctuary of his cathedral at St Alban's in Hertfordshire, wears his badge of office, which shows the three-masted ship instituted as the symbol of the Royal Almonry by Cardinal Wolsey in 1512. He is girded with towels in remembrance of the days when monarchs, who were anxious to follow Christ's mandate of humility, washed the feet of the destitute. Bishops have filled this post since 1103.*

High Almoner

No SINGLE ISSUE IN the United Kingdom has lasted for as long nor been so full of pain as the divisions that still exist in Northern Ireland. With optimism the people of the world watched the signing of the Good Friday Agreement at Stormont, the seat of power in Ulster, in 1998. It marked a significant step, but few believe that the divisions, which are based upon a long history of antagonism and countless cruelties, will quickly heal. It is ironic that, in a land where many of the political differences have attached themselves to two separate denominations, the religious leaders of each are both committed to the tolerance preached in the Gospel. Both also share the inheritance of St Patrick, the undisputed Patron Saint of Ireland.

St Patrick, who was born in England in about 389, was captured in a raid and taken to Ireland aged sixteen. Here he tended the herds of an Irish chieftain before making his escape. Later he returned to Ireland, determined to convert the people in the northern part to Christianity; other enclaves of the faith already existing elsewhere. The *Book of the Angel*, which was written around 640, claims that Patrick established his Cathedra at Armagh. In 445, it is said that he became Primate and Metropolitan of Ireland, which made Armagh the principle Christian seat in the country.

Some 700 years later, Pope Adrian became dissatisfied with the behaviour of the Irish church and issued a Bull, called the *Laudabilitier*, which gave Henry II of England leave to conquer Ireland in order that Rome's authority might be re-established. In 1169 a bloody campaign of subjugation took place, like so many other interventions in the following centuries. In its wake came Norman administration and a new Church establishment controlled from Canterbury, with Dublin as its senior church: this was a direct challenge to Armagh and the inheritance of St Patrick. The rivalry between these two cathedrals continued until Edward III intervened: first siding with Armagh in 1349, then favouring Dublin but finally suggesting a solution whereby Armagh's bishop became Primate of All-Ireland while Dublin became Primate of Ireland.

In 1551, in the first stages of the imposition of the Protestant faith in Ireland, Edward VI transferred primacy again to Dublin, and then appointed Bishop Hugh Goodacre as the first Protestant bishop of Armagh. In 1553 the king died and his half sister, Mary, restored Catholicism as the religion of the state together with its bishops. With Elizabeth I's accession, the period of twin Prelates began in Armagh: one Protestant, the other Roman Catholic. For long periods it was necessary for the latter to live in exile because of the level of oppression during the 17th and 18th centuries. This period, called the Protestant Ascendancy, enabled the established Anglican Church of Ireland to secure its foothold but it never won over the whole population. Even the Penal Laws, designed to discriminate against Catholics in almost every way, failed to convert the vast number whose loyalty remained with their own Archbishops. Stripped of the income from historic estates, which were now in the possession of the Protestant landlords, and without the right to education, to buy land or to enjoy free worship the Catholic diocese nonetheless built its own new Cathedral. The Catholic Emancipation Act of 1829 revoked the Penal Laws, but the memory of this period would not be forgotten. With the division in 1922 of Ireland into the Irish Free State, in the south, and Northern Ireland, to the north, Armagh remained a city within the United Kingdom. Today, the two identically named do what they can to effect reconciliation and peace.

Opposite: *The Cathedral of St Patrick in Armagh, Northern Island, was built by Roman Catholics long before the Reformation divided Irish Christians into separate denominations. It was here that St Patrick (seen in the right hand portrait) established his bishopric. Both churches claim the same title for the successor to the Saint. The Church of Ireland* ARCHBISHOP OF ARMAGH AND PRIMATE OF ALL IRELAND *(sitting) and the Roman Catholic* ARCHBISHOP OF ARMAGH AND PRIMATE OF ALL IRELAND *(standing) work for unity in troubled times.*

Archbishop of Armagh and Primate of All Ireland with the Archbishop of Armagh and Primate of All Ireland

IT IS SIGNIFICANT THAT THE LEGENDARY English folk hero Robin Hood challenged authority in the form of the Sheriff of Nottingham. For the medieval English yeoman, the sheriff had power over life and death. As the King's representative in the shires, he could preside over the shire court in the Earl's absence, arrest and imprison criminals to preserve the King's peace, collect taxes and fines, raise and lead the local fighting force (*Posse Comitates*) and enforce regulations covering trade, currency, weights and measures, fairs and markets.

The foundations of local administration in England were laid towards the end of the 10th century. Reeves, or bailiffs scattered around the kingdom gathered taxes and enforced the King's writs. During the reign of Aethelred II (978-1016), the senior shrieval position in each shire was the Shire Reeve. The holders of this post became the 'sheriffs' inherited by the Normans victors in 1066. The Anglo-Saxon Sheriff of Norfolk, Toli, retained his bailiwick for several years. but by 1076 Normans had been installed in every shrieval post. Roger Bigod, who held the Norfolk office in 1086, acquired extensive lands in East Anglia after the Conquest.

The function of the Sheriff's office that most concerned the reigning sovereign was gathering taxes. In the 12th century Henry I made his new Exchequer Court responsible for supervising the shrievalty of England. To avoid disagreements over what was due, many sheriffs paid Sheriff-Geld, a set sum. Any excess produced by tax in the shires, they would keep as profit. Families became wealthy on shrieval income and took over more shires. Monarchs found other ways to improve their finances: Richard I auctioned off sheriffdoms to the highest bidder to raise money for the Crusades, and gave a clutch, including Nottingham, to his brother John, in order to secure his loyalty.

Magna Carta, the great charter that John was forced to sign at Runnymede in 1215, curbed the power of the King, thereby controlling the sheriffs. Their position was eroded further in the 14th century by the introduction of Justices of the Peace, and in the 16th century by the appointment of Lord-Lieutenants to deal with military and administrative matters. As the Sheriff's workload gradually increased and the income declined, the position became less attractive: people would even nominate their enemies, in the hope that the job would bring financial ruin.

The Sheriffs Act of 1887 redefined the duties of the post, but it remains virtually unpaid and consequently attracts people with private resources. Every year, lists of three new names are still prepared for each shire. The Sheriffs Roll is subsequently taken to the Queen, in Council, and she 'Pricks the List' with a bodkin, a tradition that may have started with Elizabeth I in the 16th century. Whilst the High Sheriff's role is now largely symbolic, certain legal duties are still attached to it: for instance, civil writs issued by the courts come to the High Sheriff, whose representatives prepare the warrant that bailiffs can bring to any debtor's door. And since 1254 it is to the High Sheriff that the monarch's writ to hold a General Election in the shire is still sent.

In 1997, the incoming Labour Government sought to update the appointment, which had been an almost exclusively male preserve and had a narrow social base. Through the Shrievalty Association, the nation's bailiwicks were encouraged to recruit more widely, achieving a greater degree of representation from ethnic minorities. In 2002, for the first time, 25 per cent of appointments will be women. The plan is to make the shrievalty much more inclusive in the future.

Opposite: *Saxon rulers had reeves to govern in the shires. The office of High Sheriff in rural post-Conquest England had extensive powers within its remit, including being able to enforce law and gather taxes in every corner of the shire. Today they act as official returning officers for parliamentary elections, execute High Court writs and greet High Court judges. The* HIGH SHERIFF OF THE BAILIWICK OF NORFOLK, *pictured here in woods near his home at Ranworth in Norfolk, wears the traditional black velvet court dress with gilt buttons, sword, jabot and breeches.*

High Sheriff of the Bailiwick of Norfolk

Opposite: *The* CHANCELLOR
OF LANCASTER UNIVERSITY
*wears a Chancellor's robe
in Lancastrian red,
embroidered in heavy gold
bullion and oak leaf lace.
Woven into the silk brocade
are heraldic roses with five
petals, each of which is
seeded and barbed: these
allude to the red rose of
Lancaster, which gave its
name along with the white
rose of York, to the Wars of
the Roses. Standing in St
James's Palace, the official
London residence of the
Duke of Lancaster, who is
Visitor of the University,
the Chancellor holds an
honorary degree that it is in
her power to confer under
the Royal Charter of 1964.*

THE UNIVERSITY THAT STANDS on the Bailrigg hill just south of the City of Lancaster was granted its Charter by The Queen, in her capacity as Duke of Lancaster, in 1964. It was one of seven new greenfield universities established in the 1960s to meet the rising demand for higher education. Because the names of these establishments – Sussex, Kent, Essex, York, Warwick, Norwich and Lancaster – quite incidentally echoed the names of heroic military figures in Shakespeare's history plays, the new generation of academic foundations was colloquially referred to as the Shakespearean Seven. Unlike previous practice, and because this was a completely fresh crop, the universities were granted the autonomy of their own Charter and Statutes from the outset. Today these new institutions have reached full maturity and stand alongside the ancient universities.

Universities have always attracted students from great distances to gather and learn. While the idea of such a community is taken for granted today, it was a revolutionary concept in the Middle Ages. The first universities were founded in the cities of Bologna and Paris, where cathedrals established safe places in which students could meet and benefit from scholarship. These scholastic communities, referred to as *stadium generale*, were supported by funds from the merchant guilds and the most senior clerics were used as teachers. Students came from courts all over Europe and, because they were a distrusted rarity, vulnerable to extortion and violence, lay-monasteries regulated by the cathedrals offered a degree of protection and order for them.

Bulls and Charters granted by popes, emperors or monarchs gave these new universities the authority to teach and the licence to permit the taught to become themselves teachers. This status in law was given after rigorous examination, with the intention that each university would seed new ones who, in time and after developing the appropriate standards, would themselves be granted the same authority as their predecessors.

The first English universities at Oxford and Cambridge derived their constitutions from the University of Paris, where the Charter required the Chancellor Scholasticus of Notre Dame Cathedral to establish certain standards of merit that students had to reach. Each student, known as a Bachelor of Arts, would learn from a Master in the faculty until he had proved his competence, whereupon a magisterial cap, or biretta, would be placed on his head and he would be led by his Master to sit in the Master's chair. The Chancellor then granted him his degree, or *licentia docendi*, and thus the former Bachelor was licensed to teach in his own right and to call himself Master of Arts. Because the degree had been granted on the authority of the Chancellor, it was universally respected.

Although these explicit ecclesiastical links have long been severed, the Chancellor of a modern university is the most senior lay member and the post includes the authority to confer degrees. Lancaster's Chancellor, first appointed in 1964 and the university's longest-standing lay officer, visits the university twice a year to grant degrees; in July for first degrees and in December for higher degrees. On each occasion she also bestows honorary degrees on a selection of individuals deemed worthy of the university's highest recognition. In addition to the academic gown, a variety of hoods that mark the different degrees, many of them drawing on the university's livery colours of Lancastrian red and Quaker grey, are worn in place of the former magisterial caps.

Chancellor of Lancaster University

Opposite: *Awaiting
completion of the new
Parliament building at
Holyrood, the* First
Minister and Keeper of
the Scottish Seal *stands
in the corridor outside the
temporary Chamber
with his* Deputy First
Minister. *The* Presiding
Officer *carries the Mace, a
gift from the Queen of Scots
to her Parliament at its
opening. Crafted out of
Scots silver, it depicts four
thistles, between which
are inscribed the words
'Wisdom', 'Justice',
'Compassion' and
'Integrity'. On its head is
inscribed the opening line
of the Scotland Act of 1998:
'There shall be a Scottish
Parliament'.*

The Government's decision to establish a Parliament in Scotland and Assemblies in Northern Ireland and Wales in 1997 led to the largest creation of new appointments in modern times. The Scotland Act of 1998 stated in its opening line: 'There shall be a Scottish Parliament'. This major constitutional step of devolving power from the Parliament of Westminster involved considerable discussion to determine what form the new parliament should take. The debate centred on the controversial division of power between the two parliaments, but thought was also given to the role of the various offices that would be needed.

It was considered important that, while Edinburgh followed many of the conventions observed at Westminster, there should be no confusion between the two parliaments or the offices held there. As a result, unique names for each post were adopted. For instance, a Speaker was needed at Edinburgh, but it would lead to confusion to call the new appointment by the same name used at Westminster: instead, the title of Presiding Officer was chosen. Equally, as a second Prime Minister within the United Kingdom would be confusing, the office of First Minister was created for Scotland. In this way, the constitutional position that the holder is the monarch's principal advisor and that the First Minister holds office 'at Her Majesty's pleasure' was retained. On appointment, The Queen passes the Scottish Seal into the First Minister's custody, so making him Keeper of the Scottish Seal as well. An impression of the Scottish Seal is what gives Royal Assent to Scottish Parliament Bills. The cabinet of Scottish Ministers that the First Minister appoints with the agreement of Parliament and the approval of Her Majesty is known as the Scottish Executive.

Particular circumstances in the Scottish Parliament led to the creation of a further post, not established in the Act of 1998. As Members of the Scottish Parliament are elected using a system of proportional representation, it is less likely that any one party will have a majority of seats in the Parliament. In 1999 Members agreed that the leader of the junior party in any coalition should be appointed Deputy First Minister. The office has no statutory basis, and there is no automatic entitlement for any future leader of the junior party to hold the office. But convention is the master of precedent.

Elections for the new parliament were held on 6th May 1999, and Parliament met for the first time on 12th May. As there is no equivalent of the Queen's Speech in the Scottish Parliament, it was the First Minister who put forward his government's programme on 16th June.

On 1st July 1999, the Queen officially opened the parliament in Edinburgh – the first since 1707, when the Act of Union had united the Parliaments of Scotland and England, so dissolving the old Scottish parliament. The Crown of Scotland, which had been hidden in 1707 – to prevent it from being spirited away to London – was carried in front of the monarch into the temporary Chamber on the Royal Mile. Here she was addressed by the suitable and traditional royal title of Queen of Scots, which had not been used formally since the Union of Crowns in 1603, when the two kingdoms of England and Scotland were first united under James I of England and VI of Scotland.

The Scottish Parliament remains subordinate to the legal and political sovereignty of the Parliament at Westminster. However, the new legislature has revived a sense of nationhood and holders of these appointments will lead the Scots democracy into the future, and will forge the next links in Scotland's history.

First Minister and Keeper of the Scottish Seal, with the Deputy First Minister and the Presiding Officer

Picture Credits and Office Holders

Appointments outlive the men and women who carry them. Inevitably, many who were photographed for this book no longer hold the office to which they were appointed: some have moved on, others were removed by the ballot box and a few have died. Their names and styles are recorded here as they were on the day that their portrait was taken.

JC denotes photographs taken by Julian Calder; MC denotes photographs taken by Mark Cator.

PAGE 2 – IMPERIAL STATE CROWN, SWORD OF STATE AND THRONE: 10 October 2001 (JC)

PAGE 5 – QUEEN'S BARGEMASTER: Mr Robert Crouch – and Royal Watermen – 20 July 2001 (MC)

CHAPTER ONE
PAGE 11 – ARCHDRUID OF ANGLESEY: Mr Robert Griffiths (Bardic name Machraeth), 24 June 1998 (MC)

PAGE 13 – THE SOVEREIGN: Her Majesty Queen Elizabeth II, 10 October 2001 (JC)

PAGE 15 – THE SOVEREIGN: Her Majesty Queen Elizabeth II (in Parliament), 10 October 2001 (MC)

PAGE 17 – HEREDITARY HIGH STEWARD OF THE LIBERTY OF ST EDMUND: The 8th Marquess of Bristol, 3 October 2001 (JC)

PAGE 19 – REGISTRAR OF THE IMPERIAL SOCIETY OF KNIGHTS BACHELOR: Sir Robert Balchin KStJ, 12 November 2001 (MC)

PAGE 20 – BOY BISHOP OF HEREFORD: Master Murray Warwick-Jones, 27 September 2001 (MC)

PAGE 23 – LORD PARAMOUNT OF HOLDERNESS: Mr John Chichester-Constable; DEPUTY WARDEN OF BURTON CONSTABLE COMPANY OF BOWMEN: Mr Graham Stark, 15 September 2001 (MC)

PAGE 24 – LORD WARDEN OF THE CINQUE PORTS AND CONSTABLE OF DOVER CASTLE: Her Majesty Queen Elizabeth The Queen Mother LG, LT, CI, GCVO, GBE, 27 July 2000 (JC)

PAGE 26 – ADMIRALTY JUDGE OF THE CINQUE PORTS: Mr Justice Clarke, 10 September 1998 (MC)

PAGE 29 – DAME DE ROSEL AND BUTLER TO THE DUKE OF NORMANDY: Mrs Emma Lempriere-Johnston, 26 July 2001 (MC)

PAGE 30 – LORD ARCHBISHOP OF CANTERBURY AND PRIMATE OF ALL ENGLAND: Most Revd. and Rt. Hon. George Carey, 1 April 1996 (MC)

PAGE 32 – LORD HIGH CHANCELLOR OF GREAT BRITAIN, KEEPER OF THE GREAT SEAL, KEEPER OF THE ROYAL CONSCIENCE AND SPEAKER OF THE HOUSE OF LORDS: The Lord Mackay of Clashfern, KT, PC, QC, November 1995 (MC)

PAGE 34 – QUEEN'S CHAMPION, LORD OF THE MANOR OF SCRIVELSBY: Lieutenant-Colonel John Dymoke, OBE, 10 July 1998 (JC)

PAGE 36 – PRESIDENT OF TYNWALD: Hon. Noel Quayle Cringle; SENIOR TYNWALD MESSENGER: Mr Frank Joughin MBE, 6 July 2001 (MC)

PAGE 37 – LORD BISHOP OF SODOR AND MAN: Rt. Revd. Noel Jones, CB, 6 July 1995 (MC)

PAGE 38 – MASTER OF ST CROSS: Rev. Anthony Outhwaite; BROTHER OF THE ORDER OF NOBLE POVERTY: Mr Harold Kay; BROTHER OF THE HOSPITAL OF ST CROSS: Mr Jim Heavens, 26 November 1996 (JC)

PAGE 41 – SERGEANT AT MACE: Mr Patrick Webb; HORNBLOWER OF RIPON: Mr Alan Oliver, 12 June 1998 (JC)

PAGE 43 – LADY MARCHER OF CEMAES: Mrs John Hawkesworth; MAYOR OF NEWPORT: Mr Jeremy George, 22 April 1997 (MC)

PAGE 45 – 31ST HEREDITARY WARDEN OF SAVERNAKE FOREST: The Earl of Cardigan, 14 July 1997 (JC)

PAGE 47 – MASTER TREASURER OF THE INNER TEMPLE: Mr Edward Nugee, TD, QC, 8 July 1996 (MC)

CHAPTER TWO
PAGE 49 – 15TH HEREDITARY KEEPER AND CAPTAIN OF DUNCONNEL IN THE ISLES OF THE SEA: Sir Fitzroy Maclean of Dunconnel Bt, KT, CBE, 19 September 1995 (MC)

PAGE 51 – LORD OF THE ISLES, PRINCE AND GREAT STEWARD OF SCOTLAND, DUKE OF ROTHESAY, EARL OF CARRICK AND BARON OF RENFREW: Colonel His Royal Highness The Duke of Rothesay KG, KT, GMB, AK, QSO, ADC(P) (The Prince of Wales), 6 July 2001 (JC)

PAGE 52 – KNIGHT COMPANION OF THE MOST NOBLE ORDER OF THE GARTER: The 8th Duke of Wellington, KG, LVO, OBE, MC, 14 September 1998 (JC)

PAGE 55 – GOVERNOR OF THE MILITARY KNIGHTS AND THE MILITARY KNIGHTS OF WINDSOR: Colonel Brian Colston; Major Jim Cowley OBE, DCM; Major Richard Moore; Lieutenant Colonel Tom Hiney MC; Brigadier Tim Hackworth OBE; Major Alan Clarkson; Lieutenant Colonel Ray Giles; Major Gordon Mitchell MBE, BEM (seated); Governor Major General Sir Michael Hobbs KCVO, CBE; Major 'Tommy' Thompson MVO, MBE, DCM; Brigadier John Lindner OBE, MC, 27 July 2001 (JC)

PAGES 56–7 – OFFICERS OF THE COLLEGE OF ARMS: left to right – LANCASTER HERALD Mr Robert Noel; WINDSOR HERALD Major William Hunt TD; CHESTER HERALD Mr Timothy Duke; RICHMOND HERALD Mr Patric Dickinson; YORK HERALD Mr Henry Paston-Bedingfeld; CLARENCEUX KING OF ARMS AND SECRETARY OF THE ORDER OF THE GARTER Mr Hubert Chesshyre LVO; GARTER KING OF ARMS Mr Peter Gwynn-Jones CVO (seated); NORROY AND ULSTER KING OF ARMS Mr Thomas Woodcock LVO; MALTRAVERS HERALD EXTRAORDINARY Dr John Martin Robinson; NORFOLK HERALD EXTRAORDINARY Major David Rankin-Hunt MVO, MBE, TD; ARUNDEL HERALD EXTRAORDINARY Mr Alan Dickins; WALES HERALD EXTRAORDINARY Dr Michael Siddons; ROUGE DRAGON PURSUIVANT Mr Clive Cheesman; FITZALAN PURSUIVANT EXTRAORDINARY Alastair Bruce of Crionaich; ROUGE CROIX PURSUIVANT Mr David White, 18 June 2001 (JC)

PAGE 59 – LORD LYON KING OF ARMS: Sir Malcolm Innes of Edingight, KCVO, 8 July 1998 (JC)

PAGE 60 – LORD HIGH CONSTABLE OF SCOTLAND: The 24th Earl of Errol; SLAINS PURSUIVANT: Peter Drummond-Murray of Mastrick, 17 May 1998 (JC)

PAGE 63 – HEREDITARY MASTER OF THE ROYAL HOUSEHOLD, HIGH JUSTICIAR OF ARGYLL, ADMIRAL OF THE WESTERN ISLES, HIGH SHERIFF OF ARGYLL AND KEEPER OF THE ROYAL CASTLES OF CARRICK, DUNOON, DUNSTAFFNAGE, SWEEN AND TARBERT: The 13th Duke of Argyll, 18 July 2001 (MC)

PAGE 65 – HEREDITARY CAPTAIN OF DUNSTAFFNAGE: Michael Campbell of Dunstaffnage, 4 July 1998 (JC)

PAGE 67 – GOVERNOR OF THE COMPANY OF MERCHANT

ADVENTURERS OF YORK: Mr Trevor Copley, 27 September 2001 (JC)

PAGE 69 – LORD WARDEN OF THE STANNARIES, RIDER AND MASTER FORESTER OF THE FOREST AND CHASE OF DARTMOOR, KEEPER OF THE PRINCE'S PRIVY SEAL AND VICE CHAIRMAN OF THE PRINCE'S COUNCIL: The 3rd Earl Peel, 5 December 1996 (MC)

PAGE 71 – SPEAKER OF THE HOUSE OF COMMONS: Miss Betty Boothroyd, PC, MP, 10 July 1995 (MC)

PAGE 73 – LORD OF THE MANOR OF ALCESTER: The 9th Marquess of Hertford (seated); COURT LEET (left to right): BREAD WEIGHER: Mr John Bull; FISH AND FLESH TASTERS: Mr Ian Taylor and Mr Michael Jackson; ALE TASTERS: Mr William Bowen and Mr Glynn Bromwich; MARSHAL TO THE COURT: Mr Jeremy Howell; CONSTABLE: Mr Ron Leek; HIGH BAILIFF: Mr David Young; SURVEYOR OF THE HIGHWAYS: Mr Bob Allard; HAYWARD: Mr Keith Greenaway; STEWARD (or SENESCHAL) OF THE MANOR: Mr John Hill; IMMEDIATE PAST HIGH BAILIFF: Mr Foster Richardson; SEARCHER AND SEALER OF LEATHER: Mr Bernard Hyde; BROOK LOOKER: Mr Hamilton Leek; CHAPELAYNE: Revd. David Capron; TOWN CRIER AND BEADLE: Mr Keith Tomlinson; LOW BAILIFF: Mr Rory Duff, 6 September 1998 (JC)

PAGE 75 – MASTER OF THE HORSE: The 3rd Lord Somerleyton, KCVO, 12 November 1996 (MC)

PAGE 77 – MASTER OF THE ROLLS: Sir Thomas Bingham, 28 June 1995 (MC)

PAGE 79 – SEARCHER OF THE SANCTUARY AND HIGH BAILIFF OF WESTMINSTER ABBEY: The Lord Weatherill of North-East Croydon; HIGH STEWARD OF WESTMINSTER ABBEY: The Lord Blake of Braydeston, 30 June 1998 (JC)

PAGE 80 – QUEEN'S REMEMBRANCER: Master Robert Turner, 11 December 1996 (MC)

PAGE 83 – CHANCELLOR OF THE DUCHY OF LANCASTER: The Lord Macdonald of Tradeston CBE, 28 September 2001 (MC)

PAGE 85 – LORD HIGH ADMIRAL OF THE WASH: Mr Michael le Strange Meakin, 4 June 1997 (JC)

PAGE 87 – FIRST SEA LORD AND CHIEF OF THE NAVAL STAFF: Admiral Sir Jock Slater, GCB, LVO, ADC, 12 July 1996 (MC)

PAGE 89 – PAGEANTMASTER OF THE CITY OF LONDON: Mr Dominic Reid, 5 August 2001 (JC)

PAGES 90–91 – LORD MAYOR OF LONDON, ESCHEATOR, CLERK OF THE MARKETS AND ADMIRAL OF THE PORT OF LONDON: Alderman Michael Oliver; (behind, from left to right) DRUMBEATER WITH MUSKETEERS, COMPANY OF PIKEMEN, then TWO OFFICERS OF THE COMPANY OF PIKEMEN AND MUSKETEERS – CAPTAIN: Colonel Richard Burford TD; LIEUTENANT: Captain David Horn, 11 September 2001 (MC)

PAGE 93 – MASTER OF THE WORSHIPFUL COMPANY OF SKINNERS: Mr David Kemp; MASTER OF THE WORSHIPFUL COMPANY OF MERCHANT TAYLORS: Mr Martin Clarke, 17 July 1998 (MC)

PAGE 95 – TOLLY-KEEPERS OF WINCHESTER COLLEGE, 15 June 1998 (MC)

PAGE 96 – PROVOST OF ETON COLLEGE: Sir Antony Acland, GCMG, GCVO; CONDUCT OF ETON COLLEGE: Rev. Charles Mitchell-Innes; HEADMASTER OF ETON COLLEGE: Mr John Lewis; COLLEGER OF ETON COLLEGE: Mr Joshua Neicho, 21 March 1999 (MC)

PAGE 99 – CHORISTERS OF KING'S COLLEGE, 17 October 1988 (MC)

CHAPTER THREE
PAGE 101 – DOYEN OF THE COURT OF ST JAMES'S: Archbishop Luigi Barbarito, June 1995 (MC)

PAGE 102 – EARL MARSHAL AND HEREDITARY MARSHAL OF ENGLAND: The 17th Duke of Norfolk, KG, GCVO, CB, CBE, MC, 9 June 1998 (JC)

PAGE 105 – MESSENGER SERGEANT-MAJOR AND WARDROBE KEEPER OF THE YEOMEN OF THE GUARD: Sergeant-Major Alex Dumon MVO, MBE; CLERK OF THE CHEQUE AND ADJUTANT OF THE QUEEN'S BODY GUARD OF THE YEOMEN OF THE GUARD: Colonel Shaun Longsdon, 11 July 2001 (MC)

PAGE 107 – QUEEN'S SWAN MARKER: Mr David Barber, 22 June 2001 (JC)

PAGE 108 – YEOMAN USHER OF THE BLACK ROD, SECRETARY TO THE LORD GREAT CHAMBERLAIN AND SERGEANT-AT-ARMS OF THE HOUSE OF LORDS: General Sir Edward Jones, KCB, CBE, 27 June 1996 (JC)

PAGE 111 – CHILDREN OF THE CHAPEL ROYAL: 2 May 1996 (MC)

Index

• Earl Marshal and Hereditary Marshal of England • Messenger S
Adjutant of the Queen's Body Guard of the Yeomen of the Guard
the Lord Great Chamberlain and Sergeant-at-Arms of the House o
Rotulorum of Gloucestershire • Master of the Corporation of Trin
of St Benet-at-Holme • Senior Grecian of Christ's Hospital • Poet
Crauford who washes the Sovereign's Hands • Hereditary Falcone
Resident Governor of the Tower of London and Keeper of the Jew
Highlanders • Gold Stick in Waiting • Lord High Commissioner o
and Lord President of the Court of Session • Chief of Clan Came
Company of Archers and Gold Stick with Officers and Members of
Fort • Sisters of the Hospital of the Most Holy and Undivided Trini
Grand Master for the United Grand Lodge of England • Queen's
Watermen and Lightermen and winners of Doggett's Coat and B
Privy Council • Knight Grand Cross of the Most Honourable Ord
the Falkland Islands • Hereditary Bearer of the National Flag
Commissioner • Gentiluomo of the Cardinal Archbishop of West
and Second Sea Lord • Governor and Commander in Chief of
Superintendent of the Corps of Queen's Messengers • Senior Co
Chancellor and Lord Prior of the Most Venerable Order of Saint Jo
and Page of the Presence • Harpist to The Prince of Wales • Lady
Corps • The Unknown Warrior • Superior General of the Tyburn
• First Lord of the Treasury and Prime Minister • Adjutant of th
Naval Reserve • Chief of the Air Staff • Counsellors of State • L
and Primate of All Ireland and the Archbishop of Armagh and
Chancellor of Lancaster University • First Minister and Keepe